Articulating Design Decisions

Communicate with Stakeholders, Keep Your Sanity, and Deliver the Best User Experience

Tom Greever

 Beijing · Boston · Farnham · Sebastopol · Tokyo

Articulating Design Decisions
by Tom Greever

Published by O'Reilly Media, Inc., 1005 Gravenstein Highway North, Sebastopol, CA 95472.

O'Reilly books may be purchased for educational, business, or sales promotional use. Online editions are also available for most titles (*safaribooksonline.com*). For more information, contact our corporate/institutional sales department: (800) 998-9938 or *corporate@oreilly.com*.

Acquisitions Editor: Mary Treseler
Editor: Nick Lombardi
Production Editor: Melanie Yarbrough
Copyeditor: Octal Publishing
Proofreader: Sharon Wilkey

Indexer: Bob Pfahler
Cover Designer: Randy Comer
Interior Designers: Ron Bilodeau and Monica Kamsvaag
Illustrator: Rebecca Demarest
Compositor: Melanie Yarbrough

September 2015: First Edition.

Revision History for the First Edition:

2015-09-14   First release

See *http://oreilly.com/catalog/errata.csp?isbn=0636920037422* for release details.

978-1-491-92156-2

[LSI]

[*contents*]

[*contents*]

[*Preface*]

The Big Meeting

ON A COLD SUNDAY IN JANUARY, I left my home in Illinois to catch a late flight to San Francisco for a client meeting the next morning. But this wasn't just any meeting. About a dozen people from different areas of the company were all presenting designs to the CEO of a giant retail website. Vice presidents, directors, product owners, and UX designers were all involved in putting together a three-hour event that would lay the groundwork for an entire season's worth of projects, as long as they could get this one executive's approval.

The whole thing had begun weeks earlier, when I sat in a different meeting about the meeting. Whereas the rest of the product teams had been planning for a few weeks, our project had been overlooked in the previous review with the CEO. He asked why our project wasn't represented, and so the rest of the team insisted that I be present at the next meeting. It was extremely inconvenient for me. I had been in San Francisco the week before and was now being asked to come back for a single day the following week. To make matters worse, I needed to create new designs to support a view for every product team that was being represented, so I had a lot of work to do to prepare. However, none of that mattered. It was obvious that everyone was willing to drop what they were doing to make this meeting successful.

After working with several product managers and attending yet another meeting about the meeting, I finally had a list of designs that I needed to provide and began working on them right away. The Friday before, I sat in on a four-hour conference call, during which everyone on the team practiced their presentation to a VP, who provided feedback and suggestions for how to best present their ideas to the CEO.

The whole charade centered around one thing: presenting design ideas to a CEO for the purpose of getting his approval. There were meetings about meetings, discussions about what he might say, late nights getting everything just right, and rearranging schedules to make it happen. I personally would spend 16 hours traveling, 2 nights in a hotel, and a full day in a conference room just for this one meeting. Fortunately, the meeting went well. The CEO was very receptive, provided great feedback, and everyone set to implementing the interfaces they had designed.

But that's not the important part of this story.

What struck me about this whole thing was the amount of effort that was going into just communicating design ideas to one person. The amount of time the other designers spent actually creating the mockups was nothing compared to the time and energy that went into finding the best way of communicating them. It was clear to everyone: if we don't get approval for our designs, our projects won't see the light of day. *Communicating about the designs was more important than the designs themselves.*

You may not have a large staff like this and you may not be working with a large company for which a meeting with the CEO is such a big deal, but the principle is still the same. The way we talk about design to our stakeholders is critical to the success of our projects.

What This Book Is About

The purpose of this book is to help designers become better communicators—to expertly explain their design decisions to the people who have influence over their project. The entire premise of the book centers around a meeting: a meeting with clients or stakeholders at which we present and talk about our design decisions. Everything is written with this meeting in mind: before, during, and even after this meeting. Everything that we will walk through focuses on this meeting and is meant to help you become better at leading, participating in, and saving the day in these situations.

Some of these meetings will involve a lot of other people, but the majority of them involve just a few. Some might take place in a conference room, whereas others are simple hallway conversations. So, don't obsess over the details of how this overlays with your own reality;

instead, focus on the overarching principles that you can apply in any situation. The goal is to remain flexible and able to adapt quickly in different situations.

I go into great detail about writing down everything, asking questions, honing your listening skills, or making multiple designs. It might seem as if you'd need weeks to prepare to talk to someone about your work. But, in reality, it all happens very quickly. Sometimes you'll have plenty of time to prepare. Other times, you'll need to form a response off-the-cuff and make very quick judgment calls. That's the reason learning these skills and committing them to habit is so important. You want articulating design decisions to be something you can do so effortlessly, that you no longer need to spend conscious effort applying all the advice contained in this book.

Talking to people about design might seem like a basic skill, but it's actually really difficult to do. In my experience, designers have a difficult time adequately communicating with nondesigners in a way that's effective. So, keep reading and learn how to better communicate to stakeholders, keep your sanity, and deliver the best user experience.

Who Should Read This Book

This book is written primarily for designers working with other nondesigner stakeholders: graphic, web, UX, interaction, interface, or visual designers. However, because the book is nontechnical and deals with many common problems in design processes, many other roles in the organization will be able to relate to, and benefit from, these tips and best practices.

DESIGNERS

If you've ever had the experience of a stakeholder insisting on a change that you were unable to defend, this book is for you. It's a common situation for designers to feel as if their own expertise and judgment is overruled by stakeholders who know little about design. This book is meant to bridge that gap and help you convince them your decisions are the best choice.

SENIOR DESIGNERS

You might think you've been doing this long enough and you're already sufficiently skilled at articulating design decisions, but I promise that there is plenty in here for you, too. Besides validating what you already know, I provide a lot of actionable tactics that you can use to augment your existing practices. Have you ever painted a duck? You have, but you just don't know it yet.

DEVELOPERS

If you've ever had difficulty working with designers or had a stakeholder ask you to change something that you thought made the interface more confusing, this book will give you a lot of great insights and tips to smooth that process. Although I don't speak directly to developers, I've found that most developers are familiar enough with design to benefit greatly from this content. It will help you learn to talk about design in a way that's accessible and practical.

MANAGERS, EXECUTIVES, PRODUCT OWNERS, PROJECT MANAGERS, AND MARKETING

Everyone involved in the design and creation of a product or service—especially on the Web—can benefit from this book because it provides a common framework for talking about design in a way that's effective. In fact, Chapter 12 is written specifically for you! Whether you're an executive concerned about what the UX team has done or a product owner in the trenches with designers every day, this book will give you practical ways to talk about design to other people.

How This Book Is Organized

Before we begin the journey of meeting with stakeholders, in *Chapter 1*, I open the book with a quick look at how web, app, and UX design has changed in recent years. Specifically, at how those changes have affected and amplified our need to be better communicators of design. It's important to look at where we've been in order to understand where we are going. *Chapter 2* then takes this one step further by demonstrating how and why communication is a critical part of the design process in today's organizations. Our designs do not speak for themselves, so we must understand how clear communication is the missing component in many design processes.

Chapters 3 through 11 are organized in a linear fashion, centered around the meeting with stakeholders. We walk through the process of meeting about and presenting design. At each step, you'll see a timeline (such as the one that follows) to indicate where we are in the meeting. Along the way, we'll cover things such as understanding stakeholder perspectives, empathizing with them, and doing the prep work necessary to meet with them. During the meeting itself, we look at both implicit and explicit listening skills as well as learning to get in the right frame of mind before responding. Next, I propose several simple tactics and formulas to help you get approval for your designs by forming the best response. Yet, even after the meeting has concluded, it's still necessary to follow up and make adjustments to your work to ensure that you maintain the best user experience. From beginning to end, these chapters cover everything you need to know about meeting with stakeholders to talk about your design decisions.

However, because working with people isn't always a precise linear process, I offer some tips and best practices that will be relevant in many other areas of your work. For example, taking good notes is discussed at length in both Chapters 4 and 10, but the application for documenting design decisions is relevant in every step of your design process.

Finally, I close the book with two important chapters:

Chapter 12

This chapter is written for nondesigner stakeholders and is intended to be a resource for anyone involved in making design decisions. Developers, executives, and product owners will all benefit from learning to work with designers more effectively. Designers are encouraged to share this chapter with their nondesigner colleagues.

Chapter 13

This chapter is a departure from the concept of convincing stakeholders that our decisions are sound, and instead focuses more on establishing a pattern for demonstrating value through a design vision that's greater than the existing scope. In other words, communicating about design extends beyond our meetings; it requires a leadership mentality that recognizes how creating and articulating long-term vision is just as important as shipping the thing you're working on today.

Why I Wrote This Book

To be honest, I'm surprised by the reception this book and its content has received. Of all the areas of my design practice that I found interesting and useful, this topic was not the first thing to come to mind when I was asked to submit a speaking proposal for a design conference in St. Louis several years ago. In fact, it seemed like the most obvious and boring topic because it was something I did every day, almost without thinking. After hearing from people that it really helped them work with stakeholders, I began to look back over my own career to try and understand how my experience could help others in this area.

That process allowed me to see how my own career was filled with examples where better communication yielded better design. I realized that all my favorite designers were people who could intelligently explain why they did what they did. I noticed that a lot of the feedback I give my own team has more to do with the way they present design than it does with their skill at creating it. It has since become clear to me that the way we talk about design with others has a significant impact on whether we succeed at creating great experiences. This is a skill many designers (even senior designers) lack. The success of our work depends on our ability to get support from everyone on the team. If we can't do that, our designs will never see the light of day.

Let me be very clear: this is not about an "us versus them" mentality suggesting that designers are always right and opposing stakeholders who would otherwise make bad decisions. Rather, articulating design decisions is about creating an environment in which stakeholders can clearly see the expertise and thought process of the designers so that they *want* to agree with them. It's about creating trust, demonstrating effectiveness, and doing so in way that's compelling and convincing.

I wrote this book because I want to help designers and companies create better experiences, but there is a large gap in communication between designers and stakeholders. To fill that gap, I provide real, practical advice that you can apply to your work right now. I did it to document and clarify my own thinking on how design is influenced by communication, but I also did it to help me be intentional about the things I do every day. This book is my own personal checklist for how to talk about design, and I am also excited to share it with you. I hope it will be a useful tool.

Follow me on Twitter: *http://twitter.com/tomgreever*

Keep up with me on my website: *http://tomgreever.com*

Safari® Books Online

Safari Books Online (*http://safaribooksonline.com*) is an on-demand digital library that delivers expert *content* in both book and video form from the world's leading authors in technology and business. Technology professionals, software developers, web designers, and business and creative professionals use Safari Books Online as their primary resource for research, problem solving, learning, and certification training.

Safari Books Online offers a range of *product mixes* and pricing programs for *organizations*, *government agencies*, and *individuals*. Subscribers have access to thousands of books, training videos, and prepublication manuscripts in one fully searchable database from publishers like O'Reilly Media, Prentice Hall Professional, Addison-Wesley Professional, Microsoft Press, Sams, Que, Peachpit Press, Focal Press, Cisco Press, John Wiley & Sons, Syngress, Morgan Kaufmann, IBM Redbooks, Packt, Adobe Press, FT Press, Apress, Manning, New Riders, McGraw-Hill, Jones & Bartlett, Course Technology, and dozens *more*. For more information about Safari Books Online, please visit us *online*.

How to Contact Us

Please address comments and questions concerning this book to the publisher:

O'Reilly Media, Inc.
1005 Gravenstein Highway North
Sebastopol, CA 95472
800-998-9938 (in the United States or Canada)
707-829-0515 (international or local)
707-829-0104 (fax)

We have a web page for this book, where we list errata, examples, and any additional information. You can access this page at *http://bit.ly/ articulating-design-decisions*.

To comment or ask technical questions about this book, send email to *bookquestions@oreilly.com*.

For more information about our books, courses, conferences, and news, see our website at *http://www.oreilly.com*.

Find us on Facebook: *http://facebook.com/oreilly*

Follow us on Twitter: *http://twitter.com/oreillymedia*

Watch us on YouTube: *http://www.youtube.com/oreillymedia*

Acknowledgments

Let's get the most obvious one out of the way. My wife thinks it would be nice if I thanked "my family," which includes all sorts of characters—including at least five children—who have put up with my shenanigans and sleep-deprived state while I wrote this book. Really, she just wants me to hold the baby while she takes a shower, which I'm happy to do. I'll be right there. Just let me finish this section.

I do owe a huge thanks to the reviewers: Dennis Kardys, Christy Ennis-Kloote, Anthony Armendariz, and Heather Wydeven. This book is much more accurate and significantly less offensive because of their help. Also, Nick Lombardi has been my biggest ally at O'Reilly Media. You may not know it, but he's much more than an editor. He's like a ninja talent scout, too. The next time you're at a conference, watch out for Nick.

Last (but most certainly not least) I have to take at least two paragraphs to thank all of my existing and previous clients or stakeholders. Without you, this book would not be possible. No joke. Barb, if you hadn't gotten ticked off at that email I wrote, how would I know about understanding relationships in Chapter 3? I figured out the importance of reducing cognitive load from Chapter 4 by working with Jenny. The CEO button was inspired by literally every executive I've ever worked with! Every. Single. One. Carrie, I appreciate how your over-the-top politeness gave me the opportunity to learn to read between the lines. Josh, you were a weird dude but I'm a better person for having learned to work with you. Really, there are too many people to mention.

Actually, I'd be remiss if I didn't mention that every person that has ever worked with me is in some way a part of this book. I became good at talking about design because of you. I had to! You gave me no choice! I learned these skills through years of working with YOU, and now it's time for me to share it with the world.

[1]

A Maturing Industry

To improve is to change; to be perfect is to change often.
WINSTON CHURCHILL

HISTORICALLY, DESIGNERS HAVE BEEN relegated to the business of making pretty pictures. Most of us transitioned into user experience design, or as is more commonly known, UX, from other areas. But now that UX is everywhere, we are thrust into the limelight of product development with our own ideas forming a critical piece of the puzzle. It's what we've always wanted! The problem? We're not used to having to explain ourselves to other people, especially nondesigners.

As we look at how to talk about design to nondesigners, I want to first provide the context to help us understand how we got here in the first place. My own career has been littered with experiences (good and bad) of articulating design decisions to stakeholders. Those experiences shaped my understanding of design and helped me to see the importance of communication in the process. In addition, the term "UX" hasn't been around that long. It's important to know how the evolution of this term affects our ability to talk about our work with others. Of critical importance, however, is the shift that's taken place in organizations from seeing design as merely a utility to being a fully engaged partner in the product development cycle. Similarly, web and mobile interfaces have transitioned from being only *platforms* for products to being the product themselves. All of these factors greatly influence design within companies, teams, and the minds of our stakeholders. So, let's jump right in by first going all the way back to the 1990s.

Talking My Way Into Design

My path to working in UX began in marketing. I studied business for my undergraduate degree and quickly realized how powerful design was to bringing products to life. During college, every class project needed something designed. Local bands needed posters and album artwork. Friends needed simple websites. So, despite the fact that I wasn't in the art department at my school, I had access to the tools (computers and software) for creating products and began my journey there, self-taught.

It was easy to get freelance work as a designer. It seemed like everyone needed a graphic or web designer, and so I did what I could to pay my way through college doing something I loved. One year, I worked part-time doing web design for a small record label. In my senior year, I was working full time at an electronic payment services company as the "Marketing Coordinator," although most of my time was spent designing print ads and the company website. By the time I graduated, I had a decent portfolio of design work and was ready to take on the world.

I know it sounds crazy, but I really enjoy interviewing for jobs. I applied for just about anything and I said yes to every interview. It was a low-risk opportunity to practice talking about my work. Sometimes, I would go to interviews for jobs that I knew I didn't want. Why? I enjoyed learning how to talk to people in those kinds of meetings and built up a vocabulary for discussing design with others. Once, I actually negotiated a salary for a web design job that I had no intention of accepting, simply because I wanted to see if I could get the manager to offer me a higher salary. He didn't (in fact, he laughed at me), but it was exciting for me to push those boundaries and see just how skillful I could be at convincing him that I was worth it.

More than anything, I loved to talk with people about my work. I loved watching people look through my portfolio, comment on what they liked, or ask me questions about why I did what I did. I got a rush from telling other people about my design decisions back then; I still do today. I love to talk about design.

After graduation, I was asked to interview for a job as the creative manager at an electronic payment services provider, the same industry I had worked in earlier. The role required me to lead the "design department," although at that time there was only one full-time web designer and a handful of freelance contractors. It was a dream job for a college graduate and of course I accepted the interview if for no other reason than curiosity. If nothing else, it would be great to show someone my work and talk about design.

I passed the first interview with someone from HR who wouldn't really know whether I was qualified or not. She was just a gatekeeper. I passed the technical interview because I knew how to use design software and could easily show my skills. I passed the third interview with the director of marketing because she liked my portfolio and I was good at talking about it. So far so good! By this point, I had a lot of confidence. There I was: fresh out of college, interviewing for a manager role at a decent-sized company, doing the thing that I loved so much. I probably thought I knew a lot about design.

My last interview was with the vice president of marketing. She was a short woman who wore her hair in a bun. She had come from Proctor & Gamble and had a reputation for doing some great work. Her style was terse and to the point. She was smart and quick to reply. This woman did not mess around. In fact, you probably didn't want to mess with her at all. It was a little intimidating, but having passed all the other tests, I thought I had nothing to fear.

She quizzed me on my portfolio, which I easily defended. She asked me about my past experience and ran through my resume, which I gladly bragged about. But then she got down to the point. She made a transition from interviewer to client and asked me the most memorable question of my career: "Let's say I have a new project for you. What's the first thing you would ask me about it?"

Having done freelance work and been on plenty of projects at my other jobs, it was an easy answer. How many times had I been in a similar situation with my other clients? I only had limited experience, but this was perhaps the most common meeting for a designer: the meeting with a stakeholder. Without hesitating, I began what felt like was a tried-and-true approach to all my previous work: "Is this a print piece or a website? Will there be color or no? Will we use stock photography or original? How many pages would the website or brochure have? And, finally, what is your timeline? When do you need it done?"

"You're wrong," she said. "None of that really matters. The most important thing you could ask me...the very first thing you should always ask is, 'What are we trying to communicate?'"

I was stumped. Silent. Not only did I know that she was right, but she had exposed my superficial design ego in a way that made me feel small and completely clueless about the thing that I was most confident in— my ability to talk about design.

The good news is I got that job, and I've had many other jobs since then, but I never forgot that mistake. I was not astute enough to recognize that my stakeholder had a different agenda than my own. I failed to understand what she needed or to address her concerns. To her, the project was about communication. To me, it was only about pixels. In that moment, I realized that my ability to talk to other people about design went far beyond my own ambitions. I had to take into consideration the needs of my audience. My designs had to *do* something for the client. They had to solve a problem. And if I couldn't communicate that, I was bound to be wrong again. For me to be successful as a designer, I had to figure out how to communicate to my clients what my designs did. I had to answer their questions in a way that made sense to them, not me. I had to express to them the rationale behind a design using words that would appeal to them and meet their needs.

If I could do that, I thought, I would be successful.

UX Is Still Young

To understand the problems we face when communicating to stakeholders, it's important to take a quick look back at how we got here in the first place. We haven't always been called "user experience designers," whatever that means. It's a new term that has evolved in meaning over the past decade and continues to evolve even now. I won't address the differences between UX, UXD, UI, IA, IxD, or any other niche player in the product development life cycle. It's my opinion that these designations are a luxury that, although valuable, have potential to confuse people with unnecessary complexity. The point is this: user experience design is a relatively new thing and we're all continually adjusting to the changing attitudes and approaches to creating great stuff. It's all design. When it comes to titles, no one really knows what they're talking about. Right or wrong, we're all just making stuff up and calling it "UX" along the way. Of course, this wouldn't be a big deal if we designers were the only ones involved, but we're not. Our stakeholders are equally confused by the terminology, and it's not their fault.

IT'S A NEW WORD

As far as I can tell, the term "user experience design" emerged in the 90s as a branch of human-computer interaction (HCI), information architecture (IA) and other software-design disciplines revolving around the practice of usability. The term itself is frequently credited to Don Norman.[1] Although the ideas and influences for UX have been around since the 1950s in Henry Dreyfuss' "Designing for People,"[2] it was not until Apple released the first iPod and then the first iPhone in 2007[3] that the term came into widespread use as the role of a designer who is creating the entire end-to-end experience using a user-centered design philosophy.

Since then, jobs for UX have been growing at astounding rates. From 2008 to 2013, the number of job titles including "UX" on LinkedIn jumped from only 159 to 3,509, growing by a factor of 22 in just 5 years.[4] ComputerWorld says that recruiters specializing in digital products are seeing a similar trend, reporting massive increases in the demand for

1   Gube, Jacob. "What Is User Experience Design? OVerview, Tools and Resources," *Smashing Magazine. http://bit.ly/1JfB6As*

2   Dreyfuss, Henry. *Designing for People.* Allworth Press; illustrated edition, 2003. ISBN 1-58115-312-0

3   Quora. "How long has the term and topic UX been around?" *http://bit.ly/1JfB63B*

4   LinkedIn. "10 Hot Job Titles that Barely Existed 5 Years Ago." *http://bit.ly/1JfB4Zt*

UX Designers.[5] UX Designer is one of the top jobs projected for growth through 2020.[6] Through a series of market changes driven by rapidly evolving technology, user experience design seems to have come out of nowhere leaving both designers and stakeholders scratching their heads about the best ways of working together.

Schools are responding to the changing demand for designers by offering courses in information architecture, interface design, and usability testing techniques, and rightly so. But, the majority of people working in UX today didn't come from a school that specialized in the field nor did we take a class to teach us a user-centered approach. We migrated into UX from other areas within the company: marketing, IT, design, research. Even human behaviorists and psychologists are finding their relevance in the explosive field called UX.

IT'S A NEW ROLE

In my experience, a typical UX designer's story might sound like this: "I went to art school and started working as a graphic designer making marketing materials—brochures, print ads, and logos. Eventually, I started making websites, too. I even learned how to write some HTML and CSS. Soon, I found myself designing more websites and apps than anything else. Now I'm a UX designer."

You might have entered UX from the development side with a highly technical engineering background. Maybe you didn't go to art school, but started in business or psychology. Whatever your path, a lot of us UXers have similar stories. Most of us didn't start out in UX, because UX didn't exist.

By the time "Web 2.0" was popularized, designers had their first real opportunity to create applications instead of just brochure websites. The functionality and interaction that was once limited to desktop software was now possible and more easily available in the browser and to a much wider population of digital designers. With the advent of the iPhone, more companies began demanding better experiences and, in fact, needed experiences specifically tailored to these new devices.

---

5   Baldwin, Howard. "Tech hotshots: The rise of the UX expert," *ComputerWorld*. *http://bit.ly/1JfBcbk*

6   Lazaro, Helena. "Looking for a New Career? Here Are the 3 Most Promising Careers of 2020," General Assembly. *http://ga.co/1JfBaAi*

Thanks to Apple, everyone began expecting everything to be well-designed. Suddenly, the demand for designers who knew how to create great experiences exploded. As design-centric social media skyrocketed, too, designers were able to create just about any interface they could think of and share it with the world. It was the democratization of design tools coupled with a free platform for sharing ideas. Almost overnight, the web designer had been transformed into a cacophony of acronyms that almost all boil down to creating the user experience.

IT'S A NEW TEAM

The awkwardness of UX's adolescence could not be any clearer than it is in our relationships and interactions with developers.

Depending on the business, the website may have been born in the IT department. The engineering-types helped to build, support, and maintain it. They've been on a similar journey. Originally, the website was just *a* thing, but now the website has become *the* thing. Previously, the website didn't need to connect to the backend, but now the website is the *primary* interface for the backend; the system was rarely exposed to the general public, now exposing the system to the public is a given.

The good news is that developers are used to helping the business solve problems with technology. They're the ones who help the help desk. They know what the common complaints are among users. They maintain the backlog of issues and bugs that need to be fixed. Do users not understand that they need to create a complex password with a combination of characters and numbers? Just add messaging that lists all the password requirements. Developers have been solving these problems far longer than designers.

The difference is that the interface they used previously for solving these problems never mattered much. As long as you could teach someone how to use it, it was good enough. We didn't need effective design, we needed documentation and training. The answer to a design problem was to educate the user. If we can help users understand the system, then they will know how to use it.

Over time, developers, too, have come to see the value of creating a great user experience. They understand that better design can result in a better application, both for them to build and for the business. They're on board to help us create the best possible experience, but they probably have different ideas about how to do it.

There is an entire ecosystem of custom-built applications with terrible interfaces that companies must support with an army of developers and training staff. Designers are now being asked to redesign these applications, work with the developers entrenched in legacy systems, and create a better product. Everyone wants it, but getting there isn't easy.

IT'S A NEW CHALLENGE

We have a design industry full of people with backgrounds that are vastly different than their current job titles. Artists, researchers, and recovering marketers are all doing the best they can in this changing scenery. The graphic or web designer as we knew it has been almost completely replaced by "UX."

Now, companies are adjusting to their changing needs in a highly competitive marketplace because great design is the expected norm. For a lot of corporate history, design was just a utility. We used to only hire designers to make our stuff look more professional, to be sure the brand was consistent, or to communicate a creative idea. Now, we hire designers because there are difficult problems that must be solved in order for our products to be successful in the marketplace. Designers today are at the center of the product development cycle in a way that previously was not thought to be necessary. More people in the organization than ever before see the value in designing a great user experience. Sometimes, that's the only way to differentiate yourself in a crowded market, and it makes an impact on your bottom line.

What happens when you take an industry full of creative, right-brained thinkers and thrust them into the middle of a product cycle with usability problems and business goals? Well, it's no surprise that there is a disconnect between what the other stakeholders want to do and what the designer has so carefully crafted.

This book sits at the intersection of the growing UX design industry and the digital product business, where designers transitioning from making pretty pictures to creating great user experiences meet with developers, managers, and executives whose agenda and perspective may, at times, be at odds. The growth of the UX designer has changed our role in so many ways, none more so than the need to explain ourselves to other people who don't share our experience in design.

Design Is Subjective…Sort of

When I interview designers, I always ask them, "What makes a good design good?" Most of the answers are predictable, and some of them are sort of right, but they all tend to sound something like this: "a good use of space," "simplicity," or one of my favorites, "when you can't remove anything else." Those are good things and they express how a lot of people approach design, but they aren't truly what make a design good in the eyes of a business. They all speak to subjectivity—to an aesthetic that not everyone will agree on.

I'm not exactly sure where these designers come up with definitions that sound like something straight out of a Jonathan Ive memoir. I don't think they learned it in art school. What concerns me is that I think they picked these catch phrases up from a social-media design phenomenon where "UX" means "something that looks as cool as an iPhone." They've adopted it from a Dribbble[7] mentality that suggests pretty things are the same as usability. It's the same culture that causes well-intentioned designers to create a "redesign" mockup of any popular website or app without any clue as to what that business' needs are. It's less about solving problems and more about popularity.

The truth is, all design is subjective. What one person likes, another person hates. What seems obvious to me might not be obvious to you. What works in one context could fail miserably in another. This is why design is such a difficult thing to talk about, especially with people who aren't designers. There is little common understanding of what design is or should be.

UX has come a long way in this regard. People understand that our decisions need to be founded in some sort of explainable logic. We are much better at using research to support our ideas so that we remove some of the subjectivity from the equation. That's a good shift, but even research can be biased, unintentionally flawed, or otherwise inconclusive. This adds complexity to the challenge of talking about design and UX.

---

7 Dribbble is a social media site for sharing designs (*http://dribbble.com*).

Businesses Don't Critique

One of the valuable things about art school is learning to critique someone else's work and to receive critique from others. When everything is subjective, it's healthy to analyze one's work in an environment where everyone is on the same intellectual page, as far as the subject goes. It's beneficial for two people who share the same vocabulary to discuss their work and make each other better. This is a great skill for every designer to have, and it will go a long way toward helping you be articulate with stakeholders.

The shortcoming of the critique in business is that it doesn't always help us address the needs of the business with our design solutions. With a fine art critique, invoking dialog is the goal. Two people can disagree and go their separate ways. "I see your point about how the red swaths in this landscape are reminiscent of the Dedocian period, but they're actually intended to communicate the flushed faces of the people through Theochronic symbolism." End of story. No more discussion. Agree to disagree. Even in schools that bring in volunteer "clients" or design imaginary products, the problems being solved have no real long-term effect. But, when the user experience of a company's product is in question, millions of dollars in revenue could be on the line. We can't simply go our separate ways. We have to find a way to talk about it and arrive at a final decision.

Further, when two designers are critiquing each other's work, they are using a shared background and vocabulary that helps them to communicate. However, it's not like that when you're talking about design to stakeholders. Designers will discuss which UI control is right for this context. They'll debate button styles. They compare their mockups to the user flows that were defined at the beginning of the project. We talk a lot about designs: the use, the form, the function, and we fundamentally understand how to solve our company's problems with design but we lack the ability to explain that understanding to people who don't share our background in design. We have yet to truly master the art of explaining these things to nondesigners.

So, even though it's valuable and necessary for teams to push one another on their work, it's not what will ultimately make a difference in the final decision for our project. It's just family chatter, an internal conversation for an in-group of designer-types. It's not at all the same as talking to someone who doesn't have the same level of interest in design. It's not necessarily the right way to talk to a nondesigner.

Ego and Intuition

In some ways, there is an arrogance that prevents us from being truly productive with people outside of our own peers. We don't always see the other stakeholders on our project as knowing anything valuable about design. We don't trust their instincts the way we trust our own. After all, we're the experts. We were hired to design things because that's what we're good at doing. Why should managers care? Can't they just trust us to do our jobs?

Designers make a lot of decisions based purely on intuition. In fact, our intuition is really good at solving design problems in an elegant and simple way. We're wired to think visually, to organize elements logically for the user, and to pay careful attention to the details. The problem is that because design is subjective and because we don't always understand how our intuition connects to the problem at hand, we're unable to adequately tell other people why we did what we did, and that's one of our biggest failures.

It's as if our brains go on autopilot when it comes to making design decisions. It's muscle memory. A dancer might have a difficult time describing how she moves because she has done it so much that she just knows how to do it. She doesn't think about it, she just does it. Likewise, we tend to create things that we just know to be the right solution; perhaps it is our preference, maybe it's based on experience, or maybe it was unconsciously picked up from observing users. Whatever the reason, when someone is good at what they do, they have a hard time telling people why they did what they did. They don't think; they just do.

To make matters worse, we may be the only people in the room without a specific, articulated justification for our choices. Developers make choices based on what's possible or how to maximize their time and code. Executives want to do what is going to make the company the most money, and so they propose things that they think will accomplish that. Marketing wants you to make changes so that everything is consistent and on-brand. But, unless you're prepared to defend your decisions intelligently, the only thing you can say is that you disagree. That degree of subjectivity has to change.

A Shift Toward Products

A designer, a developer, and a CEO walk into a bar—three different bars, on opposite sides of town. The designer orders a pale ale with an oaky flavor and a hint of citrus. The developer asks for his favorite beer on tap. The CEO goes for the day's special but without too much foam, in a cold-frosted mug, and with a glass of water.

They all drink the same beer.

ATTITUDES HAVE CHANGED

To understand how designers fit into corporate culture, we need to understand the changing shift and attitudes toward design as something more than just an aesthetic. When our job was to make the company look good, it didn't matter as much who got their way on the final design. Now that we're solving problems that affect the bottom line, everyone has an opinion on the best way to solve it.

When the web took over everything, organizations, large and small, were on a much more level playing field in terms of reaching their audience. Everyone wanted and needed a website, designers hurried to meet the need, learned basic skills, and began pumping out websites to meet demand. For the first time, the world of HCI and interface design that started in the tech companies of Silicon Valley was available to a much wider group of creators who had no idea what they were doing. That's how the majority of the web was built.

THE WEB HAS CHANGED

All organizations embraced the web because it was an inexpensive mass medium, first, for communicating your message, then for selling your product, and now for actually being the product itself. This evolution caused a shift in how organizations think about design.

When designers were only communicating messages, companies didn't need to micromanage a design process that was just meant to make the company look good. Executives were typically happy if the website didn't look like crap, or at least that it looked better than their competitors. But for the most part, design was this other thing, over there, off in the corner. It was nice to have, we liked it, but we didn't need to get involved much.

As the web shifted and made it possible for us to sell our products, the focus was still on aesthetic with the addition of utility. As long as the website worked, management didn't need to care too much about the details. Something just needed to exist and get the job done. "We need filters. Those are the filters there? Great! We need an 'Add to Cart' button somewhere—I don't care what the color is; what difference does that make?" And in this world, as long as the stakeholders knew where to find the thing they thought was important, that was all that mattered. We might even set goals for the website or hire a salesperson to monitor and grow our "eBusiness," but it was less about strong opinions and more about getting the job done.

In the past 10 years, there has been a dramatic shift in attitudes toward what the web and web-like interfaces (like native mobile apps) represent. You know the story about the explosive growth of social media, the proliferation of native and web apps, and the proclivity of people to carry these things around in their pockets to be constantly engaged, consuming whatever the next thing is. Researchers believe web revenue will continue to climb as a percentage of overall retail,[8] and that as much as 60 percent of all retail transactions will involve the web in some way in coming years.[9] Mobile revenue has crossed the 50 percent mark for many of the largest companies,[10] what Luke Wroblewski calls their "mobile moment."[11] The most successful business stories nowadays are of companies who created a product that was focused on the design.[12] Heck, there is even a movie[13] and book[14] about how design is changing the business world! Great design has taken center stage as an asset, a competitive advantage, and a must-have in order to survive in the market.

8   Enright, Allison. "U.S. online retail sales will grow 57% by 2018," *Internet Retailer*. *http://bit.ly/1JfBbEj*

9   Dusto, Amy. "60% of U.S. retail sales will involve the web by 2017," *Internet Retailer*. *http://bit.ly/1fwVX2r*

10   "Mobile now over 50% of Facebook ad revenue, crosses $1B," *Vator News*. *http://bit.ly/1JfBizL*

11   Wroblewski, Luke. "The Mobile Moment," LukeW blog. *http://www.lukew.com/ff/entry.asp?1841*

12   "Design Is Changing How We Innovate," FastCo Design. *http://bit.ly/1JfBkrv*; "Design as business change agent," Designers DNA. *http://bit.ly/1JfBlLO*

13   *Design the New Business* (*http://www.designthenewbusiness.com*)

14   Brown, Tim. *Change by Design*. Harper Collins, 2009.

BUSINESSES HAVE CHANGED

Closely aligned with the growth of the web to serve products and experiences is a new business approach in which entire organizations arrange themselves to value design and make it a part of their core culture. As startups and big corporation CEOs are beginning to value design, we see an organizational model that makes it possible for businesses to really hone in on and make product design their primary strength. To complicate matters, businesses are quick to adopt buzzwords, especially those that seem to help them solve a problem they see in their organization. An executive might read an article about a successful business that has a design-centered product approach. The quote from the "user experience designer" is the tipping point. Maybe that's what he needs! His web designer now has a new title. This is why UX continues to be misunderstood, even by the designers doing the work. Businesses are changing to adapt to this new reality, but none talk about UX in the same way.

As a result, you have designers who started out somewhere else, creating stuff that was mostly focused on the look and feel. And then you have managers and executives who cared more about the utility and function of their thing—but more and more these two primary players are moving toward each other in a way that has incredible potential to change their organizations for the better. Executives now realize just how important design is, and they want to influence the process because their business is on the line. Likewise, designers have come to understand the value of creating an experience that is based on solving problems and backed up by research. And the two meet in the middle, in a meeting.

That's where we find ourselves today. In a meeting with people who have no idea how to do our jobs, yet consistently find it their place to tell us how to do it. It's enough to drive any designer insane.

Digital Experiences Are Real Life

The organizational transition to understanding and valuing the UX of digital products is maturing. From these original attitudes and approaches to design comes a mutual understanding that a great user experience will create a great product. A great product will sell, be easier to support and maintain, and be good for the bottom line. These historical attitudes—the stereotypical personality types that create these roles in the organization—all come together for a single purpose: to create the best possible products. The way that we now realize we can create the best possible products is through design. The problem is that only one of these players is a designer.

But why does this matter? If we are the experts, why should we have to justify our decisions to nondesigners? The reason is that UX has gone "mainstream," in the organization and even within pop culture. The most popular and interesting companies have put design at the forefront of their product offering, creating a buzz culture that drools over every new release and a fan following that promotes their brand for them. I'm not only thinking of Apple, but also brands such as IKEA, innovators like Tesla, and unique problem-solving designs from Dyson, Segway, or Nest. These brands command respect, elicit strong opinions, and foster loyalty from the people who follow them.

SOCIAL MEDIA HAS CHANGED HOW PEOPLE VIEW DIGITAL PRODUCTS

It's not only physical products that have transformed our understanding of the value of UX within the organization. Regular "websites" have proven that UX is a critical component to a company's success. Millions of people use Facebook every single day. Each minor tweak to the UI or change to the design incurs the praise or wrath of every user. Why? Because Facebook (and other services like it) is a very personal part of our lives. Never before have we had a platform for sharing the most intimate and mundane details of our everyday lives. For many, social media is their window into the world. It is the lens they use to connect and communicate with their friends and family. It's a powerful social engine that frames every modern conversation. And so it's no surprise that the details of how the interface works elicits strong reactions from people who perceive it almost as an intrusion into the way they live their lives. For the first time, people who previously barely noticed the design of their favorite website now are obsessed with the smallest interface details of other apps. They notice them, they touch them, they interact with them, and those elements become part of their lives. Changing those things means changing the way people interact with the world. This is why so many people have an opinion about your work.

POLITICS HAS CHANGED HOW PEOPLE VIEW DIGITAL PRODUCTS

Also notable was the reaction to the failures of the 2013 launch of the *healthcare.gov* site in the United States. Usability was a core factor in the demise of that initial launch. But why did that matter to people? If the website "worked," why did it matter if it worked well? For the same reasons as social media, the healthcare website was an intensely personal, deeply intrusive interface that threatened to change the way people lived their lives. I might argue that even the best UX might have still resulted in failure if for no other reason than the sociological implications that a "designed system" was representative of the massive changes facing the American people. An interface was responsible for people's private healthcare. Changing the way people managed their healthcare meant changing their perception of their health. But the point is this: the president of the United States was talking about usability in public forums to a mass audience![15] It's no wonder that UX has become a central focus of many organizations.

To take it a step further, we don't have to look far to see how digital products have fueled uprisings and revolutions in places such as Syria, Turkey, Egypt, and even Ferguson, Missouri in the United States. In these situations, the use of digital products became the voice of the people and upset the political balance. An interface designed by someone in a meeting with stakeholders became a tool for empowering an entire population toward revolution. *This* is why so many people have an opinion about your work.

PERSONAL DEVICES HAVE CHANGED HOW PEOPLE VIEW DIGITAL PRODUCTS

Perhaps the biggest factor, though, in the explosive growth of UX as a discipline is the personalization and shrinking of the devices we use to interact with the world on a daily basis. Sitting at a computer is not a terribly personal experience. It is a separate device at arm's length, with physical controls that one must learn to manipulate. The input methods are indirect: what I do down there with the mouse changes what I see up here on the display. And at the end of the day, I have to

---

15 McCalmont, Lucy, "10 top Obama quotes: Healthcare.gov," Politico. *http://politi.co/1iv7mZQ*

put my computer away and move on with my life. Something as simple as looking up the weather on a computer must be done purposefully and intentionally.

As mobile phone growth turned powerful smartphones into touch-screen super phones, our ability to interact with products and services on a regular basis shifted from being an intentional, arm's-length, conscious choice to an automatic muscle-memory involuntary jerk of the wrist. Like social media, our devices are intensely personal and are becoming more intimate. Our interface with the world is no longer the machine at arm's length. It's the touchable glossy display that we always have with us. Always on, always connected, always shaping the way we see our world. As a result, universal understanding of the importance of UX has grown, too. Every software update introduces new ideas and elicits strong opinions from every user. *This is why* so many people have an opinion about your work.

STARTUP CULTURE HAS CHANGED HOW PEOPLE VIEW DIGITAL PRODUCTS

Today, businesses and even entire industries are built around the "disruption" of creating a better user experience. The way that you succeed in business is to find an existing category and then tweak the user experience to the *n*th degree. It's not necessarily about being original, but about being the best—and design is usually the great differentiator.

The most prominent example I can think of is Uber. The entire business is built on creating a better end-to-end experience for taking a cab. A simple task with incredible implications for improving the user experience, Uber did what any good "disrupter" should do: it looked at the process of taking a cab, broke it down, and solved all the problems with better design. No one likes standing on the street and waving their arms? Fixed. Actually, no one likes waiting out in the rain either. Fine, stay inside. Cabs aren't clean or reliable? Uber guarantees that they are. Payment and tipping annoying? They fixed it. Want to provide feedback? It's baked in. The entire process of getting a cab has been upended by one company that looked at the problem and found design solutions to everything. *This is why so many people have an opinion about your work.*

THIS IS WHY SO MANY PEOPLE HAVE AN OPINION ABOUT YOUR WORK

Our entire culture has shifted its thinking about design, specifically the design of interfaces, devices, services, and products. Everyone has a personal device now, and they are only getting more personal. The *Internet of Things* will continue to push UX into (and onto) our faces at every turn. Everyone has apps they use, love, and hate. The people in your meetings are probably participating in another user experience while at the same time reviewing and considering your own. It's no wonder that everyone everywhere at every level of the organization is intensely interested in and has an opinion about the UX that you are trying to create. How are you going to deal with it?

As a result, more people than ever before are interested and involved in the design of your product. What was once relegated to the "Oh, that's nice" category of insignificance is now the center of everyone's attention. People from all over the organization see the value of creating a great user experience and they all want to participate in the process. Marketing, executives, developers, customer service, even people in accounting will want to tell you how they think it should work. People are excited about UX because they recognize the long-term effect it has on the product, the business, and the bottom line. The good news? You're a very popular person!

Great Designers Are Great Communicators

Words: so innocent and powerless as they are standing in a dictionary, how potent for good and evil they become in the hands of one who knows how to combine them.

NATHANIEL HAWTHORNE

TRYING TO NAVIGATE THIS new reality that designers are at the forefront of the digital product business can be a real challenge. We creative thinkers are now thrust into the middle of a process with business people, expected to be the experts on design, and then asked to tell everyone else what we think should be done. Like a fish out of water, we struggle to breathe. To make this mental shift and be effective in our new role, it's critical that we understand just how important good communication is to design.

Too Many Cooks

Designing in this new reality called UX would all go really well if it weren't for the fact that other people on the project might disagree with our decisions. Actually, they will!

There are now a lot of people who may know little or nothing about design, yet who have the authority to oversee and dictate our design practice. They have a vested interest in participating in the conversation, but they aren't trained designers and they don't have the same depth of knowledge in design or technology that we do. What used to be a somewhat obscure conversation between graphic artists is now open and available to many other players in the business.

What's more, these people will often gladly admit that they aren't the experts. They know that they don't know, yet they still insist their ideas and opinions are right. This is one of the most bizarre parts of our relationship with stakeholders. People who have influence over our project readily admit they are not good at our jobs, yet insist on making changes that we believe will be detrimental to the user experience. They say that they trust us and yet frequently overrule us. It can be incredibly demeaning and confusing, but the problem may not lie entirely with them.

These stakeholders have to be part of our process, but we struggle with including them in a way that's helpful and doesn't derail our objectives. This is what we need to figure out.

Everyone Is a Designer!

Everyone knows good design when they see it, even if they don't know how to create it. That sounds frustrating (even ridiculous), but it's actually true. The same can be said for other arts, such as music. I may not know how to play an instrument, but I can recognize a pleasing tune. I can decide what music I like (and don't like) even if I can't tell you how to create it. Although there may be different preferences, we're all able to choose music we want to listen to, regardless of whether we know how to reproduce those sounds ourselves.

The phenomenon that a nonexpert can have an opinion about your design work is something that is almost entirely unique to design within today's organizations. Accounting practices are fairly standard, and few employees would complain about how money is tracked as long as it is being tracked—that is, unless it ever affects them personally, as in their paychecks: the way they're paid or the details on their pay stub. In accounting, the paycheck is the user interface for most people in the organization.

The same could be said for development. Few people look at the code except the developers, right? No one cares what the programmers are doing unless it actually affects them. For example, if the performance of a network, website, or computer were so slow as to render it unusable, suddenly everyone will have an opinion: we should make it faster. Yet, the details of how to accomplish that are obscured to the end user; the only part we "see" is the speed. That is the main interface for development.

If engineers were treated like designers

Andy Zelman, Skeleton Claw Comics. (Used with permission: *http://skeletonclaw.com*)

The Interface Is Your Interface

No passion in the world is equal to the passion to alter someone else's draft.

HG WELLS

Similarly with design, people only care about the part that affects them. They care about the interface. However, when you're in the business of doing nothing but creating the user interface, everyone is going to care about everything that you do! All of your work is exposed, so it naturally conjures more opinions and ideas than many other areas in the organization. More than that, your work is now becoming the interface of the entire company like never before. Not surprisingly, the people who run the business have strong opinions about how your work reflects on them. Few people will tell you how to create those interfaces. The process or tools you use to create the designs are obscured to them. Unlike accounting or development, though, the vast majority of your work is exposed to every stakeholder.

It's a strange feeling: what could be more rewarding than to know that our work and expertise is so highly valued that so many people want to be a part of it? Design is being held up on a pedestal! Finally getting the recognition it deserves! We knew that we could solve real business problems and make our mark in the world. It's what we've always wanted, right? Maybe, but be careful what you wish for! If we want our work to be the center of attention, we must also take responsibility for showing people how and why our work is valued. That part doesn't come automatically. It takes work, it takes practice, but more importantly...it takes good communication.

Tom Chi & Kevin Cheng, OK/Cancel (Used with permission: *http://bit.ly/1Nkl7pl*)

There Is No U or X in Team

Collaboration seems like it should be the pinnacle of great design work: different opinions coming together to form the best possible solution. That's what everyone really wants. The image is of a handful of respectful intellectuals, passionately debating the right solutions, ultimately leading to a collaborative discussion and an ideal design that no one could have thought of on their own. Teamwork at its best! Everyone leaves satisfied, fulfilled, and respected—ready to take on the next design challenge, right? We think we want that kind of collaboration, but it becomes far more complicated when we disagree with one another. When we disagree, we tend to become defensive. When we become defensive, we fail to focus on the real issues. The meeting ends, not with collaboration, but with grumbling compromise and, often, a crippled user experience.

In situations like this, meetings can easily turn into design-by-committee. Everyone has a suggestion for how to solve a problem. We hear different opinions on every side and are unable to defend our own choices against this barrage of feedback. One suggestion evolves into an idea for something else. That idea spurs a thought about something different. Unchecked, the conversation can spiral out of control into a hodge-podge of well-intentioned tweaks that collectively spell doom for the overall goals of the project. The thing we came together to accomplish has been muddied by group think and mob mentality. Remember, teamwork always ends with work.

THE CEO BUTTON

Because of this, we see things like the *CEO button*.

> The CEO button is an unusual or otherwise unexpected request from an executive to add a feature that completely destroys the balance of a project and undermines the very purpose of a designer's existence.

It's funny because it's true. You might spend weeks or months building the best possible app. Your team has poured in all the best practices that you learned at that one conference. You've done usability testing to prove it works. Your mom was even able to use it without incident! And yet, one executive can come in and blow up the whole thing. We want to avoid this.

HOME PAGE SYNDROME

Another common problem is the *home page syndrome.*

> The home page syndrome is a condition whereby the home screen of an application or website becomes a catchall for everything, creating a garage sale of links, buttons, and banner ads that unravels the fabric of usability, causing designers to cry themselves to sleep.

You see, sometimes no matter how hard we try, the home page just becomes a huge mess. Everyone wants their business unit represented on the home page. It's as if something doesn't exist if it isn't on the home page. That new thing we're launching? Put it on the home page. And that other thing that isn't performing well? Maybe if we put it on the home page, it will get better. Sound familiar? We have to learn to deal with this phenomenon.

Communication Matters

The good news is that it doesn't have to be this way. It's possible to avoid the disruption and compromise that happens so frequently in organizational design through better communication with our stakeholders. I've found that the majority of issues or concerns that our stakeholders bring to our attention are often just a matter of misunderstanding or miscommunication. The way that we talk to them about our designs is the key to ensuring that we always end up with the best possible user experience.

It makes sense when you think about it. All human relationships are really nothing more than a series of bound-up understandings and *mis*understandings. We don't always have control over how other people understand us in the beginning. Everyone brings their past experiences into conversations we have with them on a daily basis. We do, however, have control over how we communicate with them in order to influence those future understandings. The way that we talk to people and the things we say will influence the future.

WORDS ARE POWERFUL

This makes our words really powerful. Throughout human history, words have had significant power to change people, circumstances, and entire systems of government. Words can spark wars, end relationships, and damage emotions. Conversely, words can also be used to build people up, change minds, and reinforce positive connections. Saying something out loud can make it real. So real, in fact, that you can make things happen simply by talking about them.

Our words have a profound effect on the people around us. As a parent, I have to be careful about how I talk to my kids because the things that I say to them are the things that they will grow up to believe, whether what I say is even true. If I am constantly berating my kids over their behavior, they will believe bad behavior is just part of who they are. If I tell my kids they're stupid, they could grow up believing that they shouldn't even try to learn. The things I say to my kids will shape their understanding of themselves and their perception of the world around them. You might think it's just impressionable children who don't know better, but all people are just as easily impacted by our words. In life, there are no adults, only more experienced children.

For decades, eyewitness testimony has been called into question because of how easily it can be influenced. Police have to be careful about what they say because a witness's perception of what happened is so greatly influenced by what they hear. A witness's memory can actually be changed by the way he or she is questioned. It's well documented that memories can be altered under interrogation by police.[1] The truth is not necessarily what actually happened, but what we think happened. We can use words not only to express ourselves and make our opinions known, but also to speak into the reality of other people. Our words can actually alter people's perception of the situation.

GOOD COMMUNICATORS WIN
Overall, being a better communicator will give you more opportunities. I'm amazed (and offended) at the number of designers who apply for a job yet lack basic communication skills. People will send me a resume without explanation, forget about interviews, or fail to follow instructions. Ultimately, I'm only going to pursue candidates who can communicate well, and so the poor communicators are passed over very quickly.

---

1 Loftus, Elizabeth. *Eyewitness Testimony*. Harvard University Press, 1996.

It's common for my clients to express that one of the reasons they hired me was because it's so hard to find people who are reliable and can communicate effectively. I've heard many stories about former contractors who simply couldn't pull it together enough to set expectations, follow instructions, or clearly articulate their work. The need to work with other people on the project, particularly developers and managers, is quite often the thing that sets me apart from other designers. When one of my clients went on vacation, he asked me to help run his business while he was gone because he knew he could trust me to represent him well. A contractor with good communication skills was more trusted than his own employees! I get more work simply because I can communicate effectively.

If you've ever hired an overseas contractor, you know how difficult it is to find quality people. They can be really inexpensive, but it's questionable whether you can justify the cost savings when it comes to quality and communication. The biggest barrier is usually communication. I have to spend an inordinate amount of time writing everything down, detailing requirements, and going over it with them multiple times before they finally understand what I need. The mistakes are almost always the result of a miscommunication. It's not that they're unintelligent; it's that there's a gap in communication. It's much easier to have a miscommunication when you don't speak the same language. Still, even in this situation, the overseas contractors with better communication skills (and better English-language proficiency) are far more likely to be chosen for work for the simple matter that they will be easier to work with because of those skills.

No matter what sort of design work you're looking for, it will be easier if you're a good communicator. Strangely enough, being a good communicator may be all it takes to set yourself apart from other designers— even designers who might be more artistically talented than you. Very simply: good communicators win.

Being Articulate Means Success

It's more than just communication; we have to turn those words into something that will enact change or compel people to agree with us. It's not just about using words with a frequency or persistence; it's about using them in a way that is compelling and convincing. It's about being articulate.

Being articulate can make you successful in any area of life. It can help you get almost anything you want: a job, a spouse, or a bargain. It is the ability to use your words, tone, and approach with people to communicate a specific message and elicit a specific response. The key to being articulate is to understand both the message you want to communicate and the response you want in return. If you can learn to craft your messages in such a way that they yield the desired response, you'll find that you're much more successful at getting the things that matter to you. You can apply the same ideas in your design practice.

THE BEST IDEAS (DON'T ALWAYS) WIN

In general, designers are pretty terrible at explaining themselves to nondesigners, yet when people disagree, the most articulate person usually wins. It's too altruistic to believe that the best ideas are the ones that always win. They should, perhaps, but the reality is far from that. The best ideas are stuffed into an amalgamation of meetings where competing needs vie for attention. The person who can convince the other that they're right is the one who gets his way. Your design might be revolutionary, but an aggressive and well-spoken salesperson is more likely to get his way if he can convince your boss that he's right and you're not.

Designers lacking the ability to explain why they did what they did end up on the losing side of the argument, forced to make changes they disagree with simply because they were unable to fend them off. This is not to say that the stakeholder relationship is adversarial. No, these discussions can feel very much like good, solid teamwork. But the inability to speak up and articulate your side will often land you in the position of making changes that won't yield the best results.

Alternately, being articulate about our designs:

Imparts intelligence
> You're smart, you know what you're talking about, you have expertise in this area, and you can be trusted with the solution.

Demonstrates intentionality
> You've thought about it, pursued it, and are logical in your approach. This isn't just a random idea; there is purpose and focus.

Expresses confidence

You know what you want and how to get it done. Having a solid argument shows that you're not wishy-washy and you mean what you say.

Shows respect

You value everyone's opinions and time enough that you're well prepared. You're not wasting time or disregarding others.

The way to be articulate about design is to offer a message that communicates why we did what we did in order to help stakeholders understand our rationale. We build trust with stakeholders by showing our expertise through logic and reason, not feelings and intuition. So, we need to harness the power of communication, be articulate, and use these skills to help people see that our decisions provide the best possible solution. Being articulate will help us be successful.

Becoming a Great Designer

To hone in on the best practices for articulating design decisions, let's look at what makes a design project successful, because that will form the basis for how we communicate about it. To overcome these obstacles, we need to boil down UX to its very core. We must understand the fundamentals of what makes a great experience and how we can reproduce that thinking and approach in others.

FOCUS ON THE PRODUCT, NOT THE PROCESS

Many teams are into the latest methodology: Waterfall, Agile, Lean. Whatever your flavor of project management or product development, don't let the details of process prevent you from being truly creative and making sure that your ideas get to market. Although these approaches can be incredibly useful for keeping projects on track and creating great results, we can get bogged down in the details of execution and less focused on what we're trying to achieve. This carries over into our meetings with stakeholders who may have no idea about the methodology we follow. These approaches use language that can cloud our stakeholders' ability to understand our decisions. Let's not burden them with a subculture that is unfamiliar. (Scrum master, anyone?) The truth is, it's irrelevant to the discussion of the designs. We need to think about our work differently if we want to talk about it more effectively.

THE BIG THREE

Let's return to the question that I ask every designer that I interview for a job: what makes a good design good? We could debate the answer to this question, but when it comes to creating the user experience for a web or mobile application, a design is really only good when it solves a problem. Mostly, we are trying to solve problems for the business; we're trying to accomplish some goal that will help the business grow. But, if we're also practicing a user-centered design approach, we must also make our designs easy to use for the people who will use it. Those two things together (solving a problem and making it easy for users) will help us create truly great experiences. This is what makes a good design good.

However, the one thing that we often forget is that there are other people involved who have influence over our project. It's not enough to simply create an incredible app; we also have to get the support of everyone else on our team. Without their support, our project can't see the light of day. The difference between a good designer and a great designer is the ability to not only solve the problem, but also to articulate how the design solves it in a way that is compelling and fosters agreement. If you can do that, you're a great designer.

So, I would say there are three things that every design needs to be successful:

1. It solves a problem

2. It's easy for users

3. It's supported by everyone

These are the basics of creating a great user experience that the average person (such as your stakeholders) can understand. Projects that fail are usually lacking in one of these areas. If you can do all three of these, your project will be a success.

Let's look at each one in more detail.

SOLVE THE PROBLEM

Designers involved in the practice of creating a user experience should already be accustomed to solving problems. This is, after all, the great shift that's taken place in corporate design practice in recent years. Of all the things we're trying to accomplish with our work, we have to solve problems: business goals, engagement, conversion, frequency, feedback. Whatever the problem is, our job is to find a solution and measure its success. How will we know if we've done our job? By looking at the results before and after, tracking some specific metric, and watching it improve. We may not all remember this in practice, but we're at least aware that this is (or should be) the primary focus of our jobs as UX professionals.

Hopefully you and your team have already established these goals, metrics, or key performance indicators (KPIs) for your project. If not, I recommend doing them yourself so that you have a measuring stick to use in all of your conversations. Projects without goals will surely languish because there is no way to convince someone else that you're right if you have nothing by which to measure its success. It just becomes a matter of opinions, and subjectivity will make it difficult to move forward. Therefore, if your team isn't set up to establish these in the beginning, do it now for your own sanity. Find out what the most important factors are for your stakeholders—impressions, conversion, account sign-ups—and then pick one or two measurable issues that you'd like to improve and write them down. Set this as your goal and use it to your advantage when talking to other people.

Although we're certainly adept at approaching these problems to find creative solutions, we're not always in tune with our own thought process to help other people understand why we did what we did. This is where our intuition becomes so vital and this is what makes us good designers: we know how to solve problems with design. It's often natural for us to see a solution without giving it much thought. Other times, we might wrestle with a solution through trial and error. Either way, we're making changes over time, morphing our ideas into something that will add value. In fact, what sets us apart from nondesigners is our ability to intuitively solve problems. The hard part, though, is figuring out what drives that intuition. What makes this "feel right" so that we can help other people see our perspective? How does this combination of small moves result in the right solution? The practice of solving problems with design must also be accompanied by an awareness that will help us explain our decisions to other people.

Let's take a step back to the first time you design a UI control or element for your app. You need to make yourself consciously aware of every decision you're making and why. You need to be constantly asking yourself, *"What problem am I trying to solve with this?"* Chapter 8 will list some of the most common ways I describe my own solutions, but for now just consider that you need to practice making yourself aware of all the changes you're making, all the new things you're adding, and all the rearranging that goes into finding the right interface. Those unconscious choices hold the key to explaining your designs to other people and ensuring that your expert perspective remains at the center of the final decision process.

The best way I know to practice being conscious of your decisions is to write them down. There is something about moving your unconscious thought to a tangible form that allows you to remember everything you've done. Because you have measurable problems you're trying to solve, write down the problem and then list your solutions next to it. Do whatever it takes to document your own thought process. I am a list maker, so I love to type lists and sync them across all my devices so that I can have access to them if needed. Some people prefer to put pen to paper and allow their hand to make the physical movements necessary to connect their thoughts to the real world. You can do this with simple notes or more complex sketches. Make a list on paper of your solutions or even draw a storyboard that demonstrates the before and after effect of your designs. The method you use for writing down your answers doesn't matter. The point is to get you thinking about your decisions in concrete ways.

Here are a few examples from my own work:

PROBLEM	PROPOSED SOLUTION
Users don't realize the filter controls have updated the list of results because it's instantaneous.	• Move the count of items in the list closer to the filters so that the user can see the number change. • Briefly show a loading spinner on each checkbox as the user selects it. • Add a Done button that closes the panel to give the user a sense of completing the task.
Users do not proceed to the next steps from the marketing landing page.	• Move the headline and hero image to the left to make space for the call to action on the right. • Change the color of the call to action to red; update the copy. • Remove background image, too distracting. • Position the "Next steps" list so that it will usually overlap on the fold, causing the user to want to scroll to the second CTA.

PROBLEM	PROPOSED SOLUTION
Users are not adding to their carts from the "search results" list view.	Reduce the number of actions required to add an item to the cart from search. One-Tap Add: • Tapping "Add to cart" will auto-add the item to the cart first without requiring a quantity or other information • On tap, the button changes to a quantity with an initial value of 1. User can increment quantity as needed. • Remove secondary "add to cart" confirmation button. • New messaging animates to indicate that the item was added. • "Ready to Checkout?" call to action slides in underneath messaging. • Items with options, such as color or size, will automatically select a default but provide the user with the option to change it within view.

It can also be useful to describe your designs using only words. So much of our work is purely visual that it can be difficult to understand what that "sounds like" in a world without pictures. Because our end goal is to tell other people about it, why not attempt to describe every detail in sentence form and assume that the reader doesn't have the ability to see it? How would you describe your designs to someone on the phone? Or by email? Writing down how you see your work will reveal many of your motivations, some of which you never realized were there. The purpose of this exercise is to help you uncover your thought process and articulate your decisions first to yourself. It's not intended to be a substitute for demonstrating your designs visually.

Here's an example from one of my projects:

> The list view is sorted alphabetically by country by default. The standard sort menu is available in the top right. I made each item in the list exactly the right height for a mobile touch target. On the far left of each item is that country's flag. We thought that would make them more easily identifiable to people. Next to the flag is the name of the country in bold and then a short description of the project directly underneath, in smaller gray type. A quick reference to the report title. On the far right of these controls are two things: (1) a summary of the data for the report type the users has selected. For example, it will show the percentage, like 34 percent for infection rate or the total in short form like 1.5 m. (2) A disclosure arrow to indicate that there is

> more content "to the right" if the user taps this item. The flag will make it quick for the user to find the right country and the short snippet of data will help him know if he needs to tap for a more detailed report. With this design, users should be able to quickly browse the list to find the correct report.

It doesn't need to be long, and it shouldn't be time-consuming. This isn't busywork. Do whatever it takes to help you identify your thinking. For example, if you find yourself comparing your designs to another popular platform, it's a good sign that your decision was based on solving a problem that the other platform might have already addressed. "When you tap the button, it loads the next set of results the same way that SocialApp does." It's okay to make decisions based on another app, but it doesn't always make the best case. What it will do is allow you to go through a new series of questions to get to the bottom of your thinking: Why does SocialApp do it this way? Is our context similar enough that solving the problem in the same way makes sense? Does SocialApp have any data about doing it this way? Every time you're able to describe your designs, you'll uncover a part of your thought process that can help you find the best ways to talk about it.

You do not have to share these notes with your client. They may never see them, and that's OK. For now, this is more about practicing being intentional than it is about communicating with others. The takeaway here is that the process of writing about what you create will help your brain to connect the dots between the problem you're working on and how your designs solve it. The better you are at making those connections, the better prepared you'll be to talk about them with others. Whatever works for you, the goal here is to find a way to turn your thought process into something real, sharable, and visible; to uncover the words that will help you to explain yourself to other people in a way that makes sense.

MAKE IT EASY

If we're truly taking a user-centered design approach, we absolutely must be designing interfaces that are easy for users. We may be solving business problems, but we must make it simple to use if we're going to create a great user experience. Like solving problems, this is another area where many UX practitioners do pretty well. Really, a focus on usability is the entire purpose of UX. In the same way that UX has become a focal point of the organizational product design process, so too has our own understanding of ease of use. We know that usability is the core issue to be faced with our designs, but it can be difficult to describe that to other people.

My assumption is that you already understand something about usability or you wouldn't be here in the first place. The purpose of this section is not to tell you how to make your apps easy to use (that's the topic of many other classic UX books), but rather to think about usability in a way that will help you defend, talk about, and evolve your designs to the point of a public release.

Just as you were solving problems and making yourself aware of your decisions, you must also do the same thing here. At every step of the process, for every decision you make, ask yourself, *"How does this affect the user?"* The trick to answering this question is that often we simply don't know how our decisions will affect our users. We can only make our best guess, try it out, and then draw conclusions from what we observe. Like the previous section, write it down. You need to be able to answer this question first to yourself so that you're prepared to give that answer to stakeholders.

One way that I capture how my designs affect users is to write a story that is either based on a user session I observed or loosely based on the overall use case. Here are some examples:

DESIGN CHANGES	HOW IT AFFECTS THE USER
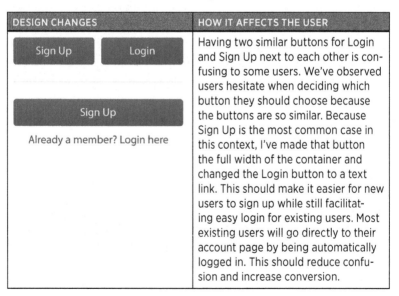	Having two similar buttons for Login and Sign Up next to each other is confusing to some users. We've observed users hesitate when deciding which button they should choose because the buttons are so similar. Because Sign Up is the most common case in this context, I've made that button the full width of the container and changed the Login button to a text link. This should make it easier for new users to sign up while still facilitating easy login for existing users. Most existing users will go directly to their account page by being automatically logged in. This should reduce confusion and increase conversion.

DESIGN CHANGES	HOW IT AFFECTS THE USER
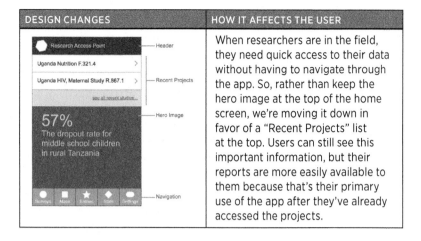	When researchers are in the field, they need quick access to their data without having to navigate through the app. So, rather than keep the hero image at the top of the home screen, we're moving it down in favor of a "Recent Projects" list at the top. Users can still see this important information, but their reports are more easily available to them because that's their primary use of the app after they've already accessed the projects.

Simplified, usability is about two things: common sense and research. When you're first beginning a project, you may not have much to work with as far as data or user observation. You really have no choice but to make your best guess about what will work for the user. As a usability expert, you have experience designing interfaces, so you're able to make informed assumptions based on what you believe will create the simplest experience. This is where common sense comes to play. There really is no reason to overthink it. Create the easiest solution you can think of. Do what makes sense and move on.

Of course, what you think makes sense and what a user does are quite often two different things. That's why we have research. After we've made some informed guesses, we need to test our ideas by using real people. We aren't doing user experience design if we haven't actually seen a user experience it. Research can take many forms, but the most common tools are either analytics or a usability study. We will talk more about this in Chapter 7, but let me say here that the challenge with analytics is that it can only tell us *what* the users did. It cannot tell us *why* they did it. The only way to actually know how your decisions affect users is to observe them. So make your best guess with the data you have, but then verify your designs with real people and make notes. You'll always be surprised by the results, and you'll be in a much better position to defend your decisions.

GET SUPPORT

It's not enough to solve problems and make our app easy to use, because if a stakeholder disagrees with our solution, we aren't going to get anywhere at all. You could have the most innovative design in the world, but if no one on your team understands what you're trying to do, you're not going to be successful at implementing it.

What happens if you don't get support? You'll constantly rehash the same conversations over and over again. When people don't remember why you did what you did (because your explanation wasn't compelling or memorable), they'll bring it up again at the next meeting. "Now, why did we agree to do this again?" When people aren't convinced that you're right, they'll continue to think of alternatives to suggest. The project scope will increase over time as people propose adding more things: a simple control, one more button, a new menu. As a result, you won't be able to move as fast as you need to because you'll be bogged down managing requests. In the end, you might have to ship a product with a compromised user experience, all because you couldn't get stakeholders on board with your solution.

Getting the support of everyone on your team is the primary focus of this book. We aren't going to be able to get anywhere unless we're able to get everyone on the same page and agree to move in the right direction. That's what getting support is all about: convincing people that the way we've solved the problem will make it easy for our users and is, therefore, the best possible choice for a great user experience. You need to create an environment where everyone understands what you're doing so that you can move on to the next thing.

To gain the support we need, we have to understand our designs by asking ourselves, *"Why is this better than the alternative?"* Implicit in this question is that we know what the alternatives are, we've considered them or even tried them, and we're prepared to explain why our solution is better.

Everything we design has another way of doing it. For each design we create, there is an alternate, often opposing, way of solving the same problem. This is the reason why we have disagreements about the solutions to begin with and a key problem with articulating design decisions. Designers can be really good at coming up with a solution for the problem, but we're less adept at coming up with *all* of the solutions to the problem. We become so myopic when we think we've found it.

Eureka! Our solution seems so obvious that there is very little need to waste time considering any other approach. (After all, we're on a tight sprint and need to get something to the client by the end of the day.) Yet, this thinking almost always creates a conversation that we're not prepared to deal with: when the client suggests an alternate idea that we haven't considered.

Ironically, we are usually cognitively aware of some of the other alternatives. We probably tried them, moved stuff around, and eventually landed on the solution we believe is best. But it's all those little movements that we failed to make ourselves consciously aware of, and so we're less prepared to help other people understand our thought process. Likewise, we often know what our clients are going suggest. If you've worked with your stakeholders before, you can make a pretty good guess about how they'll react (this is addressed at length in Chapter 4). Yet if you can guess how they'll react but you fail to consider those alternatives and understand why your solution is better, you will have a difficult time winning them over.

The point is this: be consciously aware of why your design decisions are better than the alternatives. Just like the previous two questions, write down your answers. Make a list of the other ways that you could solve this problem. Create a bunch of alternative designs, don't throw them away, and have them available if you need them. With those alternatives, make a short list of why you think they don't solve the problem as well as your proposed design. Thinking critically about these other options will help you to be prepared to discuss your decisions with other people.

Sometimes, I create very simple wireframes of the alternatives in addition to my recommendation. When the client begins asking questions about my proposed solution, I can quickly show these to visually demonstrate why my recommendation is better.

MAKE IT HAPPEN

If we're going to be successful at communicating with people about our designs, we must be able to answer these three questions about our work:

1. What problem does it solve?

2. How does it affect the user?

3. Why is it better than the alternative?

The purpose of answering these questions is more of an exercise in getting you to understand your choices than it is a prescriptive method for documenting them. Don't worry too much about the details of how you write them down. If you can answer these three questions, you'll be well on your way to defending your decisions with the people who have influence over your project. These answers will form the basis of your response to every stakeholder concern about your designs.

Your ability to be thoughtful about a problem and articulate *any* solution is more important than your ability to design the perfect solution every time. When other people realize that you've put thought into it and are being intentional, they're more willing to trust you, even if they disagree. That's how you become a great designer: by describing and expressing your designs to other people in way that makes sense to them.

In that sense, being a great designer is just as much about communication skills as it is about design chops. You need to understand your decisions and then articulate them to someone else who doesn't know design as well as you do. Using these questions as our guide, you can find better ways to explain your design decisions for the purpose of convincing people you're right and ensuring the best experience for users.

Even though it's easy to see exactly how being more articulate will help us succeed, in practice it's far more difficult and complicated than that. Being articulate is more than just learning to say the right things, because nothing we say will have any affect if we don't first consider our audience. Recognizing the importance of communication in design makes it natural for us to take the next step on this path toward being a great designer: to begin seeing things from the perspective of our stakeholders.

[3]

Understanding Relationships

I don't like that man. I must get to know him better.
ABRAHAM LINCOLN

BEFORE WE GET INTO THE DETAILS OF LISTENING TO AND TALKING TO
OUR STAKEHOLDERS, I want to take a moment to look at the relationship.
The single most important thing you can do to improve communication between you and your stakeholders is to improve those relationships, earn trust, and establish a rapport that will speak more for you
than the words that come out of your mouth in a meeting.

So much of life and work is built around relationships. It's not just *who*
you know; it's the quality of those relationships, too. If we're going to be
effective with communication, we begin with the relationship. We need
to see the world through the eyes of the people who have influence over
our project. We have to get in their heads, find out what makes them
tick, and use this information to help us approach them in a way that's
productive and valuable for everyone.

What's ironic to me is that UXers are so good at putting the user first, at
garnering empathy for and attempting to see the interface from the perspective of the user. Yet, we often fail to do the same thing for the people
who hold the keys to our success. We think carefully about the users of
our applications but less so about the stakeholders on our projects. Let's
apply these same principles to the people we work with so that we can
create a better product together. We need to take the time to understand
our stakeholders. More than that, we need to engage with them on a personal level and improve the quality of our interactions. The same care

and detail that goes into demonstrating user interactions also needs to be applied in our interactions with stakeholders. When it comes to relationships, you are truly an interaction designer!

The purpose of this chapter is to take a step back from the process, before we get bogged down in a cycle of meetings. We begin here, with a high-level view of our stakeholder relationships so that we can approach them in the right way. In order to do that, we need to:

See them as human
Everyone has other things going on that we simply cannot predict.

Create shared experiences
Finding common ground is important to earning trust.

Develop empathy
Get to know their viewpoint so intimately that we're driven to action.

Ask good questions
Understand how their interests outside of the office affect their perspective.

In addition to getting to know our stakeholders, it's important to look at the individuals on our team and work to improve the quality of our communication by:

Identifying influencers
Based on what we already know about their role on the team, we can understand the values that drive their reactions to our work.

Building good relationships
Simple things can go a long way in establishing rapport: be yourself, do stuff, and give stuff. Communication is easier in good relationships.

See Their Perspective

To know how to approach people and respond to them, we must first see their perspective. We have the opportunity to learn to speak their language, to get to know them better, and to keep our project on track. It's not easy, but we can get a better sense for where people are coming from when we remember they're human, find common ground through shared experiences, develop empathy for their viewpoint, and ask questions that give us insight into their world.

SEE THEM AS HUMAN

The trouble with people is that we're all so unpredictable and yet so incredibly predictable at the same time. Often the people in your meetings are dealing with things, in both their personal and professional lives, which are more important to them than your current design project. People are too busy (or at least they think they are). "I have too many things going on right now," or "I have to get to another meeting," or "I've got to make this deadline." Whatever the case, a lot of people you need help from are not always focused on the thing you want them to be. More than that, their attitudes and responses to your work might have more to do with the things happening outside of this meeting than what you're showing them.

Before we go any further, stop for just a minute and think about the people on your project. Call to mind their faces, names, and even their role in the company. Now, pause and consider this: each one of them is a unique individual. Each person is a human with feelings, emotions, and a past that speaks into their present every single day. They all have relationships outside of work that include friends, spouses, parents, and children. When they're finished with your meeting, they're going to go visit their mother in the hospital. One of them has to shuttle his kids to an athletic game. And someone else on your team will go home to an empty house, lonely with nothing but the TV for company. Despite the fact that we spend so much time together during working hours, all of these people's most important relationships are somewhere else.

We can't pretend to ever really know what's going on inside their heads, but we *can* take the time to realize that the way they respond to our ideas and work might have (or probably has) nothing to do with us at all. There are just too many other factors, distractions, and problems in the average person's life for us to ever assume that the thing we want from them is the thing they care about. In psychology, the concept of attribution describes how people see one another, and specifically, how we understand other people's behavior. Interestingly, most people tend to see other people's behavior as a reflection of their particular personality traits, whereas we see our own behavior as being primarily situational. You see, we already have an unfair view of our stakeholders' reactions. It's natural for us to believe that their personality ("They're not a designer") is what causes them to disagree with our solutions, but that's not true.

Was your colleague short with you in the hallway about the new interactions you made? Maybe she's dealing with some issues in her personal life. Did that guy in your last meeting throw you under the bus and blame you for a problem that he was actually responsible for? Perhaps he's feeling pressure from his boss. Has an executive ever shown up and declared that everything had to be changed? It's possible he just came from a meeting and his budget was slashed. Stakeholder reactions to our design work often have an underlying situational explanation that we might never know about.

I will never forget the time when a manager came to our team late in the day with an emergency request. Suddenly, everything we were working on had to be stopped so that we could put together some concepts for a completely new, different idea. He was aggressive and rude, out of the ordinary. The only explanation was that it had suddenly become a high priority. I tried to understand the situation, but it just didn't make sense nor did it line up with what we had agreed on previously. We did our best to appease him and shifted focus to this new thing, but then a few days later he dropped the project and told us to go back to our original work. Later, I found out that he had lost one of his biggest contracts and was on the verge of missing his financial goals near bonus time. This new project was a last ditch effort to make something happen, but he would never have told us it was because of his own bonus.

Of course, it wasn't appropriate for him to treat our team that way just because his own financial incentives were on the line, but that's not the point. The point is that there was something else going on that we didn't understand at the time. And actually, there are *always* other things going on in the room that you will never know about. There are *always* things that are influencing people's behaviors that we are not privy to. And there will *always* be things that we simply can't predict. Always. The more often you remember that, the better off you'll be.

Our job as articulate designers is to recognize just enough of that reality so that we can talk to the people that we work with in a way that pushes past all the extra distractions and gets down to the core thing we need to know to be successful. We need to recognize that the way people react to our work may not have anything to do with us or our designs at all. So, as often as you need to, stop, take a look at the people around you, and remember one thing: they are human.

CREATE SHARED EXPERIENCES

Our inability to see the perspective of another person often results from a lack of shared experiences. We simply don't have enough in common with the other person. Why do some people seem to get along better than others? Why are we immediately drawn to some people, but not others? It's because we have something in common with them. When we have shared experiences, we have something to talk about. When we don't have anything in common with another person, it's nearly impossible to talk to them. Everything we think of falls flat. However, everyone has *something* in common with another person; this is why the weather is such an easy thing to talk about. And although the weather is a perfectly fine experience to share, if we want to understand our stakeholders, we need to be willing to go deeper than that.

That's not to say that we should dig into people's personal lives. Actually, there are plenty of ways in which we can create shared experiences with other people on a professional level. It can be something as simple as going to lunch together or grabbing a drink after work. It doesn't matter what you talk about: work, life, or the TV show you watched last night. The point is that you're removing yourself, your ego, and the pressure of the minute-to-minute business of work. You're out of the office—out of your usual context and experiencing something with this other person that you would not have otherwise.

Many companies organize team building and informal gatherings of employees for this very reason. But, if that's not built in to your culture, you can make it happen on your own. Other ways of creating shared experiences include going to a conference, volunteering at your company's annual charity, or asking that person's advice. "Hey, I was thinking of buying a telescope for my kids and I know you're into astronomy. What would you recommend?" Finding ways to create connections with other people is an important step toward understanding them.

THAT'S SO JOSH!

I will never forget how drastically my relationship with and approach toward a colleague changed after I had a shared experience with him. Josh was in a similar role to mine, but in a different department. As a result, we used a lot of the same shared resources and our paths would cross on projects occasionally. My impression of him was that he was a troublemaker: he was unorganized, inconsiderate, and not respected within the organization. It was especially difficult to work on a project with him because I knew he would have lots of different ideas, and those ideas always seemed as if they were just creating extra work for me. He was my nemesis. But by chance, one year we both ended up working at the same conference. We drove together, about three hours one way. We stayed at the same resort, which happened to be a paradise of relaxation. And we spent every day out of our usual context setting things up, talking to people, and eating most of our meals together. Very quickly, I got to know him through our shared experiences.

Almost immediately, my opinion of Josh changed. From then on, his suggestions were innovative! He was no longer inconsiderate, but just a little busy and less mindful of the details. "That's so Josh!" Nothing had changed, except my own perspective of him and our shared experiences. From then on, it became much easier to work with Josh and get his buy-in on projects simply because we had those shared experiences. In fact, he became one of my greatest allies.

You don't need to go on a road trip with stakeholders to create shared experiences. Finding that common ground can be as simple as pointing out something interesting in the hallway on the way to a meeting. You might notice that they have the latest mobile device, are wearing a brand you like, or have a souvenir from Paris on their desk. Anything you can do to explicitly call out common ground between you will go a long way toward reminding everyone (yourself included) that you have common interests. We are more than just pixel pushers. We are people. Often, the only thing keeping us from developing good relationships is ourselves.

DEVELOP EMPATHY

Empathy is a big buzz word in UX. If we can develop true empathy for our users, we'll build better applications. But what about our stakeholders? We need to empathize with them, too, if we really expect to get through to them.

Empathy drives behavior. It is so much more than just understanding another person or seeing their perspective. It's the ability to actually share in their feelings and experience so much that you have to help them: to get to know their viewpoint so intimately that we feel their pain. Empathy is what drives people to defend civil-rights injustices. It's the reason why we have events to raise support and awareness for causes such as cancer. It motivates us to care so much about the challenges of another person that we're driven to action. Empathy is the ultimate form of understanding.

Developing empathy for our stakeholders means attempting to look at our project from their perspective so that we're no longer defensive and protective of our own ideas. We realize their reactions and suggestions are based in a reality that, for them, is more important than our own. When you have empathy for stakeholders, you not only understand their perspective but you're actually driven to action; you want to make changes to your designs because you feel their pain. You see the urgency of meeting their needs and want to do something about it. That doesn't mean that you do anything and everything they say. It simply means that your priority for communicating with them has shifted from a position of defense to one of solidarity. You still might disagree on the solution, but at least now you're better prepared to talk to them about your choices. Having empathy for our stakeholders is important to establishing a foundational mindset that will allow us to form the best possible response to their feedback, as we will see in Chapter 6 and beyond. We cannot expect to listen to and respond to their feedback without first empathizing with their situation.

LEADING WITH VISION

I once worked with an executive who was very much a visionary thinker, but we were building a basic minimum viable product (MVP) for the first release. At the first couple of meetings, he was underwhelmed by our basic functionality. He knew the constraints of the project, but we needed him to be on board to get his approval. He was always present, but never very excited. In the process of working with him, I tried to see our project from his perspective. As an executive, he always had a high-level, 30,000-foot view of everything going on, yet we were showing him a minute detail that might only be a small blip on the radar of this product. He was looking toward the end-game, a massive release with fanfare, but we were focused on this intermediary step, the here and now.

So, from that point on, I chose to bring two different mockups to each meeting. One was this baseline MVP, which was modest and simple. The other was an innovative, no-limits picture of awesome that we would never be able to pull off, at least in the short term. But I was able to hold his attention by keeping both concepts in front of him. I was able to lead our conversations with this incredible vision of a preferred future, while also showing and getting approval for the thing that would allow us to take a step in that direction. He could see where we were going and so he was more likely to approve our MVP.

I could not have been prepared with this approach if I wasn't able to empathize with his position. It took more work on my part, but it was worth it in the long run because it meant keeping our designs moving. He trusted us more because he could see our vision. Actually, I've found that it's often a best practice when working with executives to show both what's possible in the short term and what's preferred for the future. This approach creates a buzz that keeps everyone excited and makes it more likely that they'll agree with you. We'll go into more detail about the importance of designing for vision in the Chapter 13.

ASK GOOD QUESTIONS

Seeing the perspective of our stakeholders requires a lot of patience and work. It's not something that comes automatically; it takes time and practice. Some people are naturally good at seeing other people's perspective, but the majority of us need to be very intentional about it. You should learn to view things from the perspective of your stakeholders in the same way that you would with users of your application—by asking questions. If we want to see our stakeholders as human, to create shared experiences, and develop empathy for their situation, the best thing we can do is to just ask.

My brother-in-law, Lars, is one of the most interesting people I know. Everywhere he goes, people like to talk to him. What's funny is that he doesn't seem like a very outgoing person. His personality is a little reserved, he's careful when he speaks, and he never talks too much. Yet it seems as if people are drawn to him. When people see him, they stop to talk. If they spot him across a room, they'll seek him out. Why? It's because Lars is really good at asking questions. People love to talk to Lars because Lars is good at getting them to talk. You leave a conversation with Lars feeling like you just met someone who was really smart, interesting, and was intensely interested in the mundane details of your life. He's a great conversationalist not because he's good at talking, but because he's good at asking questions. Talking to Lars makes me feel smart and that makes me want to talk to him more!

Lars' skill at getting people to talk demonstrates that we need to be better at asking people questions about themselves so that they feel valued and are comfortable talking to us. This approach to relationships and conversations will help us build a reputation that makes people want to talk to us more and, as a byproduct, listen to us more when it matters the most.

GET PERSONAL

As Lars has shown me, people love to talk about themselves. Even people who are more humble and less inclined to volunteer information still enjoy chatting about the stuff that's important to them. So, take the time to know a little bit about each person so that you can begin to see that their life doesn't revolve around work. Don't ask yes/no questions, and don't get so personal that you overstep normal social behavior. Keep it light, but let them tell you what they're willing to tell. Questions like:

- What did you do this weekend?

- How was your holiday?

- Have you seen any good movies lately?

- So what's new?

These questions are simple, open ended, and allow the person to divulge as much or as little as they're willing. They are general enough to be safe with any audience and can create conversation to help you see their perspective. They'll create a path for you to get to know them better and eventually ask more specific questions.

If you know they have kids, ask about their kids. Everyone will talk to you about their kids and it's something many people have in common. The same goes for pets; people love to talk about their pets. I was having a one-on-one meeting with a stakeholder. While we walked to the conference room, I asked her if she had pets. She pulled out her phone to log in to the remote camera she had mounted in her outdoor cat enclosure. Conveniently, the conversation quickly turned to technology and the app that controls her camera. That naturally shifted to a discussion of the UX. Asking her about pets gave her something she loved to talk about and gave me an opportunity to demonstrate my own expertise in the process, earning some trust and respect regarding the project we were about to discuss. You never know how asking good questions will improve your relationships and help you to earn the trust you need to communicate about your designs.

OFFER YOURSELF

But it's not a one-way street. You should also offer some information about yourself to get people talking. Find something that you're interested in and ask them about it:

- I went camping this past weekend; do you like camping?

- We hosted my family for dinner last night; do you like to cook?

- I saw this great movie yesterday; have you seen it?

Offering people a glimpse into your own life is a great way to create a sense that they are just like you. No matter how they might respond to you in the moment, you may find that you have a lot in common. I was visiting a client in New York who offered to take me to lunch in his car. It was a small car, but I happened to notice that it had an upgraded exhaust system. I asked him about it because I am restoring a classic car myself and was curious about his interest in cars. I told him about my project and we started chatting about cars in general. That conversation turned into a story about him borrowing money to buy a plane when he was only in his twenties. He still owned that plane and loved to fly. I had been working with this guy for several months, but I had no idea he was a pilot! In fact, every time I talk to him now, he always gives me the latest update on flying because he knows I'm genuinely interested in his hobby. Revealing some of my own interests made it possible for us to establish some common ground.

GO PRO

But seeing our stakeholder's perspective requires that we understand how they approach their jobs and our project, too, not just their personal life. So, it's important to get to know how people think in our work-context, as well. Ask things like:

- What did you think of the meeting last week?

- How's your work going on the other project?

- Do you have a lot going on this week?

If you find that you're butting heads with the people in charge, it's common that the stated goals or priorities for the project actually differ from the individual's. In that case, I suggest being as direct as possible when trying to uncover people's viewpoints and perspectives in situations where they can be difficult to read. For example:

- What's your opinion on this project?
- How does this project affect your job?
- What is your priority for this project?

Allowing people to express what might be their own opinion or perspective gives them permission to deviate from the party line because they can speak freely without the pressure that they'll upset the process or misrepresent the company.

I was having some difficulty with a manager who was pushing us on some priorities, and his suggestions seemed to conflict with our goal of improving conversion. I asked him how our project would affect him, and he told me that his highest priority was migrating off of the old platform as quickly as possible, because during the transition he was paying for the development of both. As long as both platforms were on his budget, he was under a lot of pressure. However, he never could have gotten approval to build the new platform if the stated goal hadn't been improved conversion. So, although our official mandate was to increase conversion, his personal agenda was to replace the platform as soon as possible. Knowing that significantly improved our ability to communicate with each other on the designs and priorities for the rest of the project.

Again, the point of asking questions is to get the other person to talk to you about what's important to them. You just want to understand more about their perspective so that you have a better sense for how to respond to them, when needed. That's how you create an awareness of the other person's viewpoint and set yourself up for a better relationship, better communication, and better success in creating the best user experience.

Identifying Influencers

Now that we've considered the best ways of seeing our stakeholder's perspective, let's look at the kinds of people who influence our projects so that we can tailor these approaches to them.

Every project has a variety of people who influence its outcome. To keep it simple, let's assume that there are only three main types of people who you need to understand:

Team Influencers
> The people on your direct team

Executive Influencers
> The people who oversee your project

External Influencers
> People outside of your team

Depending on where the person sits in relation to you, it can be difficult to get to know them well enough to understand them and their perspective. But our job is to identify these people and seek to understand them as best as we can.

TEAM INFLUENCERS

People who are within your immediate influence are the people you see and interact with every day. This probably includes other designers, developers, and project managers or product owners. It can be more difficult to work with these people on a regular basis simply because, well...you have to work with them on a regular basis! However, the benefit is that you have plenty of opportunity to learn about them, find out what makes them tick, and tailor your approach to them in a way that appeals to their needs.

Healthy companies have healthy teams, and so your work with this group could feel like hanging out with friends on a daily basis. Unhealthy teams have difficult people and relationships that make it hard to accomplish much at all. Most of the time, I find that there's a mix of team dynamics: there are people you most identify with and who will come to your aid. And then there are some people who you don't understand or who have difficult personalities, and you need to learn to handle them better. Whatever the mix on your team, the goal is to find ways of understanding them so that we can better communicate with them.

In general, your team is the best source of people who can help you on your project. You have daily opportunities to pour into these relationships for the benefit of the user experience. The more time you can spend with these people describing solutions, communicating value, and establishing a foundation of vocabulary, the better off you'll be as far as creating a culture that follows your lead on important UX decisions. It is hard work because you have to put on your game face every day and find ways to lead, even if you're not the leader. Your team influencers are your most important allies.

EXECUTIVE INFLUENCERS

The people outside your immediate influence, but who have a stake in and influence over your project are the executive influencers. Most commonly, this is an executive or manager who oversees your team, perhaps one or two levels removed. This is the boss: the person whose approval you most need. On small teams and in startups, this might be the CEO, whom you also work with in close quarters. In larger organizations, it's a manager or VP, and you may not have regular access to them. Either way, these people are the most important people on your project. Without their final approval, you can't get what you need to be successful. In many ways, communicating with these people is the primary purpose of this book.

Hopefully there isn't more than one or two major executive influencers on your project. The difficult part about understanding this group is that we don't usually meet with them often enough to easily size them up and understand their perspective. They are probably busy, late to your meeting, short and to the point, and may not have much time or brain space to devote to your carefully thought-through presentation. In this case, you have to use keen observation in every meeting, get to know the people who know them (like an administrative assistant or direct report) and do your best with the limited information you have. In short, you need to figure them out and respond to them almost instantaneously. Over time, you'll develop a rhythm that can add to your bucket of understanding and help you communicate with them.

EXTERNAL INFLUENCERS

A third group of people, who matter less to your day-to-day decision making but who can also help or hurt your efforts, are the external influencers. This group lives in a different part of the organization, probably unrelated to your work or project, but they may have the ear of anyone in the other two groups and speak into your project via proxy. Often, we may not even know who the external influencers are because we only hear about them secondhand. But just as often, they are people who have access to and/or use our project and therefore have an interest in seeing it become the best it can be.

These might be people in accounting and finance, IT, customer service or call-center employees, or HR, depending on the kind of app you're building. They could be people outside the organization, too: a spouse, friend, or former colleague of an executive influencer. It's not uncommon for people in meetings to say things like, "I was showing the app to my friend in accounting and he seemed to think the button was not obvious enough. He didn't even notice it until I pointed it out to him!" They then expect that we should make design decisions exclusively on this anonymous person in accounting. Even worse is the external influencer who is deemed to be part of the user base for the product. "I was showing it to my wife because she's part of our target audience and she didn't like the grid view at all. She thinks we should default to the list view instead." Now you have to find a nice way to tell this person that not only is his wife wrong, but she's not even part of our user base either! It's no small challenge, for sure.

Stakeholder Values

I tend to see people in different roles as individual *people* and try to avoid creating stereotypes in my head based on their job title. Everyone is unique, and you must consider them in different ways no matter what their role. Although that's true, our stakeholders' viewpoint of our project is still influenced significantly by how they spend their time and energy every day. To the extent that it's possible, let's look at some of the more common roles on the team, what the people in those roles value, and what that means for our approach. This is just a starting point to help you understand how different roles will affect people's perspective of your project and what you can focus on when working with them.

EXECUTIVES OR MANAGERS

It's no exaggeration that executives and senior managers have a lot on their plate. But it's less about being too busy and more about brain capacity; they're constantly switching between completely different topics, projects, and challenges. Walking into your meeting might even be disorienting if they can't remember where you last left off. Your job is to bring them up to speed as quickly as possible, present your solutions, and solicit their feedback. They want to know that you've thought about it and have made smart decisions that align with their vision for the organization.

BECAUSE THEY VALUE...	YOU SHOULD FOCUS ON...
• Concise information	• Getting to the point
• Growing the business	• Accomplishing goals
• Solving problems	• Describing the solution

DEVELOPERS OR ENGINEERS

Working with developers can be one of the most challenging relationships for designers, simply because they think so differently about our projects than we do. Developers are usually looking at a backlog of bugs and enhancements on the one hand, and a roadmap for future development that's bigger than they can manage on the other. They tend to be more analytical, so they don't even "see" some of the UI details you've designed. They may even be concerned with "over-designing" something that they think is not worth the extra effort. Your job is to help them see the value in everything you've done so that they're excited about the end result, while also demonstrating that you understand the effort involved.

BECAUSE THEY VALUE...	YOU SHOULD FOCUS ON...
• Building it once and minimizing rework	• Understanding all of the use cases up front
• Efficiency and maintainable code	• Maximizing existing scope and reusing UI patterns
• Understanding the effort involved	• Communicating the value for the users or business

PRODUCT OWNERS

If your organization is large enough to have a dedicated product owner, working with them will be one of the primary things you do. The great news is that product owners tend to want their products to be the very best they can be, so they're usually one of our greatest allies and get really excited about all the creative designs we can produce. Taking direction from a product owner is challenging, though, if they don't have a good understanding of design, what's technically possible, or if they have an unclear vision for the product roadmap.

BECAUSE THEY VALUE...	YOU SHOULD FOCUS ON...
• Innovation and creativity	• Finding new approaches to solving problems
• Meeting business goals	• Connecting your designs to the business objectives
• The big picture, long-term roadmap	• How your design moves them forward

PROJECT MANAGERS

Most projects will have a project manager, even if this is a combination of people from other roles. This is the person in charge of ensuring the project stays on track, on budget, and on time. They like things like Gantt charts, deadlines, and meetings. Your job with PMs is to be sure they always understand where you're at in the process, alert them about any concerns as soon as possible, and allow them to negotiate between everyone else to get stuff done.

BECAUSE THEY VALUE...	YOU SHOULD FOCUS ON...
• Deadlines and staying on schedule	• Possible efficiencies of reusing design elements
• Managing scope and budgets	• Managing expectations on any changes
• Keeping everyone in the loop	• Updating them on your progress

MARKETING, CONTENT, AND CREATIVE

I hate to put all three of these roles into the same category, but there is plenty of overlap in these roles from the perspective of a designer. Only the largest companies will employ separate people for each one of these roles. The point, for designers, is that there are people who will be concerned more with the content, look and feel, and copy of your application. There may be branding guidelines, style guides, or a defined design language that drives most of these conversations. Your job is to already be aware of these requirements, find out what the standard content and copy is, and incorporate it into your designs as early as possible.

BECAUSE THEY VALUE...	YOU SHOULD FOCUS ON...
• Brand consistency across the organization	• Creating styles that match the brand or communicating any differences
• Consistent voice in copy and messaging	• Ensuring that the copy you use is already approved, or if it deviates, why
• Creating a product that provides value to customer and is sellable	• Specific value proposition in features or microinteractions

Stakeholder Stories

Writing user stories is a popular method for designers and developers to understand their users, but have you ever written a story like that for your stakeholders? As we seek to understand the people we work with, perhaps it will be useful to write out stories so that we can understand the project from their perspective. Here are a few examples to get you started.

EXECUTIVES

- As an executive, I want to see what my team is working on so that I can provide a report back to upper management.

- As an executive, I want to provide feedback on the design of my products so that I can help you make them better.

- As an executive, I want to provide a vision and roadmap of the future so that my team can be excited about where we are headed.

DEVELOPERS

- As a developer, I want to build a solid application so that I can be proud of my work.

- As a developer, I want to write quality code so that I don't have to deal with so many bugs or a lot of maintenance.

- As a developer, I want to understand all the requirements up front so that I can plan my work and maximize my time.

PRODUCT OWNERS

- As a product owner, I want to create the best possible product so that I can create value for our customers and for the company.

- As a product owner, I want to deliver new and creative ideas so that I can make an impression on the company with my leadership.

- As a product owner, I want to make a product that is simple and elegant so that people will want to use it.

PROJECT MANAGERS

- As a project manager, I want to meet with everyone on the team so that I can ensure that we're on track.

- As a project manager, I want to cut scope so that we can stay on schedule and under budget.

- As a project manager, I want to plan carefully so that I can ensure that we have the time and resources we need to be successful.

MARKETING, CONTENT, AND CREATIVE

- As a marketer, I want to provide feedback on the product design so that we will have a product that is competitive and will sell.

- As a brand or content strategist, I want to ensure that all of our products communicate the same look or tone so that our customers have a consistent experience across the entire organization.

- As a creative director, I want to be involved in your project's design so that I can ensure that it aligns with all of the other initiatives I oversee.

These are meant to be casual examples to make the point that each person on our team has a different perspective. We could probably write many more. You could take the time to write your own user/stakeholder stories for the people on your team, too. The more we can do to get into their frame of mind, the better we'll be at articulating our design decisions to them.

Build Good Relationships

The overall lesson is this: communication is much easier in good relationships. Good relationships take work. In fact, building good relationships is a pretty basic and straightforward process—you get out of it what you put into it. So, let's take a practical look at some things you can do to improve the quality of your relationships with stakeholders.

Technology has improved the speed at which we're able to communicate, but not necessarily the quality. Text messaging and emails are incredibly useful tools for getting work done, but we need to be careful not to go to an extreme of limiting our capacity to communicate to a few hundred characters. It might be necessary for you to fire off a short response to people on your team for the purpose of getting it done, but don't let that be the only way that they ever interact with you. Whenever possible, seek them out and have a friendly and casual conversation with them. This is more difficult when working remotely, but not impossible. Take the time to do the simple things that will help you to improve your relationships and, as a byproduct, your communication with each other.

BE YOURSELF

The best advice I can give you is to just be yourself around people. Too often, people are serious about doing serious work seriously. In an attempt to be professional, some people (maybe you) never let anyone see who they really are. We may put up fronts, never let our guard down, and always focus on work, work, work. This is no way to maintain a rapport with your peers and bosses. You need to show people you're human and reveal your own personality, when it's appropriate. There are absolutely times when we have to put on our professional hat and get things done, but there are also in-between times, break times, and coffee times when we can learn to be human with those around us. Finding that balance is important; people appreciate getting to see the "real" you.

DO STUFF

It's also important to do things for other people to make them feel valued. Pretty much anything you do that is outside of the usual way your team communicates and relates to one another will make an impression on people that you care. Typically, this is just checking in with people regularly to see how they are. That might be stopping by their desk, inviting them to coffee, or leaving a note. Sometimes, just saying hello to someone for no reason at all is enough to express this. To take it a step further, ask if there's anything you can do to help them. Any of the questions in the previous section would be a great fit here, but the key is to express that you're on the same team and you care enough to ask.

When I'm visiting one particular client's office, I always stop by Jennifer's desk because I enjoyed working with her on a previous project. She's almost never there, so I leave her a note to say hello on a Post-it. Later, I found out she had been keeping all of my notes stuck to her display because she appreciated them so much. On another client, I sometimes work directly with the CEO, so whenever I'm onsite I always walk by his office even if I don't have an appointment. Once, he was in another conversation but he waved me over, stopped his meeting briefly, shook my hand, and thanked me for being there. Another time, I was reading an article that reminded me of a client I had worked for months earlier. I watched his online status for a few days to see when he was available and then sent him a short message with a link to the article. Even though we didn't have an active project together, it was important for me to maintain the relationship. I want people to know that I'm there to serve them, to help them do their jobs better, and to make them successful at designing great products. Going out of my way to do these simple things helps me to express that to them and makes it easier when talking to them about design.

GIVE STUFF
Taking it a step further, relationships will be improved when you actually do things that show a genuine interest in people by giving them something useful or meaningful.

Handwritten notes
I sometimes send handwritten thank-you notes or cards to people after we've worked together. Not often, but occasionally. When all of our communication is electronic, a handwritten card is especially notable and always makes an impression. But don't misunderstand me; I'm not much of a letter-writing person to begin with. I'm not the person who sent you a thank-you note for a wedding gift the same day that you gave the gift. I've never been that guy. This is a real stretch for me to remember to do, but I think it's always valuable and I probably don't do it enough. If you have trouble with something like this, set your goals

low: write one hand-written note to a client or stakeholder every two to three months. Hopefully, that will help you establish a pattern of expressing your gratitude to the people you have the privilege of working with.

Simple, Inexpensive Gifts

Another simple way to build your relationships is to send simple gifts to people, when appropriate. These aren't meant to be bribes, but just small tokens of appreciation to show the other person that you care. Some companies have policies about gift giving, so be sure you understand the environment and always use good judgment. But as a rule, giving a small gift is a great way to show the other person that you're more than just a defender of buttons.

For individuals, the best gifts are the ones that show you listen to them. One of my clients was a hobbyist photographer, so I sent him a coffee cup that looks like a lens. To my client who loves to fly, I sent a license plate frame that said "My other car is a plane"—he still talks about it to this day and has offered me to fly with him next time I'm in New York. I gave a coworker who was getting married a humorous book about what bachelors need to know before the wedding. And my boss who had a reputation for always ordering a Jack Daniel's with water got just that. I bought one bottle of each, designed a custom label for the package with the title "Joan's Regular," and had a friend shrink wrap them together so it looked like a real product. All these things were inexpensive, simple ways to let the other person know that I value them. The gifts were not generic, but tailored to something specific I knew about them. The sentiment was not in the gift itself, but in the thought I had put into choosing it. They knew I listened to them and understood something about them.

If you're concerned about showing favoritism or if you're not good at giving individual gifts, one simple way to give people a gift is to be the person who brings snacks or food. If everyone is groaning about an early morning meeting, bring breakfast with you. You can also put a communal jar of candy on your desk to give people a reason to stop by. Occasionally offer to make a coffee run for the team during the 3 p.m. slump. This way of giving gifts doesn't favor one particular relationship, but it still shows people that you value them.

It might seem like focusing on stakeholder relationships has nothing to do with design. Cultivating good relationships is a great skill no matter what your job is, but it's one area that I think designers can improve upon. Many designers expect their designs to speak for themselves, especially as it relates to user experience. "If your design requires an explanation, then it's not very good." As if you could expect to just hand your stakeholders some mockups and wait for them to give it a stamp of approval. It's surprising just how much a good relationship can affect another person's view of our work. Having good relationships really does make our designs more acceptable to the people who matter.

People may view us for the utility we provide, specifically related to our roles as designers. We are actually making something that they need, and they may, unintentionally, see our interactions with each other as the way to get things done. But when we don't have that human connection, meeting with stakeholders can sometimes be downgraded to nothing more than an exchange of skills. The more we can show them that we're people, too, the more value and stock they'll put into our ideas, suggestions, and proposals. We're not robots churning out stuff just to get a paycheck; we're smart people with great ideas working together to create great products. Focusing on these relationships is more than just being nice and making sure people like us. It's reminding them that we're people, too, and that we can be trusted to create great solutions. Having good relationships will help ensure that this happens.

STAKEHOLDERS ARE PEOPLE, TOO

If we really expect to communicate effectively with our stakeholders, we need to use the same skills with them that we use in identifying with our users. We have to understand people by the roles and position on our team, recognize what's important to them, and make a note of the best ways of approaching them. Part of this process involves remembering that they are human, that they have other things going on in their lives, or being intentional about creating shared experiences so that we change our view of them personally. Finally, developing empathy for stakeholders drives us to act and to want to position our approach toward them in a way that agrees with their needs, rather than our own. At the end of the day, a focus on building good relationships is the most important factor in establishing good channels of communication.

[4]

Reducing Cognitive Load

Before anything else, preparation is the key to success.
ALEXANDER GRAHAM BELL

WHEN IT COMES TO USABILITY, getting users to successfully complete a task is all about their available brain space: their *cognitive load*. The more clutter, options, or roadblocks we put in front of them, the more we fill their head and make it difficult for them to complete a task. The same is true when it comes to the task of meeting with stakeholders. Our goal should be to remove as much of the clutter, options, and road-blocks as possible so that our stakeholders' brains are freed to focus on the primary task of the meeting: getting approval for our designs. If they are distracted by an incoherent outline, grumpy coworkers, or a derailed conversation that has nothing to do with the project, it will be much more difficult for us to complete that task. Our goal is not to just have a meeting, but to make the meeting productive, valuable, and successful.

To that end, understanding our stakeholders would be of little use if we didn't use that knowledge to break down these barriers and make our meetings more "usable." This chapter looks at how to remove any distractions from the conversation, how to anticipate what the stake-holders might say, and ways to bring in other people who can help us move things forward. In addition, you can never be fully prepared for these meetings without first rehearsing them, either in your head or out loud. The time you spend preparing for the meeting makes you that much more likely to be successful at making a case for your design decisions, because you can focus more on being articulate and less on the agenda. Our goal is to reduce the cognitive load for our stakeholders, our team, and ourselves.

Remove Distractions

When you're in a meeting to get approval for your designs, staying focused is critical. It's very easy for design discussions to go off on a tangent or be taken in an unexpected direction because of one small thing. There's just something about design that elicits so much more clutter conversation than other disciplines. One way to keep focused is to remove anything that you think will be a distraction. A lot of people are easily distracted by things that simply don't matter to the goal of the meeting. They can be so distracted by one thing that they'll identify a different, unrelated problem or be unable to discuss the real issues. Consequently, part of your job is to pay attention to those things that derail the discussion and remove them from the equation altogether.

A common example involves the use of placeholder content: stock images and *lorem ipsum* copy. I can't tell you how many times my clients have obsessed over the placeholder content I chose. And yet, here are some examples:

- I was designing a site for a diesel manufacturer and chose a product image to use on the home page. The client spent an inordinate amount of time talking about how that particular engine part was not their best seller and, in fact, was being discontinued because of engineering flaws. He then proceeded to educate me on their entire line of engine bits.

- I was working with a retailer who did not have any readily available images of the interior of their stores, so I found a placeholder image online and included it in the mockups. It turns out that I had chosen a photo from their closest competitor and rival. It was difficult for the stakeholder to move past the fact that he was looking at the competition in a mockup for his own store's site.

- On a mapping application I used a Google Maps screenshot as the background placeholder for where the map would be. My client used a different ("enterprise") mapping service provider and he had a difficult time reconciling that the image did not look like the maps they would see in the real application.

- On an app for a pharmaceutical company, my client was confused about why she couldn't understand the ipsum copy even though she had studied Latin in college. She spent part of the meeting trying to read it aloud, and I had to explain to her why we use ipsum copy in design.

In each case, my placeholder content created an unnecessary distraction.

The challenge is that removing these distractions often requires more work on our part. We use *ipsum* copy because it easier than writing real copy. We use stock images because a quick search will give us tons of options. In fact, an Agile/Lean approach values fast iterations, MVPs, quick work, and short sprints. The prospect of being required to dig deeper and go two extra steps with your wireframes might seem to go against these philosophies. Worse, it might slow you down, right? Not necessarily.

I was working with a guy who was very sensitive to everything being perfectly lined up in a grid. My wireframes were a little messy because, well, they're just wireframes: quick and dirty, just enough to communicate the intent, right? He began making suggestions for changing the layout: "move this call to action over here, drop this element down there." Not minor tweaks, but overall rework. I began to realize that he was so distracted by how misaligned some of the elements were that he was trying to make the design feel more balanced. I paused the discussion and took a few minutes to go back and ensure that everything was properly aligned. Almost immediately, his reaction changed. Many of his objections over the placement of major elements had gone away. We could now focus on the real business. But I learned that with this particular person, it was important that I take the time to clean up my wireframes so that I could save time in a meeting as well as avoiding any possible suggested rework.

However, it might not be quite as simple as removing placeholder content or aligning elements. Some people are really distracted by any use of color, so it's better to avoid color as much as possible. Others will be distracted by legacy UI elements that aren't the focus of the meeting, such as an old navigation element that they've never liked. So, you can't just use a screenshot of it in your mockups. Everyone is a little different, and our job is to figure out these distractions.

At this point you need to weigh whether the extra time that you spend up front removing these distractions will give back time when it comes to getting approvals and agreement from stakeholders. I personally think it's worth the extra effort to discover and remove distractions for the sake of keeping the project moving than sacrificing the time and effort involved in bringing a conversation back to its core purpose. If your client doesn't discover a missing business requirement because they're distracted by something else, that missing requirement will eventually surface, usually after it's too late in the process, causing everyone to run around trying to make it happen at the last minute. The takeaway here is to work with your team to do what it takes to keep the stakeholders focused even if it takes some extra time and preparation.

One client of mine really loved the left panel that Axure creates when a prototype is generated. It's just an iframe that lists every single page in the prototype, a site map of the entire project.[1] She liked it so much, in fact, that she would comment on it during each of our calls, "Oh, it's so convenient to be able to see all the pages right there." I usually just ignored her infatuation and moved on with the meeting. Finally during one call, she actually suggested we use it as the navigation of the app. "I just love how you can see everything all the time," she said, "We should use that for our navigation, instead!" All of the previously agreed upon design work we had done to create a consistent, meaningful hierarchy for the app was on the chopping block! Again, I chose not to respond in the moment but instead, after that, I began going into the Axure folder structure and sending her the link, not to the index.html file, which would show the left panel, but to the direct HTML file that would open outside of the iframe so that she would not see that left panel any more. After that, she never mentioned it again.

---

1 This was an early version of Axure that did not provide the option to turn off the display of this panel. In more recent versions, you can remove this panel from the prototype.

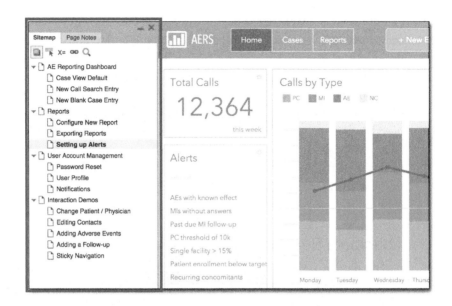

One of my clients was so distracted by the left panel that Axure generates (highlighted here in red) that she suggested we use that for the navigation of the app we were designing.

One app that I was designing needed an icon for the user's account, and we chose a silhouette of a person. The software I was using had a limited set of icons available and that particular user icon was really bubbly, a terrible expression of a user. Still, for the sake of time, I used it as a placeholder because I didn't think it was worth creating my own just for these mockups. After the *third* meeting during which a different person addressed how terrible the icon was, I finally decided to take the extra effort to make my own and get that out of the conversation. Had I used a better icon to begin with, I could have saved myself from explaining the limitations of my installed icon set each time.

The default placeholder icon that was easily available to me (left) was so terrible that it was distracting to everyone who saw it, so I finally took the time to design one that would be better (right), and the conversation went away.

The point here is that as you get to know people, you should be able to identify what is distracting to them and remove those things from the conversation. Too often, people (especially nondesigners) obsess over things that don't really matter for the goals of the website or application. Even after you help them understand that those things are temporary or off-topic, I find that they still keep coming around to it again and again. "I know we talked about this last time, but I still think we need to redesign that menu." Just get rid of the distractions altogether! Distractions should only happen once. If you go to two meetings and the same distraction comes up both times, you're doing it wrong. Take the time to discover the distractions and remove them so that you can focus on the real issues regarding the effectiveness of your designs.

Anticipate Reactions

Based on what you know about the people you're working with, you should be able to anticipate how they will react to your designs. In the previous chapter, we identified the influencers on our projects and called out some of their values and motivations. When we combine what we know about their perspective with the values they carry in their role, we can make some pretty good guesses about how they'll respond to our designs. The good news is that most people are fairly predictable. That is, they tend to obsess over and react to the same kinds of things every single time. If you've met with them before, anticipating their reaction becomes much easier. It will take a few meetings to really hone in on how people are wired, but I've found that anticipating reactions is much more formulaic and predictable than you might expect.

The manager who asked about the color you used is going to think more critically about the details of the UI. The developer who wanted to see the analytics for the current app values the use of data to back up your claims. The executive who thought the call to action wasn't high up enough on the page needs to know how your choices affect conversion and sales. We can expect to hear similar ideas, recommendations, and objections from these people each time. What seems like a fuzzy, soft skill might actually be more of a recipe: personality + role / values + observed reactions = predictable behavior! Although it's not actually that simple, it gets easier and more predictable over time.

So go through each of your designs, look at the agenda for the meeting, and decide the best flow for presenting your ideas. In the same way that we create a flow for our users through the application, we also want to curate the flow of our design discussion. Now match up those needs with the people in the room. For each person, ask yourself:

- What do they care about the most?

- What are their personal goals for this design?

- What do I already know they want or don't want?

Answering these questions should give you a good picture of what to expect from them and make it possible for you to take notes that will prepare you to respond in the moment.

For some people, you might not know the answer to these questions because their participation is unclear. People are sometimes invited to meetings because they have a unique perspective on our product, even if they aren't directly involved. In those cases, you have to decide how important their input is and engage them at an appropriate level. They're at your meeting for a reason. Figure out that reason and make it relevant for them so that you can get the most out of everyone's time. Think about their particular role and make your best guess about how their viewpoint can help you. If you're not sure, ask them directly what they hope to get out of it or how they see themselves contributing. It's appropriate for you to tell people that you want to be sure you're making the most of everyone's time. Understanding their involvement helps you structure the agenda and sets you up to anticipate how things will play out.

WRITE DOWN OBJECTIONS

Once you've considered all the people involved, write down any objections you expect them to have along with your own response. Until you get really good at responding off-the-cuff, it can be difficult in the moment to remember how you were planning to reply. Make a list, and read and reread that list over and over until you're fully prepared with your best guess about how people will react to your designs. Even if you can't associate each anticipated reaction with a single person, it's still a good idea to make a simple list of objections that you think might come up. These could be in the form of questions that might be asked or opinions you think will be expressed. It's a fairly straightforward and simple practice. Just jot down what you think people will say.

Here are some examples of how you might write down anticipated objections:

HOME PAGE	PRODUCT PAGE
• Why did we remove one of the CTAs?	• Why isn't the image larger like we discussed?
• Does the carousel advance automatically? (Justin)	• Do we have to use two different buttons? Can we get the CTA above the fold?
• The utility nav is too crowded. (Kristen)	• Why are Reviews further down on the page?
• What happened to the Recommended Item feed?	• The fixed nav interaction should automatically add the item to cart. (Kristen)
• We can't "hide" the Join button under the menu. (Mark)	• This flow has more complex use cases than I think you've considered. (Mark)

CREATE ALTERNATIVES

Part of anticipating how people will react is preparing in advance the alternatives that you considered or that you think will be suggested. You'll remember from Chapter 2 that one of the questions we're trying to answer for our stakeholders is: *Why is this better than the alternative?*

Bringing alternatives (especially those that aren't the right solution) complicates the conversation because it forces us to have a well-articulated explanation for our choices. Many designers avoid this by not presenting alternatives that aren't recommended. The fear is that the client will prefer the "wrong" concept and insist it be used. Even though this is always a risk, approaching our meetings with this fear actually undermines the purpose of articulating design decisions. If we aren't able to convince stakeholders that our solution is better, either we aren't doing a good job of communicating to them or we don't understand their needs enough to create a design that solves the problem. What we really need is for them to agree with our solution, even after considering all of the alternatives. We can't protect them from all the bad ideas that might be suggested. Instead, we arm them with the knowledge and language for why our decisions are best. That's the only way we're truly going to earn their long-term support and get them on board with our solution.

You'll want to bring these alternative designs and mockups as evidence that you've tried these other approaches and they weren't as effective as what you're proposing. For example, if you know that someone is going to ask you about the icon you chose, then bring a batch of alternative icons that might also communicate the same concept. It demonstrates that you've thought about it and chose what you believe to be the best one. Sometimes, the design we've come to discuss was suggested in a previous meeting. The stakeholders asked you to make some changes (despite your best efforts at convincing them otherwise), and now you must show them that design. In these situations, bringing alternatives is absolutely critical to demonstrating why your proposed solution is better. However, you still have to lead the conversation with the design that they're expecting. So present the idea they asked for, but also prepare alternatives that you think better address the problem.

More than simply addressing someone's suggestion, bringing alternatives creates a common place to discuss the merits of each option—a place, by the way, that you created and you control. If you come to the meeting with no alternatives, your stakeholders are going to search the Internet from their phone and propose the first option they find. You make a much stronger case if you have a set of clearly well-prepared ideas than whatever they find by spending a few seconds online. It's much easier to keep the conversation moving forward if you have these alternatives to discuss rather than trying to address new ideas and suggestions on the spot. Don't toss out all the rejected ideas; bring them with you. In fact, you should try the alternatives you think people will suggest so that you're prepared in the moment to demonstrate the differences. We'll look at presenting alternatives again in Chapter 7, but remember that having more than one design always creates a conversation that demonstrates there is more than one way to solve this problem.

PREPARE DATA

Likewise, prepare data (analytics, usability reports) to support any part of your proposal. It's one thing to make a suggestion, but it's another thing altogether to show the data that supports your ideas. Most of the time, it's enough to simply let everyone know that your decisions are based on data, but you must also be prepared to show that data, if it's in question. Actually, I don't recommend pulling out the data unless it's necessary to make your case. Using data to bolster your position is helpful when people disagree or when they react to your designs with skepticism. Because you're only anticipating how they will react at this point, have the data available, prepare it in advance, and know that you're basing your decision on it, but don't slap it on the table during the course of your presentation. Data is very powerful (almost too powerful) and using it all the time can create an environment in which no one wants to suggest anything different. You may stifle the conversation before it even gets started. So, be prepared to defend your decisions with data, but don't use it unless it's necessary to make your case.

During the course of working with stakeholders, your job is to learn what makes them tick, identify what things they care about, and then come up with a plan for how you'll respond to them in the moment. Writing down anticipated reactions, bringing alternative designs, and having data available are important parts of this process. You won't be able to do it perfectly each time, but it will help you to be prepared. Often, just knowing what to expect in a meeting can go a long way toward being articulate in the moment.

Create a Support Network

One of the best things you can do to ensure that your stakeholders agree with your recommendations is to get other people to support you in your decisions. That is, you want to be sure there are other people in the room who will back you up, help you make your case, and tip the scales when it comes to the final decision.

Getting other people to support your decisions is about showing that you're not alone in your ideas. It demonstrates that there are other smart people in the room who agree with you (and who may have more relational capital than you). It's about bringing out the best practices that the experts agree is the right decision. If 9 out of 10 designers agree, why shouldn't your clients? The majority doesn't always rule, but it's definitely more compelling than an individual making his case alone to an unsympathetic manager.

THE RINGER

In television, it's common to have prearranged "ringers" on programs. Whether it's a news broadcast, talk show, or reality TV, there are always people whose answer or reaction the show's producers have prearranged. They might need help building energy and momentum to make the show feel more interesting. The ringer might be the anchor who asks a good question of a reporter that he didn't cover in the initial story. Or the ringer could be an audience member asking a question to communicate something that's more effective coming from an average person than the expert host. Whatever the case, a ringer's purpose is to bolster support for an idea.

In design meetings, we want to be certain that there are other people who are prepared to ask good questions, point out specific important elements, or otherwise support our proposed designs. We may not remember everything that needs to be communicated, and a ringer can jump in to cover anything we forgot. They can ask you a question that sets you up to provide a well-articulated answer. Sometimes the ringer will just reinforce what you already said.

Often, ringers happen naturally on teams that are close-knit. After practicing the presentation with the rest of your team, it's common for a ringer to naturally emerge during the course of the meeting. When your coworker realizes that you forgot to demonstrate an interaction, he might ask, "So what happens when you click the button?" even though he already knows the answer. Or if more than one design is presented, your ringer can speak up, "The first option is better because..." as if the two of you hadn't talked beforehand.

I recommend being forthright with people about your need for support. It's okay to ask people to be your ringer. It may seem underhanded, but the purpose is not to deceive people or bowl them over with unauthentic enthusiasm. The purpose of getting people to back you up is to build a case to demonstrate that other people agree with you. Be open with people about your need for support, ask them to help you, and tell them to speak up when the situation calls for it.

IDENTIFYING PEOPLE

The process of getting people on board with your vision takes place more in one-on-one meetings than it does in a conference room. People can be reluctant to agree in a group setting if they're aware that the executive in charge has a different idea. Your job is to work with people beforehand and figure out who is on board with your designs before that conversation even takes place. You want to find the swing votes that will build a majority or ask other people to be prepared to help you. Make sure that you build into other people and relationships enough that you already have these go-to people available. It's not something you should expect to pull off right before the meeting.

The easiest place to get this support is your team: other designers or developers who have already been part of the discussion and design process. They're already on board and they were part of the discussion that led to the decision you'll present. These people should always be prepared to come to your defense if things take a turn that you're not expecting. But it's not enough to just assume that they will. If there is a concept, idea, or design that you think will meet resistance, be up-front with them and let them know that you might need backup.

Ask them to help you with writing the justification for the decision so that everyone is on the same page about your rationale. This is critical because when you're the one presenting, you may not be able to look away to check your notes and remember everything that went into the design. Your teammates can be there with the same list and interject when they see an important part of the logic is missing from the discussion.

However, your team cannot be your only source of support because everyone in the room knows that you share the same perspective. It's also necessary for you to seek out other people in the organization who have a stake in your project and may have some influence, clout, or reputation that you can use for support. There are almost always other people who understand what you're doing, are excited about the project, and can't wait to see it succeed. This might be someone you used to work with in a different area or it's the person who stopped by your desk, saw the designs, and seemed excited about the project. When people find out you're working on something they're interested in, they might even contact you themselves to express support and interest.

Find these other people and pull them aside. Invite them to the meeting, if it's appropriate, and prepare them to speak up if needed. Explain to them what the meeting is about, give them a copy of the agenda and designs in advance, and ask them directly for their support. It's okay to go so far as to tell them you might want them to speak up if there is any disagreement. If possible, point out the specific problem areas that you think will be a point of contention and help them understand how to respond. Give them any data or other rationale you have. Explain everything to them so that they have the same understanding that you do and are on board with the vision of your designs. You want this person to be your representative, to feel confident in their ability to support you, and to agree that your solutions are the best.

PEOPLE GET IT

I was in a meeting with the president of a large ecommerce site and we were presenting some recently implemented designs as well as a few new concepts that were in the works. The meeting went well; there were a few questions from him that I was able to address, and we walked away from the meeting with good vibes and a list of items to consider for another round of revisions. Immediately afterward, one of the other executives pulled me aside and said, "Hey, I'm sorry I haven't made myself available much, but I really want your project to succeed and I'd like to help, if I can. Maybe we can go over everything before these meetings so that I can back you up and we can all speak with one voice."

Here was someone who understood the value of communicating to stakeholders. Although she was one of the stakeholders herself, she saw that there was an opportunity for us to work together to achieve the best result. She liked our ideas, trusted our expertise, and wanted to ensure that we wouldn't be blocked. Needless to say, she became part of my support network. And even though she wasn't involved in every meeting about the project, I made a habit of keeping in touch with her regularly, pulling her into the loop on our designs, and allowing her to be our advocate in conversations that took place outside of our formal presentations.

Always remember that other people can help you accomplish what you want. Learn to build into those relationships and allow them to add value to the conversation. Find the people who can help you accomplish your vision, and set them up for success right alongside you. Having this small group of people who support you in a meeting creates an atmosphere of consensus. It demonstrates that you know what you're talking about because other people agree with you. It spreads the responsibility of the decision across the entire team. This is not just one person's idea, but an idea that is supported by other people, too.

More than that, it gives other people the opportunity to speak on your behalf. You may find that you don't have to do nearly as much talking to express yourself because other people will do it for you. It is much more difficult for an executive who disagrees with your solution to insist you change it when the other experts in the room agree with you.

The Dress Rehearsal

Now that you understand your stakeholders, have removed the distractions, anticipated their reactions, and gathered a group of people to back you up, it's time to go through the meeting step by step, practice your presentation, and prep everyone involved. The level of importance of the meeting often determines how much practice you need, but I've found that you should still make a habit of doing these things even for less important meetings. Whether it's a daily standup to review yesterday's work or a big presentation for an executive, each one of these following action items provides structure and a framework to guide your conversation. I recommend doing all of them every time, but the degree to which you spend time on it differs in each situation.

MAKE A LIST

Most people understand the value of having an agenda for a meeting and it cannot be underestimated when meeting with stakeholders about designs either. For an executive presentation, you probably already have an elaborate outline of the content you'll cover in a slide deck. That's good, and it will probably keep you on track. However, I'd still recommend having a separate printed version of your agenda for your own reference. Design discussions naturally wander around topics and can be difficult to keep on task when multiple people have ideas or suggestions that are not immediately relevant or may be jumping ahead. Storing the agenda in an accessible place is important for everyone else on the team (as we will see in the next chapter), but a paper agenda gives you a physical base you can quickly refer to. Printing to paper seems so low-tech these days, but you'll be more confident if you're not fumbling with technology (even a separate tablet or phone) to find your place.

Even for short meetings with your own team, like a daily standup, I still recommend putting together a quick agenda. It's so easy to forget the thing you meant to talk about or become sidetracked on details about something else. If you're like me, you go throughout your day working on multiple designs (perhaps even multiple projects) at a time. A coworker will stop you to ask you about an interaction, which causes you to rethink it on the spot. In the middle of the night, you wake up to the realization that there is a very important use case that no one had considered. You need a place to write these things down so that you don't forget to review them with the people who matter. I personally like to use a simple notes app that syncs with all of my devices so that even if I'm out shopping, I can add an item to my constantly evolving agenda for the next meeting and then release my brain from the burden of needing to remember it.

If you're not a note-taker or if it isn't your responsibility to remember everything on a project, there is still tremendous value to quickly jotting down an agenda for every meeting. You don't have to create an elaborate outline; just a simple list will suffice. Even if your meeting is with one other person, a list like this will be your guide and help you to know whether the meeting was a success. When I'm in a rush, I will still take five or so minutes before the meeting to jot down a few things I want to discuss. Even the smallest amount of preparation will help you know what to talk about. Always make a list.

PRACTICE OUT LOUD

It's also important that you practice having the meeting out loud, beforehand. That's right, like the dress rehearsal for a school play, you need to go into a room, talk through your entire agenda as if there were already people present, and even anticipate and answer mock questions out loud. You've already anticipated how people are going to respond, so play out the meeting in your head and verbally answer their questions to an empty room. Practicing what you'll say gives you the opportunity to hear your words. Hearing yourself speak aloud is very different from how it sounds in your head. Plus, you'll catch yourself saying things that could be worded differently, aren't helpful, or are repetitive. This is your chance to practice using the phrases and tactics you'll learn in Chapter 7 and Chapter 8 as well as catch yourself saying the things you shouldn't, which we'll see in Chapter 6.

The idea of holding a mock meeting might seem silly, but it's actually a critical part of preparing to be articulate. The more you practice going through the content, the less your brain will have to think about the agenda and the more mental capacity you'll have to be focused on being articulate and responding. You commit it to memory. We want to reduce our own cognitive load to the point that holding the meeting is a breeze. But also, design decisions can be particularly difficult to understand and there may be underlying reasons for your choices that you haven't even uncovered yet. I've found that I can identify some of my own motivations for design simply by talking out loud to myself.

I've spent countless hours of my career practicing meetings out loud: pacing the floor of my office, presenting my content to a picture on the wall, and even answering questions from invisible audience members. I've done the same thing in my car, in line at the grocery store, or waiting for a plane. Any onlooker might think I'm crazy, talking and gesturing as if there were someone else with me. But the habit of practicing for a meeting is one of the only ways you'll know how you sound. You anticipate reactions and then you practice how to reply.

As with agendas, the degree to which you need to practice will vary depending on the importance of the meeting. A big presentation with the CEO should be practiced a lot. A daily meeting with your boss will require less, but it's still a good idea if there are issues that might be difficult to discuss or if you're unsure how you might say it. For a big meeting, I might book the meeting room the day before so that I can practice in the same environment as much as I need to. For a simple phone call with my boss, I might stand at my desk and talk through the agenda once or twice to build my confidence. You have to decide how much practice is necessary to ensure you have the mental capacity to be articulate in the moment.

Overall, hearing yourself say things out loud gives your words new meaning, commits them to memory, and is the perfect testing environment. Practicing for a meeting is the usability test of being articulate: you get to run through everything and make sure it all works as expected. If not, there's still time to tweak it before the meeting begins. But regardless of the importance, always practice your meetings.

PREP EVERYONE

Finally, before you head to the conference room, have a short huddle with everyone involved in your support network. Review the agenda, go through each point, and note the items that are of importance. Ask people to jump in at specific points and confirm that there isn't anything missing. This is a great opportunity for a peer to check your work and verify that you're on the right track to getting your designs approved. It also ensures that everyone is on the same page, knows their part, and is ready to help you be articulate. It doesn't need to be long. Even just 5 or 10 minutes before the meeting will do, but it will help you and your peers to be prepared to present and respond.

Remember that the main purpose of taking so much care to prepare for discussing design decisions is to reduce the cognitive load both for your stakeholders and for you. Just as we would approach the usability of a design, our meetings have the same opportunity for refining what people see, optimizing the flow of the conversation, and testing our assumptions before it all begins. When our stakeholders have the mental capacity to focus on the most important decisions, we're far more likely to have conversations that are productive and helpful for the user experience. When we ourselves have the mental capacity to be free from remembering the agenda, we too can focus more on being articulate and carefully respond to feedback.

"Practicing for a meeting is the usability test of being articulate."

If you find your meeting happening exactly as you expected, that's a good sign that you did your homework and are well prepared to defend your design decisions. Allow it to build your confidence in the moment because confidence, too, will help you be articulate and give you the perspective you need to really listen to the feedback that's about to come.

[5]

Listening Is Understanding

No man ever listened himself out of a job.
CALVIN COOLIDGE

NOW THAT YOU'VE PREPARED yourself to present your designs and anticipated what the responses will be, you have the opportunity to actually meet face to face with the people who have influence over the project. This is where our skill at communicating really begins, but not because of anything that we say. The first thing we need to do is *listen*.

Listening is an important skill for every relationship, and it's no different when discussing design decisions. Listening isn't just waiting for the other person to stop speaking so that we can begin our response. The entire purpose of careful listening is to ensure that we understand our stakeholders before responding.

A proper and articulate response requires that we use implicit skills such as listening without interrupting, hearing what they're not saying, uncovering the actual problem they're trying to solve, and then pausing before moving on. We also must use more explicit techniques like taking notes, asking questions, and repeating or rephrasing what was said. Using these tactics, we can outwardly demonstrate that we understand what they're saying. Because most stakeholders don't speak our designer jargon, we must listen closely for the clues that will help us to attach their words to our designs, and when we respond, we need to use language that will be effective for everyone. We want to understand exactly what they're saying so that we can form the best response.

Implicit Activities

Implicit listening is applying skill in understanding what people are saying without outwardly doing anything specific to demonstrate that we hear them. An implicit listener is one who can quickly organize what's being said and derive meaning without any other external clues or further information. For the purpose of listening to design feedback, I'd like to highlight four ways we can implicitly mine stakeholder feedback to get at the core information we need to respond.

LET THEM TALK

The first thing you should do is to let your stakeholders talk as much as they want without interrupting. That's right, allow them to say as much as they need to and don't cut them off. People like to hear themselves talk, and they need enough space and time to express themselves without feeling rushed.

It can be difficult not to interrupt someone providing feedback on your work, especially if they're saying things you know to be incorrect or uninformed. Besides, we *also* like to hear ourselves talk! It's difficult to hear someone talk about your design work without feeling the urge to jump in and contribute your own ideas. After all, it's *your* design they're talking about. But don't stop them. It is to your advantage to let everyone finish first.

There are a variety of reasons why people need to talk so much. Some people just want to sound smart in public. It could be that there are other people in the room who they're trying to impress. As I mentioned in Chapter 3, you never know what sort of politics are at play. Other people are audible learners, and the process of talking about something helps them understand it more clearly. In fact, because design can be so difficult to talk about (especially for nondesigners), the process of talking through one's thoughts may allow stakeholders to arrive at their opinions over time. They might even eventually explain your design to themselves in the process without you having to say a word. Whatever the reason, allow your stakeholders to say their piece before moving on.

There are three main benefits to letting them talk as much as they want:

They will make themselves more clear

As people talk, they naturally repeat themselves and rephrase what they mean in an effort to communicate clearly. Because your job is to understand exactly how they see your designs, it's critical that you give them the space they need to describe them. Not everyone knows the vocabulary to use when discussing design, and it can take them a few tries to fully express themselves.

It gives them confidence that they were understood

The more people are able to say what they need to get a point across, the more confidence they'll have that they did just that. You want your stakeholders to know that they communicated effectively so that they can't blame a misunderstanding on their inability to communicate (or your inability to listen). Letting them talk gives them room to have that confidence.

It demonstrates that you value what they're saying

No matter what you say in response, allowing stakeholders to talk as much as they want communicates to them that you appreciate what they're saying and you're listening to every word. When you make them feel that way, it builds trust and they'll be more likely to agree with you later if they know they've been heard.

While they talk, present yourself as valuing their input by maintaining eye contact and nodding your head in agreement. Be sure to listen for specific words they use; for example, pay attention to any jargon they use and terms they prefer when describing your designs. Most people won't use language such as UI control, input element, drop list, popover, carousel, or tooltip. Part of your job with listening is to figure out what words they're comfortable using to describe your designs so that you can use those terms, too, when you respond. It will be difficult to earn their approval if you're using a different vocabulary; therefore, adopt the words that they use and also (eventually) find ways to teach them terms that will be more effective in the future. We'll look at this more in the section "Repeat and Rephrase."

Overall, allowing stakeholders to talk freely creates an atmosphere in which your stakeholders know they can express themselves without being interrupted, which makes them more likely to tell you what they think every time. They know that this is a safe place for them to express themselves and be heard.

HEAR WHAT ISN'T BEING SAID

Not everything that our stakeholders say will be immediately clear. Sometimes, we need to look deeper than their actual words to derive their intended meaning. So, another important part of listening to your clients and stakeholders is to *hear what isn't being said*. You have to try to understand both what they've expressed out loud as well as what never came out of their mouths. What's the subtext? What is the elephant in the room that no one really wants to mention? Often, what people say and what they mean can be two completely different things.

This might be more important in design than any other field simply because design is more subjective and people aren't always sure how to express themselves. Further, your stakeholders realize this is something that you made. You created it. It's your baby. They may be sensitive to that fact and try to tell you about a problem they see in indirect ways. If this is the case, people commonly respond with questions rather than direct disagreement. "Oh, that's interesting. Why did you use the primary call to action here instead of the secondary one?" The subtext might actually be that this person thinks the secondary call to action is a better choice but they just don't want to come out and say it that way. Any time someone uses the word "interesting" in a response to your designs, that's a big clue that they disagree with your approach.

As I've mentioned before, there are other factors going on in every meeting we're simply unaware of. If one person is being disruptive about something benign, perhaps he's trying to make a point to someone else in the room. Or, when your manager didn't care about the dashboard graphs last week but is now suddenly insisting that they be changed, maybe she's reacting to the meeting she just returned from with her own boss. We can expect that there is often something else going on.

Polite Paula

In one of my previous roles, I pitched an idea for a web interface that was a little unusual. My manager responded with enthusiasm because she knew I was excited about the idea and wanted me to succeed. She was the kind of person who was always supportive. She agreed to let me spend Fridays working on this side project so that it didn't distract me from my regular work during the week. For several months, I worked on this new idea, and when it was ready I brought it to her for feedback. She was so nice but rather than tell me outright that it was a disaster, she instead asked me questions about it in a way that showed me the flaws in my design. Because it was my pet project, I was naturally a little defensive. I answered her questions as best as I could, but in the end it was unclear to me what she wanted me to do. Looking back, I realize now that she was just trying to tell me indirectly that she didn't think it was worth pursuing. I would have preferred if she had been up-front with me about it, but I couldn't control how she chose to respond to my work. We have no choice but to hear what they're not saying if we have any hope of knowing the best way to respond.

Discouraging Dan

At another company, I worked on a marketing site for an online service. The site was completely broken: bad links, missing images, and outdated copy. It looked like an abandoned house. As it turns out, an unusual number of support questions were related to simple problems with this site. I knew the product owner didn't have the resources to redesign it. To me, it was low-hanging fruit: a simple five-page brochure site that could quickly be templated and updated. Because it really bothered me that the site was broken, I decided to redesign it while I was in between projects. My thinking was that an improved and functional website would be better than a perfect and infinitely delayed one. The first design I showed to the product owner was met without enthusiasm. "Oh...um, wow, Tom. That's really nice, thank you. It looks much better, but you really don't need to be spending time on this," was his reaction. I assumed he was just being nice. He wasn't my boss and didn't have the authority to ask me for help, but the site clearly needed some TLC. What could it hurt? I finished the designs, created the pages, and put it on a staging server. Again, the product owner wasn't excited. He appreciated my effort and gave me the green light to put it in production, but it seemed like he couldn't care less that I had done him this *favor*.

A few weeks after putting it into production, our group received an email announcing that this service was being shut down immediately, the marketing site would be taken offline, and existing customers would be given a transition period to find a new service. I can only assume that this product owner could not tell me that the service was being discontinued at that time. He tried to discourage me from working on the site, but I was not astute enough to read between the lines. Although I don't regret the time I invested in it (because I am proud of the way it turned out), I could have redirected my effort to something else that would have had a bigger impact if I had been skilled enough to hear what wasn't being said. I should have dived deeper to understand his lack of enthusiasm before blindly moving forward on my own. These kinds of subtle cues are easy to miss and require a keen understanding of our stakeholders.

UNCOVER THE REAL PROBLEM

While you're listening to your stakeholder's feedback, work to uncover the real problem they're trying to solve. Often, our stakeholders see a need that isn't being met with our designs and they may express it with a suggestion that isn't the right solution. So, don't focus on what they think needs to be changed or the specific words they use; instead, focus on the underlying problem they're trying to solve by suggesting that change.

People naturally think in terms of solutions rather than first identifying the problem. Because design is visual, it's much easier to say "Move this button over there" than it is to recognize that the problem is the proximity between the button and the date picker. Other times, people use vague language simply because they don't know how to express their reaction to a design. When someone says, "There's way too many colors here! It's like a rainbow," what they're actually expressing is, "The number of colors are distracting and I don't know where to look or what's important." We can help our clients understand the real problem by asking questions and repeating it back to them (in the following sections), but first we need to be on the lookout for this situation.

Reordered Inputs

A client once asked me to change the order of some text input fields on a form. It was a simple request. She just wanted to move some things around, but it struck me as odd because we had already agreed on the most efficient way for a user to enter the data. Although simple, her request was contradictory to what we had previously agreed upon. When I asked her why, her response was nothing more than an expressed preference: she simply preferred that the data be entered in that way. I asked her for an example of another application that did this and she sent me the spreadsheet that she gets as an export from the system, which she uses to generate reports for her meetings. Now, she didn't actually think that our app needed to look like a spreadsheet; that's not what she was trying to accomplish. However, in her explanation she mentioned that the order of the columns in the spreadsheet needed to match the data entered in the system. She thought that the way the user entered the data in the form would be reflected in the exported file that she would get from a dump of the database. She had no idea that we could customize the order of the data in the report for her, independent of the user's input. Had I made the simple change she originally requested without question, it would have resulted in a less optimal experience for the user. By digging deeper and understanding the real problem she was trying to address, I was able to respond and address her concerns without changing the design at all.

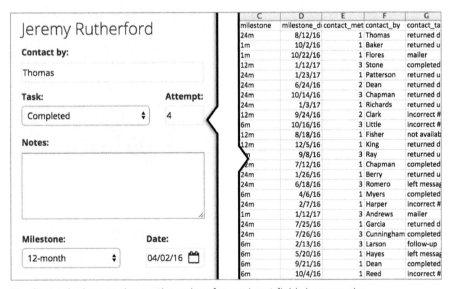

My client asked me to change the order of some input fields because she didn't realize that the exported file could be independently ordered from the user's input.

Duplicate Data

Another project I worked on had a complicated series of forms that were presented to the user as multiple steps. Each form could be different based on the options chosen in the previous step. First, the user would enter some information about the people in the report such as name, address, height, and weight and then choose the next form. When the user chose the second form (the event category in the figure that follows), we decided it was best to take them to a completely new page without the whole app navigation because the forms were so complex. We wanted the user to focus on the task and not be distracted. On that second form, the user's previously entered details were plainly visible at the top of the view.

When our client saw it, she said it was fine but the user needed to be able to edit the patient's details on this second form as well as the first. I questioned this because the user had just entered that information. Why would they need to immediately change it? Her response was confusing: she went on a tangent about a paper government form she was used to filling out, she expressed that she didn't want to train employees, that the details had to be entered correctly the first time, and that sometimes you might want two different addresses for the same person. Paper forms? Training? Duplicate data? None of it made any sense, so I pushed back.

 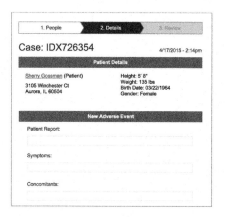

This is a simplified version, but in my original design, the user moved horizontally from one step to the other, but my client expressed frustration at not being able to edit the information from Step 1.

For several meetings, she continued to insist that we allow the user to edit the patient details on the second form, until finally I began to realize that she saw this app as a digital version of the paper form she had mentioned earlier. I had indeed designed it to be similar and she was distracted by what she saw as the differences. After some tough choices, we decided that the second form would not load on a new page but would instead simply load inline on the page directly below where the user had entered these details. We moved from a horizontal progress status to a vertical one. It was effectively still the same, but not having to return to a previous step to see the information gave the user a greater sense of control.

In the final design, the user moved vertically, which gave my client a better sense of control over entering the data.

When she saw our solution, she agreed it was better and we moved on to the next design. Had we made the changes she suggested initially (allowing users to edit the same data in two places), it would have resulted in a host of other usability problems. Listening to her and working hard to uncover the real problem she was trying to solve helped to ensure that we maintained a better user experience.

In summary, the visual nature of design naturally lends itself to changes in those visuals in order to accomplish the desired result. People make suggestions on how to change those things rather than describe the problem they see. It's hard for most people to think concretely about and express design problems. They only know that it doesn't feel right. Consequently, we need to be adept at listening to their solutions and connecting the dots in order to uncover the real problem.

THE ART OF THE PAUSE

The right word may be effective, but no word was ever as effective as a rightly timed pause.
MARK TWAIN

One last implicit listening skill is mastering the art of the pause—when you think your stakeholders are done talking, just wait. Don't immediately jump in with your response. Instead, pause for several seconds (maybe two or three) and allow for silence, however uncomfortable that might seem. This can actually be a little awkward, especially on a conference call or video chat where there are frequently delays and it might be difficult to tell if you've dropped off. (My own clients commonly ask if I'm still on the line, unsure if I was disconnected.) But whether you're on a call or face-to-face, it's worth risking the awkwardness to be sure that your stakeholder is finished talking and that there is a small gap in the discussion.

The purpose of the pause is threefold:

- First, you want to be sure they're actually done talking and that they haven't just paused themselves. Sometimes people stop and then immediately think of something else or a better way of saying it. If there's a better way for them to give you their feedback, you will want to hear it, because people don't always express it correctly the first time. Give them a chance to be articulate themselves. They need to feel good about what they said so they can't blame a misunderstanding on poor wording.

- Second, it gives you a chance to let the air settle; to let your stakeholders' words sit on everyone's ears for just a moment. You're letting the conversation simmer briefly, which gives you a chance to very quickly consider how to respond. You're not jumping directly into a defensive posture, but instead taking a moment to consider what was said and form an appropriate response. Just these few seconds of waiting will make you much more prepared to respond.

- The third (and most important) benefit to pausing is that you communicate to the other person that what they said is important enough for you to really consider it and think about it. Because you didn't jump directly to a conclusion that might conflict with theirs, you create a sense that what they just said was really valuable. People want to be heard (or at least to *feel* that they've been heard), and pausing gives you a chance to show them that you take their feedback seriously. If the silence is too deafening for you, say something like, "I hear what you're saying. Let me think about that for a second."

All of these implicit listening skills should establish a framework for how you see and hear your stakeholder's feedback. As you listen to them, you're making a conscious, nonverbal effort to truly understand what they mean. These internalized activities give you an opportunity to better organize your thoughts so that you can find the most effective response.

Explicit Activities

In addition to the internalized activities we use to listen to design feedback, there are also several explicit activities we can use to improve listening. Explicit listening includes verbally demonstrating that you're listening as well as doing things that outwardly show you are engaged in the conversation. For design meetings, taking notes, asking questions, and repeating back or rephrasing what they say are all important ways to effectively listen to our stakeholder's feedback.

WRITE IT ALL DOWN

The first thing you need to *do* to listen is to take notes. You're not going to remember everything your stakeholders say or suggest. One of the best ways to listen to them is to write down what they say. Record everything, especially the items that need to be followed up on. Even in smaller meetings, it's important to write down what was discussed and save it somewhere. I've already recommended writing things down and taking notes at different stages of the process, and you should always have a way to take notes in your meetings. You might never reference your notes after the meeting, but that's okay. Taking notes is more than just having a place to record what was said:

Notes prevent you from having the same conversation again.
Taking notes is the only way you're going to remember what was discussed and create a history that will help you to avoid the same conversations again in the future. I've found that a lack of notes is frequently responsible for miscommunications, repeat conversations, and changing requirements on many projects. Having notes avoids the rework that will prevent you from being successful in communicating about your designs.

When it comes to design, notes are critical because opinions and ideas about the right decision will change over time. If you don't have notes, you don't have a paper trail to understand what logic went into the original decisions. You only have "he said, she said" and a bunch of rehashed conversations. When design decisions are made verbally in a meeting, it can be nearly impossible to remember later why decisions were made. Additionally, there may be team members who aren't present at the meeting. Having notes helps you to quickly bring them up to speed without recounting the entire meeting.

I am, admittedly, not the best at keeping my notes organized, but I do keep them, and there have been multiple occasions when we chose a path for a specific interaction that was called into question after the public release. "Hey, why did we do it this way?" I was able to find my notes from months earlier and follow up with everyone and even remind them of the person who suggested the change, why, and the date. When you can do that, it usually shuts down the conversation, saves everyone time, and allows you to move on. With detailed information like that, you can either address the problem and discuss a better solution or remember that the decisions were right the first time and move on.

Notes free you to focus on being articulate.

For the same reasons discussed in Chapter 4, writing things down reduces your cognitive load and frees your mind to focus on being articulate in your response. When it's written, you no longer need to think about it. If you allow all their ideas and feedback to float freely through your brain, you'll have a difficult time organizing those suggestions in a way that will yield the best response. Write down what they're saying so you can take the next step and form your responses without needing to actively recall everything from memory.

Notes build trust with your stakeholders.

Another benefit to taking notes is that just the act of writing things down will make you look attentive, smart, and, as a result, more articulate. Taking notes makes you look like a good communicator. It makes the other person feel valued because you care enough about what they said to write it down. This gives them confidence that you heard what they said and you're planning to follow through.

When people have that impression of you, they do a much better job of listening to and considering your own response later. It's a shared respect that goes both ways. As a result, I often use note taking as a way to tell people that I'm listening and bring out the best in the discussion even if I disagree with their suggestion. Verbally saying something like, "Oh, I see your point. Let me write that down," earns trust and shows that you're a safe person to talk to.

I don't mean to suggest that you should write things down that you have no intention of following up on only to make the other person feel good. Taking notes can create a positive perception, but you shouldn't be disingenuous. For instance, if I'm not sure I really want to do what that person is suggesting, I might write it down but leave a question mark next to it so that I can follow up later. Taking notes is more than just remembering what was decided. It has intrinsic value above and beyond what you will actually do with the notes after the fact.

Notes keep the meeting on track.

Writing things down is also a great way to ensure that your meeting stays focused by giving you a place to record parts of the conversation that get off topic. People will think of just about anything in a design meeting, and it's easy for it to get derailed by something that isn't the core focus.

Suppose that you're showing the home page to discuss the interaction on the category menu, but when your boss notices that the login form is messed up, suddenly the meeting is headed in a different direction. Because you're taking notes, you can suggest delaying the discussion of the login form if that's not the purpose of the meeting. "Yeah, I noticed the login form this morning, too. Let me make a note of that and I will follow up right after this meeting, but for now let's stay focused on the category menu." Taking notes gives you a natural place to put stuff that might otherwise be distracting.

Writing things down feels more permanent than only saying it out loud. It gives everyone a sense of security that what's being said was important and will not be discarded.

TAKING BETTER NOTES

The best way to take notes is to ask another person to do it for you. This frees up your brain to be focused on listening and being articulate. If you're trying to write down what people are saying, you'll miss important parts of the conversation because things can move quickly. If you don't have the authority to tell someone else to take notes for you, find a note buddy who is willing to help. Offer to swap note taking responsibilities at each other's meetings. It could even be someone from a different department or project, any willing person who can be trusted to capture the conversation. You might also consider recording audio or video of the meeting, but I've found that I rarely have time to review the video afterward to recapture lost notes. The best practice is to write down what people say so that you have an immediately accessible history to reference, even if you do it yourself.

To get the most of your notes from a design meeting, they should be:

Accessible

Store your notes in a place that everyone can access. As we will see in Chapter 9, following up with your notes afterward is an important part of the process. Here in the meeting, you just need to be sure that everyone can see or has access to them. This might be a wiki page in your project's repo, a separate page on your design mockups, or a shared folder or document. Your notes should always be available to everyone on the team, even during the meeting itself.

Organized

Write your notes within each agenda item so that it stays connected to the design in question. Usually, this would be by page, UI control, or interaction. Attach your notes to one specific thing. I usually create a bullet list of notes under each agenda item as the meeting progresses.

Specific

Write down the names of people who make the suggestion you're noting as well as the names of people who agree or disagree. This is not always an exact science, but something as simple as "Cynthia suggests changing the color; Brian isn't sure" comes in useful later when you're trying to remember who was responsible for suggesting the change.

Definitive

When a decision is made, make that explicitly clear so that you can find it later if you need to remember it; for example, "Final: drop-down control should be a pop-over menu." Items that are still undecided should also be marked so that you can follow up on them later. I add a question mark to anything pending a decision: "Reconsider placement of sort options (?)"

Actionable

Nearly every item should have a follow-up action or person associated with it. Writing down ideas is useful, but if there's no action, there is almost no point. For example: "To do: update prototype w/ new control," or better, "Chad to update prototype w/ new control." If there is a lot of follow-up to be done, it might be useful to create a separate section in your notes just for documenting it so that you don't miss it in the list of other notes. I often create a separate heading below the agenda called "Follow-Up."

Referenced

Add links, URLs, screenshots, or other reference material to your notes so that it's easier to communicate what the point of the discussion was. When people suggest other websites or apps as a reference, add that information to help you remember the conversation. Without references, it will be difficult to recall what you meant by "See how SocialApp does it." Adding inline screenshots or URLs with the agenda makes your notes much more valuable in the long term.

Forward-looking

Aside from the agenda items that you need to cover right away, there are always other design decisions that will come up during the course of the conversation. You need a place in your notes to add items to be discussed at the next meeting, or in a different context. I do this by simply adding a new heading in my notes called "Next Meeting." Having this real-estate set aside gives me a place I can quickly organize discussion that might be off-topic and note it for the next time around.

To summarize, taking notes is a critical part of listening to stakeholders. It's important to write things down so that we have a history of what was decided and avoid having the same conversation twice. But notes are more than just a place to record our decisions; they also allow us to focus more on being articulate in our response because we no longer need to rethink everything that was said previously. With our notes in hand, it's much easier to go through each piece of feedback and prepare the best response. Regardless of the size or importance of the meeting, always take notes.

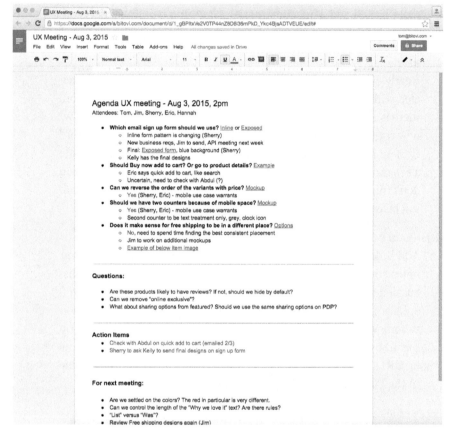

I don't always take good notes, but when I do, they're Accessible (Google Docs), Organized, Specific, Definitive, Actionable, Referenced, and Forward-Looking!

ASK QUESTIONS

The challenge with talking about design to stakeholders is that they often don't know the best words to communicate their meaning. In the same way that we designers have difficulty expressing our decisions to them, they, too, have difficulty expressing their own thoughts to us. Yet, so much of listening is just about getting the other person to talk. We need to pull the words out of them that will help us do our job better.

It's not usually enough to just let someone to say their piece and then move on. Some people will have plenty to say that is difficult to interpret, whereas others won't have much to say at all. We need to get them talking more, to say it in a different way, and to express their thoughts more carefully. The way that we do that is by asking good questions.

Here are a handful of common questions that are useful to ask in any situation to get people talking more and help you to understand their suggestions or feedback:

- *What problem are you trying to solve?* Like the previous section, it's okay to be direct if it's not clear what stakeholders are trying to accomplish with their suggestions. Just ask them outright.

- *What are the advantages of doing it this way?* This gives stakeholders a neutral way of explaining why they think their suggestion is better without explicitly labeling one as better than the other. Giving them a way to express these differences will reveal a lot about why they think it's the right solution.

- *What do you suggest?* Often stakeholders will say something needs to change without any idea about how that will be done. Even though it's our job is to find the solution, giving stakeholders an opportunity to propose something helps us understand their needs and gives them some context to realize the difficulty of the problem.

- *How will this affect our goals?* Stakeholders often have our goals in mind, but they don't always realize how what they're saying is connected to them. You want them to directly connect your designs to the goals every time. Often, just the process of answering this question helps them see why their suggestion won't work as well as they thought.

- *Where have you seen this before?* Asking for reference material (other apps and websites) is one of the best ways of seeing your stakeholder's perspective. The point isn't to suggest that their idea won't work if it doesn't exist already, but to find out if it's rooted in a known design pattern from some other app or website.

The main purpose of asking questions is to get your stakeholders to explain what they mean so that you can be sure you understand. Asking questions also has benefits beyond simply getting the other person to clarify what they mean. Even if you already understand what the other person is trying to say, asking good questions shows that you're listening. By repeating back to them what they said in your words and in the form of a question, you're reinforcing that you understand. This creates more trust. The other person feels respected, valued, and understood. Just like letting them talk, they're much more likely to agree with you later when they feel good about being heard now.

REPEAT AND REPHRASE

The beginning of wisdom is the definition of terms.
SOCRATES

The words we choose to talk about our designs can make or break the conversation. If we aren't using the same vocabulary to talk about our work with other people, there will inevitably be misunderstanding, confusion, and missed expectations along the way. Our stakeholders don't always know or use the same words that we do. Finding that common ground is a balancing act of meeting them where they are, while also helping them take steps in the right direction by teaching them to talk about design. If we're going to agree on a solution, we need to get everyone using a shared vocabulary that facilitates understanding. Part of listening is identifying the words our stakeholders use to describe our designs and then repeating it back to them in way that helps everyone get on the same page.

Rephrase: Convert "Likes" to "Works"

The most important way we can do this is to help our clients move from talking about what they like and don't like (which are their preferences) to what works and what doesn't work (which is the effectiveness of the design). It's too easy for someone to say they simply don't like something. A subjective response like that gives us no way to address our stakeholders' concerns because it's not possible to tell them their opinion is incorrect. We can only have a different opinion.

Instead, listen for opportunities to convert "likes" into "works." Repeat back what they said by rephrasing the statement to focus on effectiveness. You might also consider following up with a question to confirm that's what they intended to communicate or for additional clarification.

For example, "I understand that you want us to move that UI control over there, but why doesn't it work to have it over here?" When people hear their concerns rephrased inside a frame of effectiveness, they often recognize that they're only expressing a personal preference. You might still have to deal with managing their request, but at least we're getting to the core issue and understanding how to respond to them more intelligently.

This doesn't mean we should teach our stakeholders, correct them, or send them a copy of Chapter 12 for homework. (Although the latter wouldn't be a bad idea!) What we should do is rephrase their response in the form of a question that forces them to talk about it in a way that's more helpful. If you're not sure, ask them directly. Encourage them to tell you what doesn't work about your design. This means that you, too, must work hard to strike the word "like" from your vocabulary and always place an emphasis on the utility and function of the design.

Getting our stakeholders to move from discussing their preference to describing the function of the application is a key skill in the process of articulating design decisions. The reality is, we don't really care about what our stakeholders like or don't like (although we could never tell them that). With a user-centered design approach, we're concerned with what does and doesn't work for the user and ultimately for the business. Flipping this switch in the minds of our stakeholders can make a big difference in our ability to communicate.

Repeat: What I Hear You Saying

Another way to train our stakeholders to communicate more clearly is by repeating back to them what they said using words that are more relevant to a discussion of design and UX. Because we don't expect that they'll know all the "right words" to describe our designs, we have to listen to what they're saying and translate that into a vocabulary that will become our common ground. Leading with the phrase "What I hear you saying..." is the best approach to accomplishing this because it emphasizes that we are listening to them, understand what they said, and will now confirm it by expressing it in our own words. This is an opportunity to bridge the language gap: take what they said in their own words and translate it into something that will be more helpful in the design decision-making process.

Here's an example:

> **Stakeholder:** I don't like how these disabled buttons look. I have no idea why they don't work! We should add some help text or a tooltip or something.

> **Designer:** What I hear you saying is that you don't think a segmented control is the best choice in this context, because the user won't understand why the disabled options aren't available to them. Is that right?

Why aren't kittens available? Teaching our stakeholders to call this a "segmented control" without talking down to them can be useful in moving toward a shared vocabulary.

Repeating what our stakeholders say, using terms that will be more helpful to the conversation, is a great step toward a common language without coming across as overtly condescending or alienating them for using the wrong words. You need to find the right balance of helping them without making them feel silly.

This is actually something I've learned with my kids. The best way to teach them is not to correct them directly, but to repeat back what they said in the correct way. When my child says, "Gimme that big red thingy," it's much more effective to respond, "Oh, you'd like this measuring cup?" than it is to say, "Silly child, this is a measuring cup! And 'thingy' isn't even a real word! Ask for it using the right words and then I'll give it to you." My child isn't ignorant. She just lacks the vocabulary to describe what seems to me like everyday objects. Our stakeholders aren't to be treated like children just because they don't use the same words we do. Instead, we can help them be more effective by repeating back to them words that are more useful.

Here are some examples of how you might craft your responses in a way which introduces stakeholders to a shared vocabulary:

Stakeholder: That button needs to be moved over here.

Designer: We purposefully placed the call to action above the fold.

Stakeholder: That arrow is too difficult to see.

Designer: The disclosure is meant to be subtle so it doesn't distract from the content.

Stakeholder: This menu is hard to use.

Designer: We're using the system's native droplist, but we could design a custom control.

Remember that an important part of listening is rephrasing and repeating back what our clients have said so that we can confirm we're on the same page and have a solid understanding of the best way to respond.

Let's review what it looks like to listen to stakeholder's design feedback. We cannot communicate effectively with them unless we listen to them and fully understand what they're saying. There are several implicit ways we listen, such as letting them talk as much as they need to, trying to hear what isn't being said, and working to uncover the real problem they're addressing. After that, pause for a few seconds to be sure they've finished talking. But there are also several explicit skills we can apply to be better listeners of design feedback. We take good notes by writing down what was decided. We ask questions to clarify and tune our understanding. And we repeat and rephrase what stakeholders say to help establish a shared vocabulary and common ground. All of these things help us be better listeners, understand what is being communicated, and allow us to form the best response. You might think it's time to tell them what *you* think now, but it's not. First, we need to get in the right frame of mind.

[6]

The Right Frame of Mind

First learn the meaning of what you say, and then speak.
EPICTETUS

YOU'VE POURED YOUR SOUL into these designs. You've taken all this time to think about your stakeholder's perspective. Plus, you just spent the better part of your mental capacity listening to them talk about why your designs don't work as well as you think they do. It would be tempting (even logical) to think that you're cleared now to launch into an epic speech about usability and wax eloquent on design patterns and data, but you're not. Before you go to the point of no return, you should get in the right mindset. You need to put on an attitude that will help you be articulate and get what you want. It requires you to give up control, check your ego at the door, and always lead with a "yes." More than that, preparing to respond is about learning to be charming and avoiding replies that will only hurt your efforts. When you're in the right frame of mind, you can set up your response by following a pattern called "Thank, Repeat, Prepare." The purpose of this chapter is to help you be mentally prepared to take on the responsibility of using your own words to win people over. Crafting an effective response requires a bit of mental exercise to do well.

Give Up Control

If you're familiar with twelve-step programs that help people overcome addiction, the first step is appropriate in our relationship to our designs, too. *The first step to recovery is admitting that you're not in control.*[1] No matter what we think, we don't usually have the final say when it comes to our designs. We have a significant amount of input into the process, but at the end of the day, there is always someone else who can overrule us. There may even be an entire team of people who disagree with our proposed solutions! We'd like to think that we can design whatever we want, but we're naturally limited by those in authority over us. There are other people involved, whether that's our team or an individual executive. The sooner you realize this, the sooner you'll see how important it is for you to learn to influence people with your words. You can't force them to agree with you. You have no choice but to find a better way.

Even if we could, would we really want to get our way every time without needing the approval of others? Would we even want to have the authority to design something against the better judgment of our peers? It would be incredibly unsatisfying as a designer to know that no one else agreed with us, and yet we still chose to go our own way. The whole purpose of user experience design is to create something that's useful—in fact, delightful—for the widest possible audience. What sort of enjoyment would we get from an experience that everyone else around us thinks is terrible? That's no way to live a designer's life, and as much as it can be difficult dealing with feedback from other people, the approval of and appreciation from the people on our team is actually far more rewarding in the long term.

This is why letting go of our designs is a healthy thing. We create it, we give it life and influence its direction, but then it grows up and goes out into the world on its own. After we show it to someone else, it is no longer only ours to cherish and coddle. When we share our designs with other people, we are letting them into our world and allowing them to influence our process. The parallels to parenting are not lost on me.

The hardest part of listening to design feedback from a nondesigner is letting go. When we recognize that we don't have ultimate control over the final outcome, we make a mental shift that exposes just how much

---

1   The 12 steps were originally published in the 1939 book, *Alcoholics Anonymous: The Story of How Many Thousands of Men and Women Have Recovered from Alcoholism.* They have been adapted and used in many different substance abuse and addiction recovery programs.

we need to communicate well in order to maintain the sanity of the user experience. Letting go of control creates an emotional release so you can keep your wits about you and not take everything so personally.

What does that look like in practice? It's nothing more than taking on the attitude that your work is not your own. It's making the simple recognition that you can't control everything. It's admitting that you need help from other people to create the best experience. It's a mental practice of taking two steps back, getting out of your bubble, and walking around to the other side of the table to sit with your stakeholder. Armed with empathy for their perspective, it becomes much more natural to allow their feedback to exist separately from your own personal interests. If you can convince yourself of those things, you'll be in a healthier place to talk about your designs with others. You cannot respond unless you've first learned to let go.

Check Your Ego at the Door

Getting in the right frame of mind is also about remembering to check your ego at the door. We need to separate ourselves from our own ideas and ambitions in a way that allows other people to inform the project without being blind to their suggestions. We can't think that we're the only ones with good ideas, that we have all the best solutions, or that there is only one way (our way) to accomplish the goals. Our egos can get in the way of our ability to respond to stakeholders effectively.

There is a tension here, though. Our expertise in design suggests that we should be recommending the best solutions. We *do* want our stakeholders to understand us and trust that we know what we're talking about. They should know that our expertise and recommendations are to be taken seriously. We want to convince them that we're right, but at the same time, we can't actually believe that our ideas are the only way. There's a delicate balance between believing that we have the *best* ideas and recognizing that they aren't the *only* ideas. The challenge is to make solid recommendations while also separating yourself from your ego and taking seriously the suggestions and ideas of other people. This is difficult to do.

The trouble with ego is that it's almost impossible to see in yourself, which is why it's a problem to begin with. If everyone could easily recognize when they're being egotistical, the world would be a much simpler place to navigate. The red flag to look for is when you find yourself thinking that your solution is *so much better* that you don't see any value at all in the other person's suggestion. In normal, healthy discussions, you can usually see the value of what the other person is saying even if you disagree. When your ego is getting in the way, that value is lost. Any time you think that you're right and they're wrong, you should be cautious. It doesn't mean that you must agree with them, it only means that you might need to reevaluate the situation.

When our egos are preventing us from seeing the value of other ideas, it will manifest itself in the form of excuses for why the other person's suggestion is not valid. For example, you might find yourself thinking, "They don't understand technology," "They're old," "They're not our target user," or "They don't know anything about design." When you begin excusing other people's ideas with glib stereotypes or by writing off their expertise, there's a good chance your ego is to blame. Be on the lookout for these kinds of subtle reactions in your own mind and find a better way to position yourself so that you can form the best response. If the only logic for disagreeing with someone else's suggestion is "they don't understand my job," you're not going to be able to build your case on that kind of generic (and egotistical) assumption. By removing your ego, you create the space you need to form a response that will be based in reality and logic instead of opinion and stereotypes. Removing your ego makes you less defensive and therefore better prepared to respond appropriately.

Arrogance Killed the Interface Star

Early in my career, I led a design team at a medium-sized company that provided electronic payment services to small businesses. The company offered a terminal-based system for customers to manage their accounts. It was expensive and clunky, so it decided to move to a web application. This was a big deal! The web version would be cheap and simple to use by comparison. In fact, the old system was so terrible that *anything* would have been an improvement. It'd be pretty hard to screw this up, I thought.

One of the first things we decided on was the resolution. (Yeah, I know how weird that sounds today.) At the time, a lot of people had 1024 × 768 pixel screens, designers' screens were in the 1,200-plus range, but some people were still stuck with old 800 × 600 screens, and even a few with resolutions as low as 640 × 480. I made the decision that we would design for 1024 × 768 because, "most people should have a larger screen by now." It seemed like a reasonable choice: it wasn't as large as my own screen, but it wasn't the smallest either. A sort of middle ground.

Another designer (who was much more experienced than I was) suggested that we go with 800 pixels because we were dealing with small companies who were unlikely to have new displays. But my arrogance got in the way. I wanted the application to *look* good, and an 800-pixel width was just too limiting for me. I even remember joking, "If anyone still has an 800-pixel screen, they don't deserve to use it," but there was more truth to my attitude than I'd like to admit. And so, we designed the entire app for a 1024-pixel fixed width screen. Can you see where this is going?

We released the app with plenty of internal fanfare. We didn't do any usability testing. In fact, we didn't really change the overall experience at all. We just took the terminal app field-for-field and put it into an HTML form. But anyway, the app was released and we could all pat each other on the back.

Later during a follow-up call, one of the salespeople was enthusiastic. It was so much better than the old system (high fives!), but it had really been a hassle for customers to scroll "sideways" to see all of the fields. Wait…what? That's right, *sideways scrolling*. He didn't even suggest it was a flaw with the design. As is common in usability testing, users tend to blame themselves. "It's too bad. If only our customers had more modern computers." However, it was a major design flaw that adversely affected the productivity of pretty much everyone who used it. And so we went back to redesigning the app for an 800-pixel screen.

This took place during a time when user-centered design was brand new to web designers, but I still see situations like this today. Well-meaning individuals are so invested in their work that they make decisions at the expense of their users. My mistake cost our company real time and money, not to mention the hassle to our customers and the damage to our credibility. Hopefully, you can learn from my mistake and check your ego at the door.

Not every design decision will cost you tangible amounts of money, but letting your ego get in the way has real consequences even if you don't realize it. Despite learning from my own mistakes, I still find it a daily struggle to keep my ego in check. There is no magic pill. It takes conscious effort, reminders from your team, and practice. So, do your best to check your ego at the door. It will allow you to have an open mind and put you in a much healthier place to respond to the people whose support you need to be successful.

Lead with a YES

One of the biggest barriers to effective communication is when people see each other as being on opposite teams. It's easy for there to be an us-versus-them mentality when discussing design with someone who is not a designer. One of our jobs as good communicators is to remember and reinforce that we're all in this together, headed toward the same goals, and with the same level of passion for the product.

There is no better way to foster this atmosphere of collaboration than to always lead with a YES.

The concept of leading with a yes was modeled for me by Dave Ferguson, one of the cofounders of the NewThing Network, a nonprofit network of churches and social-justice organizations whose mission is derived from the passion, charity, and volunteerism of others. Dave and I worked together for many years in the suburbs of Chicago, and I absorbed much of his leadership style into my own routines. Since the beginning of Dave's leadership, he wasn't often in a position to pay people salaries to accomplish the mission and vision of the organizations he leads. Because he relied on donations, he simply couldn't do everything that other stakeholders thought was important to the mission of the organization. Instead, he had to learn to influence people with his leadership style and the passion they had to do good things for others. When he was first starting out as a pastor, people would come to him with great ideas that he wasn't able to pull off on his own. Rather than turn people away, he chose to always deliberately say yes to people who had ideas that might be seem impossible given his resources.

He found that people were more motivated, empowered, and passionate when their ideas were given permission to succeed. Even if they didn't fully accomplish their goal, it was far better to empower people to do great things than to shut them down at the outset. Dave says, "We have learned that if we want to be involved in innovative and creative new things, we have to 'lead with a yes.'"[2] He has been helping other people learn to do this by always looking for the opportunity to agree with and empower them with a positive reaction to their ideas and suggestions. Dave references an article from *Fast Company* magazine titled "My Greatest Lesson" by Katherine Hudson. In that article, she says, "When someone offers you a challenge, don't think of all the reasons why you can't do it. Instead, say, 'Yes!' Then figure out how you'll get it done." This is the foundational principle for leading with a yes.

This principle also has roots in improvisational comedy. One common rule for improv is that each actor must agree with the other: whatever one actor brings, the other must go along with. Why? Because if one actor says no, it will completely shut down the sketch; they'll have nowhere to go. Our meetings with stakeholders are also improvisations. If we expect to head in a positive direction, then it's critical that we always lead with a yes. Otherwise, we risk shutting down the conversation or sounding like we're making excuses for why their suggestion won't work.

This idea has had a profound effect on the way I communicate to people about design. It means to always stay positive and never refuse someone, regardless of the implications their suggestion might have on the project. It's about stating directly that you value the other person's perspective. It's about being open to new, innovative ideas even if you're not sure they will work. It's a positive, life-giving word that will change the way you communicate about your designs to other people.

---

2   *The Big Idea* by Dave Ferguson, Jon Ferguson, and Eric Bramlett. Page 180. Used by permission.

DEVELOPING A YES REFLEX

Leading with a yes means that you always begin every response with a positive affirmation of the other person's idea or request. It is a mindset that this person isn't wrong. They have just as much potential for good ideas as you, and they're a valued part of the process. Dave calls this the "yes reflex":

> Most of us have a "no reflex" to new and creative ideas that seem impossible. But you can change this...the next time someone brings up a new opportunity, make sure the first word that comes out of your mouth is *yes*....The yes mindset gives outrageous, seemingly impossible ideas a chance to live and breathe and sometimes be implemented in whole or in part.[3]

The purpose of honing your "yes reflex" is not to give in to every request from our stakeholders or to just let them have their way with the experience we've so carefully crafted. Instead, it creates a space where everyone recognizes that we're all on the same team, accomplishing the same goals, and we can work together toward the best solution. As Dave writes, it gives you more time to figure it out:

> Training yourself to have a yes reflex doesn't commit you to actually implementing the idea. Before "Yes" ever commits you to doing something, it actually buys you time to figure out how you are going to make it happen. Often we say yes and then take time to regroup and consider the opportunity's potential benefits and liabilities. Leading with a yes gives you time to figure out if you can really pull it off... We're not making the case for having no boundaries; we're describing how innovation happens. *And innovation happens in places where 'No' is seldom heard...*[4]

Leading with a yes is much easier when you agree with the other person's suggestion. "Yes, that's a great idea. I completely agree that this control should be a text link instead of a button." It's even easier when

---

3 Ibid.

4 Ibid. Emphasis mine.

the other person can do the work they're suggesting, like another designer on the team. "Yes, let's make that happen! Please go ahead and update the documentation to reflect this new design. Good idea!"

However, it's not always easy to say yes when you disagree. If you understand the problem your stakeholder is trying to solve, but you disagree with the solution they propose, leading with a yes might sound like, "Yes, I completely agree with you that we need to reconsider the placement of this UI control." We're not saying that their precise solution is correct and that we will implement it in that way. We're only agreeing on the problem because it might still be possible that another approach will solve it. Further, it leaves the conversation open-ended so that their idea can live in the room for a while, giving other people the opportunity to contribute to a solution.

Leading with a yes also means finding a way to say no, while actually (verbally) saying yes. For instance, the change they're suggesting will take more time or money than your team has, and you know it's not possible even if everyone agrees with the solution. Perhaps there is a trade-off for another feature. In those cases, leading with a yes might sound like this:

> Yes, I agree that the interaction for "add to cart" should be updated. With the release next week, we will need to postpone implementing the new search template so that we can get this in. Do you agree?

You know that your stakeholders aren't going to budge on the new search template, but you can start the conversation about what needs to happen to move things forward. You've started off on the right foot and allowed them to participate in the process in a positive way. You're empowering other people to take part in your project at a level that is necessary for them to see the realities and decisions in your world. Often, people outside our immediate influence simply don't understand everything that goes into our decisions. Leading with a yes invites them to be part of the decision so that they can help us navigate the process. This often results in them agreeing with our point of view.

> Yes, you're right that our documentation isn't where it should be, and we need to fix that. If you'd be willing to help me oversee that part of the project and audit the existing docs, I think we can arrange our priorities to make it happen.

It's a common problem for people to offer ideas without any responsibility. The more ownership you propose, the less likely you are to encounter resistance. It's too easy for people on the outside to criticize something they have a limited view of. If you give people the chance to be part of the solution, they will either take you up on it or they will decline and retract their suggestion. In either case, you've remained positive and helped them to see that their opinions are valuable and appreciated.

Sometimes, leading with a yes alone can get you the trust you need to move forward without even having to discuss it further. Often, our stakeholders just want to know that we value their time and feedback. I was in a meeting with several people, including the president of the company. He was very hands-on and wanted to participate in the details of the new application we were designing, so we had scheduled a regular design review with him to provide input on the project. During one meeting, he began nitpicking one specific UI control—a menu the user could use to sort and filter a list of search results. It was an important part of the experience, but his feedback evolved from a casual question to very specific suggestions about the placement, copy, color, and interaction. Although I was happy to address his concerns, the details of his feedback seemed misplaced to me. Why would an executive care so much about these little details? Rather than get into a discussion about it or offer my own opinion, I said "Yes, I agree with you that we need to reconsider the implementation of this menu." Abruptly, he stopped, looked directly at me and said, "Great, I know you guys will find the right solution. Let's move on."

You see, he didn't actually want to get into the details of design minutia. In hindsight, he was probably "just talking"; he saw something, had a suggestion, and chose to go down the path of working with us to make it better. He knew that it wasn't his job to come up with all that stuff. So, what seemed at first to be an unusual or concerning series of suggestions was actually just a casual conversation. My agreement with him that there was a problem to be addressed reminded him that we could be trusted with the solution. He wanted to know that we were listening to him and considering his feedback. After that, he was happy to let us do our jobs. Leading with a yes reinforced this and let us get on with the meeting.

As you develop your yes reflex, remember:

- It reinforces that you're all on the same team and facilitates collaboration.

- It allows you to be open to new ideas, even if you're not sure how it will work.

- It keeps the conversation open-ended, giving you time to find the appropriate response.

- It gives you the opportunity to consider ideas in light of limitations and resources.

- It shifts responsibility for new ideas onto others, making them participants in the solution.

- It builds trust and confidence with stakeholders that you value their input.

Be Charming

One challenge that we designers face in receiving feedback is that we simply don't have a good rapport with nondesigners When we go into a meeting with a stakeholder, we might assume the worst, prepare for a battle, and put up our guard to protect us against an onslaught of negative feedback. We can become defensive, which can be reflected in both our posture and our response. Yet the surest way to get what we want (the best possible user experience) is to go into the meeting with an attitude that will convey our expertise so that our stakeholders will want to trust us with the decisions. We have to be likable, approachable, and project a sense of self that's appealing to others. In short, we have to learn to be charming.

Charm is something that can be learned and honed for any relationship, but is equally valuable in our interactions with stakeholders. It's the ability to communicate to other people in a way that appeals to their needs and compels them to agree with us. It's about presenting ourselves in a light that reflects our best qualities and demonstrates an earnest effort to show an interest in helping the other person. This puts us both on a path toward mutual benefit. If you can do that, you've mastered the ability to be charming.

In our relationship with stakeholders, being charming is the best way to assume the attitude we need to respond to them appropriately. A grumpy and defensive remark isn't going to woo them into agreement. Instead we can smile with confidence, be authentic, not take ourselves too seriously, and orient ourselves toward them.

HAVE CONFIDENCE

The most useful tool you have in being charming is confidence. If you have confidence in yourself and your designs, people will trust you and give you the freedom to decide. When you lack confidence, you convey uncertainty, which leads stakeholders to question your solution. To be certain, having confidence is not about being arrogant, cocky, or asserting that you're always right. It is allowing the knowledge that your skills are valuable to overflow into your tone, body language, and attitude when you talk about your work. Being confident is being proud of your work while also understanding that you're not the only smart person in the room.

To build your confidence, consider this: you got this job for a reason. Maybe it was your beautiful portfolio, your impressive resume, or your past work experience. Whatever it was, your stakeholders chose you for this job. That conveys a certain amount of trust, belief in your expertise, and a willingness to let you make decisions. Although you should always have to work to earn their trust, you're already in a great position to communicate your message with confidence.

The best way to communicate that confidence is to smile. Most people think of smiling as expressing happiness, but smiling expresses a lot of other emotions, as well: agreement, enjoyment, appreciation, connection, and yes, confidence. When we smile, we show that we expect to be in agreement with others, we appreciate their time and attention, and we are confident in our ability to solve difficult problems. People without confidence don't smile; they look concerned, worried, upset, or distant. If we want to convey confidence, we must smile as much as possible. A.J. Harbinger, who runs a coaching business and podcast called The Art of Charm, suggests practicing in the mirror. Says Harbinger, "Smiling makes you look more confident and approachable. You should practice this in the mirror, especially if you're not super smiley by nature. Remember that you want to smile with your whole face, not just with your mouth."[5] When you're meeting with stakeholders, make a conscious effort to smile even if it feels a little unnatural. Smiling will show your confidence and build theirs in the process.

What's interesting is that confidence, in general, has so many benefits and can make a huge impact on your success in life, your salary, your relationships, and, yes, even your ability to communicate to people about your designs. Harbinger adds these points about confidence:[6]

- Confidence is a self-fulfilling prophecy. For example, children who think of themselves as the smartest in the room get the best grades.[7]

- The same study found confidence had more to do with lifetime earnings than IQ. In short, it's better to be confident than smart.

- Not only can overconfidence make you successful even when you know you're bluffing, it might eventually become just regular old confidence.[8]

- Sitting up straight in your chair will increase your overall confidence. This applies to posture overall. What's more, behaving confidently will make you feel more confident over time.[9]

JUST BE YOURSELF

A challenge for designers in corporate settings is being authentic: learning to be ourselves around stakeholders. No one likes it when they have the feeling that the other person is being fake. We are at our best when we are ourselves. We are relaxed, natural, and able to think more clearly. Too often, designers put on airs in a meeting. They puff themselves up to protect themselves from negative feedback but having that attitude will only backfire. Instead, use your strengths to your advantage and be confident in your ability to communicate.

---

5 Harbinger, AJ. "A Daily Checklist for Staying Confident." Used by permission. *http://bit.ly/1JfCG5w*.

6 Ibid.

7 Callaway, Ewen. "Confidence as important as IQ in exam success." *http://bit.ly/1JfCL96*.

8 Weisul, Kimberly. "Study: Better to Be Confident Than Right." *http://cbsn.ws/1JfCLpR*

9 Ohio State University. "Body Posture Affects Confidence In Your Own Thoughts, Study Finds." ScienceDaily. *http://bit.ly/1JfCLWH*.

Additionally, being yourself helps everyone else relax, too. They can relate to you more easily when they see you for who you really are. Harbinger notes that being yourself will help other people be authentic, too, because you've shown them "that it's okay to relax and be genuine" and it makes people feel good to be around you.[10]

Part of what makes us so great as individuals is our own unique way of winning people over. Everyone is different, yet everyone has a way with people. What is it that you do to make people smile? How do you get someone's attention if you need to? How did you win the heart of your spouse or the class election in grade school? Whatever successes you've had in the past, now is the time to mine them for meaning and use them to your advantage in projecting a persona that is uniquely you.

Some people are witty or funny. Some are good at hospitality and making people feel welcome. Others are great at listening and following up, giving gifts, paying compliments, or remembering important dates. Whatever your thing is, you have an opportunity to use that unique gift with the people who you want to influence. There is no better way to influence people than to use your natural-born tendencies to appeal to the needs of your audience. The point is this: relax and be yourself. You'll be better for it, and your stakeholders will appreciate your authenticity. Just the act of being "normal" with other people contributes to your own unique way of being charming.

DON'T TAKE YOURSELF SO SERIOUSLY

One of the biggest killers of any conversation is someone who is so serious about their work, their project, or their task that they're unable to relax and respond with a posture that makes them seem human. Sometimes, we act like robots: unable to grasp a lighthearted comment or show simple kindness. When we get in this "getting things done" mode, it can be really easy to have tunnel vision and become too focused on what we're trying to accomplish. That can be fine (and really effective) when we're heads down in our computers creating awesome stuff, but it's much less effective with a group of people who we want to agree with us. When you meet with stakeholders, more than any

---

10 M., Brian. "How to Be Charming to Women." *http://bit.ly/1JfCLWT*.

other time during your work, you need to stop taking yourself so seriously. Learn to relax and take everything with a good dose of reality: not everyone thinks as seriously about your work as you do.

Another key element to learning charm is finding ways to specifically convey that we're okay with critique of our work. Doing this requires that we be ourselves, as we saw in the previous section. It also means that we have to take a step outside of our project and remember that the people we work with are human, as we saw in Chapter 3. Most of all, though, we should be kind, lighthearted, and even funny around the people that we want to agree with us. Put simply, we need to be likable.

Using humor is a great way to be likable and exude charm. Humor disarms uneasy situations, and laughter reduces tension. Breaking the ice with a benign joke or lighthearted comment is a great way to get everyone to relax and focus on the purpose of the meeting. Plus, it reminds everyone that the decisions we're making are not life or death.

However, there's a delicate balance of knowing what's appropriate, what's actually funny, and what's completely off-limits. It can be good to poke fun at the elephant in the room, especially if everyone is particularly uptight about it. However, it's not okay to focus jokes on one specific person, no matter how funny or relevant it might be.

Harbinger says that humor is a great way to be charming, but that the goal is not to make other people laugh. He explains, "Focus instead on making yourself laugh. Be self-amusing and have fun first; then look to share that enjoyment.... By focusing on having a good time yourself, you'll generate a fun, positive attitude that will infect those around you and make you more charming."[11]

It's not my place to advise you on using humor, but with the right exposure and good inputs you can learn to use humor to make people smile, disarm them, and keep the conversation moving forward in an upbeat way. The goal of using humor is not to have stakeholders in raucous laughter, but to break the ice, help everyone relax, and maintain a good

---

11 M., Brian. "How to Charm Women with Humor." Used by permission. *http://bit. ly/1JfCSle*.

spirit. Humor is a solid way to not take yourself too seriously and to be charming with the people whose support you need in order to be successful.

ORIENT YOURSELF TOWARD OTHERS

The last skill we need to learn to be charming is to have a posture that is oriented toward other people. When we align ourselves with the needs of others, we create a connection that can overcome any obstacles to our communication. Harbinger says this is about making someone feel as if they are the most important person in the world.[12]

The opposite, of course, is being egotistical—focused only on ourselves. Just as we are checking our ego at the door, we are also turning our minds to our stakeholders and thinking critically about what they need to hear to agree with us. It's not a selfish attempt to pander to them to get what we want, but an honest look at how we can talk to them in a way that will make them (and us) successful. When we put on an attitude that orients our response toward the needs of our stakeholders, we are addressing their concerns in a way that (combined with all of these other approaches) turns on the charm and presents our response in the best possible light.

When I do something to hurt my wife's feelings, I know it can take time for her to forgive me and to move on. However, I can accelerate that process by being charming. I have confidence that she *will* forgive me, so I can approach her with a smile and an assumption that reconciliation is possible. I can be myself by being honest about my intentions and provide my perspective. I also don't need to take myself so seriously, so I will always break the tension with a joke or witty reference to my own stupidity. All the while, my response is oriented toward her needs: what does she need from me to reconcile? If I do that, we are usually able to move on pretty quickly and focus on the most important things together.

My six-year-old son is remarkably good at being charming for his age. His younger sister loves to play with him so much that she never wants to stop. He's learned that if he just stops playing and walks away, she'll burst into a fit of tears. Rather than endure that over and over again,

---

12 M., Brian. "Developing Charisma is Possible." Used by permission. *http://bit.ly/1L5T8eg*.

he's found ways to redirect, distract, or entice her with other things that meet her needs. After they've played the same game a dozen times, he doesn't outright say he's tired of playing *with her*. Instead, he proposes something more transitional that meets her needs of having more play time. I've overheard him say things like, "Hey, this is a really fun game but I have to go to the bathroom. Let's take a break for a few minutes and then we can play again later. Like after lunch!" Usually, she has moved on and is occupied with something else after he's returned from the bathroom. He is applying charm through an orientation toward her needs.

Using charm in our response to stakeholders is not really all that different from a marital spat or two children playing together. As I mentioned in Chapter 2, we are all only more experienced children. We have to approach our stakeholders with the same care that we would our loved ones. Getting into the right frame of mind requires that we use charm to our advantage and are conscious of how to apply it to our conversations. Learning charm is critical in our approach to stakeholders. It helps us exert a positive influence and ensures that they are working with us to create the best user experience.

Change Your Vocabulary

As you make the transition to a mindset that is positively focused on yielding a great response to stakeholders, it's important to commit some things to memory about what you should and shouldn't say in the process. Before you respond, you need to change your vocabulary.

"YOU'RE WRONG"

Don't say "you're wrong"—no one likes to be told they're wrong (even if they are), and you'll only make them defensive. Remember, your goal is to stay positive and always lead with a yes. Even directly telling them you disagree can be a flash point for the conversation. If you need to disagree, find ways to communicate that disagreement as an alternate idea or a different perspective. Even though there might be times to put your foot down and explicitly stand up for something you believe in strongly, it's almost always better to project yourself as being in alignment with the stakeholders as much as possible. Finding those opportunities for outright disagreement are difficult and probably not worth the risk.

"FROM A DESIGN PERSPECTIVE…"

Don't start any sentence with "From a design perspective…" because that's usually just another way of saying "from my perspective." Remember, we don't care about *your* perspective; we care about the user's perspective. Plus, this sounds like you're trying to one-up them with your expertise in design. Although your expertise and perspective is indeed valuable, it's not usually necessary to point it out. Our stakeholders understand that what we say is our perspective. Sometimes we use this phrase to mean "the reason we did it this way…" If that's the case, say that. You do not want to create a separation between your expertise and that of the stakeholders. We're all on the same team. "From a design perspective…" doesn't reinforce that, so strike it from your vocabulary.

"LIKE" AND "DON'T LIKE"

Don't talk about what you like or don't like; instead, focus on what works and what doesn't work. Remember, our interest is in the usability and effectiveness of the application, not our own personal preferences. In fact, remove the word "like" from your vocabulary altogether. If you catch yourself saying it or asking other people what they like, stop and correct yourself. It will be worth emphasizing that you shouldn't have used "like" at all.

This is more difficult if you're discussing the visual design of an application, rather than specific flows or general usability. Visual design matters less to the utility of an application, but it conjures a lot of opinions about what looks good and what doesn't. A lot of people are visual, and the specific look and feel of those UI elements will be front and center. If the express purpose of the meeting is to review the visual design, you still need to find ways to communicate why you think the visuals work or don't work rather than why you like or don't like them. For instance, because specific colors and styles contribute to the user experience, you can keep your comments focused on how the visuals affect branding, perception, or emotion. Hopefully, the visual design of the UI is defined by branding guidelines, a documented design language, other existing applications, or a style guide. Even if that's not the case, keep in mind that our purpose is to ensure that the experience is consistent, thoughtful, and delightful. A rightful focus on avoiding the word "like" will help us be effective in our response.

TOO MUCH JARGON

Finally, avoid using industry-specific jargon as much as possible. Instead, find words that the average person can understand so that we're all on the same page. It is easy in our UX designer bubble to become accustomed to referring to specific processes (Agile, scrum, sprints), tools (Git, Bootstrap, Axure), or elements (accordion, CTA, modal). Many stakeholders don't share in our design-web-app culture of vocabulary, so before we respond, we should take the time to filter our response for words that might be unclear. Instead, use the knowledge you have from listening to them and adopt the words that you heard them use, as we saw in Chapter 5. This is your opportunity to repeat and rephrase what they said in an effort to both communicate clearly as well as teach them to talk about design, too, but you can't start off by using words that are unfamiliar. Always be cognizant of the vocabulary you use and make sure it's something your stakeholders will understand.

Make a Transition

Now that you're in the right frame of mind, you need to provide a transition to your response that will set you up for success. This transition will set the stage for everything you're about to say and help determine exactly how your stakeholders listen to you. You have the opportunity to get their attention and let them know what to expect. It's critical to ensuring that your stakeholders listen to and accept your response in the best possible light. This is the response *before* the response.

However you decide to structure the actual response, remember to keep this transition brief. The point is to provide a transition only, not a long introduction. I recommend a simple approach called "Thank, Repeat, Prepare." Each of these three elements should be part of one quick statement.

THANK

The first thing you should always do is thank your stakeholders for the feedback they just provided. It's the most polite way to get from what they said to what you want to say and it recognizes that their time is both valuable and appreciated. We always want our stakeholders to know how much we appreciate their time and attention. They're the reason we're so fortunate to have this incredible job! As briefly as you can, form a word of thanks as you begin this transition.

REPEAT

Next, briefly summarize what the stakeholders just said if you haven't already. I don't mean that you should go over each point line by line from your notes. Instead, make a statement that describes what they've just done for you in a way that is flattering and complimentary. This will naturally build off of the "thanks" that you've already led with and remind them that you were listening.

PREPARE

Lastly, tell your stakeholders that you're about to respond to their feedback. Perhaps it seems obvious (and it is), but the transition is meant to provide a segue for everyone. However unnecessary it might seem, setting the stage in this way will create the right kind of vibe and prepare them to listen to and absorb what you're about to say.

It's not enough to just tell stakeholders that you're going to respond. You need to give them some insight about the content of your response; you're foreshadowing what's to come. You should tell them not only that you're going to respond, but how and what you plan to say. This is an opportunity to let the cat out of the bag, to clue them in as to what your feedback will be to ensure that there are no surprises. You're trying to avoid beating around the bush by being direct and getting straight to the point.

Here are some examples:

- "Thanks for sharing your thoughts with us about this project. Your insights are really valuable, and I appreciate you going through all that with us. I'm going to go back through all of your points so that we can discuss them, but I want you to know that some of the things we decided on have an explanation that I think you'll agree with once we start talking about it."

- "Thank you for sharing your feedback. I appreciate the opportunity to go through all of this with you because it's important for us to be on the same page. I'd like to go back over everything you said because there are some important points where you need to be aware of our decisions in more detail and it will help you to see where we're coming from."

These are somewhat general and can be used in about any situation, but you can see how they all create an air of respect, reinforce the team mentality, and let the stakeholder be prepped for what's going to come next. In both cases, I've told the stakeholder that our ideas have an explanation worth considering. Maybe it seems like communications mumbo-jumbo, but the practice of telling someone what they should or are likely to think is actually very effective. Interestingly, people will often believe what you tell them, so tell them that they will agree with you! Even if they don't, you've at least set the stage in a positive way.

Here are some other examples that might deal with more specific feedback:

- "Thanks for pointing out the differences between the existing app and our new designs. You're right that there are some important things we should consider, and I want you to know we put a lot of thought into how we designed it, so I'd like to explain to you why we did what we did with the grid views."

- "Thanks for being up-front that you're concerned about our implementation of the cart and checkout flow. I'm going to address each of your points because we had some very specific reasons for doing it this way that I want you to be aware of. I think you'll agree that this is going to increase conversion once you understand our thought process."

- "Thanks for your viewpoint on the home page. You've definitely given a lot of great feedback and I'd like to go through it all, if that's okay. Our thinking about the layout had more to do with our long-term vision and some other initiatives that we expect to see down the road, so it's important for you to know why we approached it in this way."

The point is this: it's not enough to just launch right into a defense of your work. You must take the time to get in the right frame of mind, stay positive, and make a graceful transition to what's next.

All this prep work will pay off. It might seem like there's a lot to consider, remember, and do to just have a simple conversation with a stakeholder about design, but the process moves very quickly in real life. Our job is to adopt these practices and make them habitual so that we can transparently navigate the conversation with this approach. We need to focus on letting go of control and separating ourselves from our ego to get into the right frame of mind. With that done, we learn to always lead with a yes and use charm, humor, and our own personality in a way that will make people want to agree with us. This step includes avoiding certain phrases, like "You're wrong," while using language that focuses on what works and what doesn't work. Finally, we can set up our response to stakeholders by crafting a short transition that thanks them, summarizes what they've said, and prepares them for what we're about to say.

In summary, to get into the right frame of mind, you need to:

- Give up control of the outcome so that we can allow other people to provide feedback on the project
- Check your ego at the door so that we can be open to other people's ideas
- Lead with a yes so that we create an atmosphere of agreement and cooperation
- Learn to apply charm so that we can win people over with our own unique personality
- Change our vocabulary so that we avoid tainting our response with potential miscommunications
- Form a transitional phrase so that we can set the stage for what we're about to say

At last, we can now jump into our own response and find the best ways of helping our stakeholders to see our perspective and win them over. The best part is that there are already some tried-and-true ways to get what we want. The next step is to respond.

Further Reading

A.J. Harbinger from the Art of Charm website (*http://theartofcharm. com*) provides great resources for learning how to be charming. I recommend these additional articles from the Art of Charm on learning to be more charming in any relationship:

- M., Brian. "Anybody Can Have Charm." *http://bit.ly/1L5TfXb*

- Harbinger, AJ. "Why Confidence Is More Important Than Looks." *http://bit.ly/1EndNme*

- M., Brian. "What a Good Smile Can Do for You." *http://bit. ly/1L5TcdL*

- Harbinger, AJ. "Confidence: Fake It 'Til You Make It." *http://bit. ly/1L5TaTi*

- M., Brian. "Developing Charisma Is Possible." *http://bit.ly/1L5T8eg*

- Harbinger, AJ. "It's Not Always What You Say, but How You Say It." *http://bit.ly/1L5T4v1*

- Harbinger, AJ. "How to Improve Your Speech." *http://bit.ly/1L5T26i*

- M., Brian. "The Importance of Confident Body Language." *http:// bit.ly/1L5T1iS*

- M., Brian. "Speaking with Confidence in Work and in Life." *http:// bit.ly/1L5SZaw*

[7]

The Response: Strategy and Tactics

Strategy requires thought, tactics require observation.
MAX EUWE

NOW THAT IT'S TIME to actually respond to our stakeholders, we need to take everything we've gathered so far and apply it on the spot. Responding to stakeholder feedback is a matter of forming your words in a way that will yield the best response by staying focused on the goal of the meeting: to get agreement from them. There is a structure and format to your response that will make it easier to get what you need out of your time together. To accomplish our goal, we break down our response into several core parts that will form the building blocks of our words. That logic will flow together and make it possible for us to present our reasoning in such a way that it will communicate the very best response. *This is the key to articulating design decisions.*

When we communicate with people about design and expect to get their buy-in on our project, it's no different than other communication mediums that demand a response, such as marketing and advertising, politics, or even military campaigns. There is a rhythm and pattern to our response that mimics these other communications approaches. As with any good communications plan, we need to have an objective or goal, a strategy for achieving the objective, tactics for delivering the strategy, messaging for employing the tactics, and, finally, a way to elicit a response from the recipient. Each one feeds back into the other to help us accomplish the goal.

| Objective | → | Strategy | → | Tactics | → | Messaging | → | Response |

In this chapter and the next two chapters, we will look at these parts in detail. For now, we'll begin by first defining our strategy for responding. We need to know what we want to say to achieve our objective of getting agreement. Next, we will look at four specific tactics for delivering that strategy. These tactics are tailored to design discussions and give us some options for how to talk about our work in the context of the user experience (UX). In Chapter 8, we will review several of the most common response types used for UX design feedback. These templates will help you identify the key messages that are important for your situation and give you a starting point for your response. Finally in Chapter 9, we will bring everything together by creating a response that touches on all the important areas and then directly asks for agreement from our stakeholders. This is what I call the *ideal response*. If this all seems a little too contrived for the average conversation, stick with me through this process, because we first need to look at all the parts individually for them to flow naturally in a real context.

At a high level, crafting a good response requires that we:

- **Define our strategy for responding.** What will we say to make a compelling case?

- **Employ tactics that will help us get there.** How will we deliver the strategy?

- **Identify common, relevant responses.** What key messages are important in our context?

- **Apply a common framework and ask for agreement.** What do we want our stakeholders to do next?

A UX Strategy for Responding

We already know our objective: to get agreement from our stakeholders. Everything we say needs to take this into account. The way we do that is to employ a strategy for responding that keeps us focused on that objective. Let's go back to the three questions I posed in Chapter 2 that will help you be a better communicator and a great designer. It's important to emphasize that all throughout this process you're going back to your answers to these questions and using them to inform how you respond to your stakeholders:

1. What problem does it solve?

2. How does it affect the user?

3. Why is it better than the alternative?

The answers to these three questions form the basis for every response you provide to stakeholders. If we can communicate these three things, we'll set ourselves up for success. Conveniently, we can craft our strategy for responding around our answers to these questions. That will lay the groundwork for the tactics we choose to use in our response. Let's see how each of these questions gives us a clear strategy for responding.

APPEAL TO A NOBLER MOTIVE

Our first strategy for responding is to *appeal to a nobler motive*. Every time you respond to design feedback, you should always attempt to attach your decisions to a goal, metric, or other problem that you're solving. This is where your answer to the question *What problem does it solve?* comes in handy. This idea of associating your decisions with an agreed-upon metric is one of the steps to effective communication that Dale Carnegie calls "Appealing to a nobler motive" in his 1936 classic *How to Win Friends and Influence People*.[1] I find that this is especially effective in design discussions and is often the missing ingredient from a designer's portfolio of communication techniques. You want to find the thing that you know your stakeholders care the most about and connect it to the proposed user experience. If you can do that, you're well on your way to being a great communicator.

With any application or website, we have an agreed-upon set of goals, metrics, key performance indicators (KPIs), or other success factors. We are trying to solve problems with our designs, and every decision should reflect that. As mentioned in Chapter 2, having these problems defined in the beginning and a metric for measuring success will be

---

1   Carnegie, Dale. *How to Win Friends and Influence People*. New York: Simon and Schuster, 1936.

critical to making your case with stakeholders. If you don't have any goals or metrics, write them yourself and present them to the stakeholder. You both need them if you're going to succeed.

Often, design feedback from stakeholders isn't taking these goals into account at the outset. People look at something and react, often without considering the original intent of the project. Art and design, after all, are intended to elicit emotion, to create a response, and so your stakeholders' knee-jerk reaction to your work may not be an indicator of failure; they just simply aren't thinking about the original goals. Your job is to keep those front and center, remind them why you're all there, and keep the discussion moving forward.

Increasing Add-to-Cart Rate

I was working on an ecommerce site with a goal of increasing the add-to-cart rate. We had created some great interactions specifically geared toward improving this metric, and the design was tailored to the unique logistics challenges of this particular business. As stakeholders compared the experience to other popular ecommerce sites, a lot of questions arose. "Why was this button so big? Did the interaction really have to use that particular control? Are we sure this is the right copy for the call to action?" Beyond the design, questions came up about other metrics: "What about cart abandonment? Overall conversion? Didn't those matter too?" In these conversations, I could point back at our goal for the phase (increasing add-to-cart) to remind them of that focus and why we believed these decisions would improve that KPI. Without this previously agreed-upon metric, we could have easily allowed the project to morph into a monster of addressing each concern that came up, and the result would have been a mess. Instead, we kept our designs laser-focused on the problem that we were asked to solve.

More than only justifying your decisions, though, appealing to a nobler motive can also help you to keep the meeting under control. In another meeting with the same team, the discussion turned to the visibility of the store finder utility and how it integrated with showing actual in-store stock levels in the search results. Although that conversation was important to the business overall and it was indeed an issue that needed to be addressed long-term, it was not something that we were trying to solve in this particular phase. Rather than allow that discussion to derail the meeting, I proposed adding this as a backlog item to be discussed for a future phase and delay the discussion. We were able to stay on track.

You see, sometimes the thing you get stuck on is not actually going to help you achieve your goals and so it's appropriate to suggest moving on and addressing it later. If your goal is to improve conversion but everyone is talking about whether the loading indicator should be a spinner or a status bar, that's a good sign that the conversation is not ultimately going to help you. The spinners might be important, but don't get stuck on it. Agree to move on. Any time you can connect your design decisions to the original goals, use cases, or metrics of the application you stand a great chance of making your case.

REPRESENT THE USER

Our second strategy is to explicitly *represent the user*. Perhaps it's so obvious that it's easily overlooked, but our response should always represent the user in a way that is tangible and real—more than just lip-service. We have to help our stakeholders understand our decisions by answering the question *How does this affect the user?*

We naturally think a great deal about the user. We probably even refer to "the user" in our meetings, but it's important to remember that our role in the design process is not just about building things that take the user into consideration; it is actually to advocate on their behalf to our stakeholders. We are the representative of our users at this meeting.

Imagine the lawyer representing a class-action lawsuit or the leader of a worker's union negotiating fair wages. We bear the same level of responsibility when we claim to be UX designers. It's not enough to only watch users in a usability study and then work those learnings into our designs. We must go one step further and see ourselves as possibly the only window our stakeholders have into the needs and objectives of our users. When we talk about them to stakeholders, we need real stories, concrete examples, and demonstrable experiences to use in our defense.

Your response is an opportunity to bring what you already know about your users and present it to your client in the form of a story that creates the kind of empathy required to drive us to action: to make the best decision for them. Instead of focusing on the mechanics of the system, we create a human connection that demonstrates a real need being met.

Adding a button

One of the great things about modern web applications is that they can update the page without the need to refresh and reload everything. However, I've discovered that this occasionally causes problems with users who expect to see the page change when they choose a different option. If it doesn't, they think the app isn't responding. In one app like this, we had a set of filters that the users could check and uncheck. The page was updated instantaneously, without even the need for a loading indicator, but some of the users we observed didn't realize the search results had been updated, so I added a Done button that closed the filter panel and gave them a sense of completion.

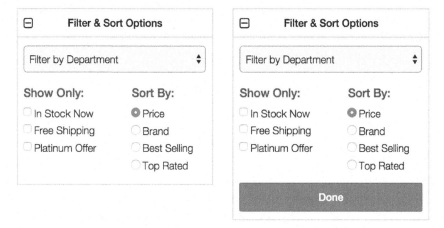

The addition of a Done button gave the user a greater sense of control, but in fact did nothing more than close the panel.

When I presented this change to our stakeholders, I had to justify the addition of a button that seemed unnecessary and did almost nothing, yet it took up space in the UI. The easiest way to represent the user in this case would be to talk about my observations in general terms:

> In our usability study, people didn't realize that the search results were being updated automatically, so we added the Done button to give them a way to explicitly indicate that they were finished.

What would be better is to present the same idea as a story (or use case) that describes a real situation for users.

> We have a lot of distracted users navigating the app while they shop, and they need a way to indicate that they've finished filtering. The Done button allows them to make that clear and gives them a sense of control over the filters.

What would be best, though, would be to tell a story of one user who makes a good spokesperson for others, using human details that encourage a connection to their needs.

> We had a mom using the app in-store with her kids. She was distracted and didn't notice the results updating, so she tapped multiple times and became frustrated that it didn't appear to respond. Giving her this Done button will make it more clear and show her products more quickly.

As I mentioned in Chapter 2, user observation and usability studies are critical to your ability to communicate effectively to stakeholders and make a case for the user. You can't represent someone you've never met or observed. So, do whatever is necessary to make yourself get up and go watch people use your project. It doesn't take very many observations to draw meaningful insights about the design of your application or website. You can then apply this understanding in your meetings with stakeholders to represent the user and make a case for why your designs are the right option for delivering the best user experience.

DEMONSTRATE EFFECTIVENESS

Our third strategy for maintaining the user experience answers the final question *Why is this better than the alternative?* and positions us to get the agreement and support we need to move forward. To do this, our response must demonstrate how our proposed solution is better than the alternatives, including any of those suggested by our stakeholders.

As I mentioned earlier, this is the part of the conversation where designers often fail to adequately make a case for their designs. Even though we probably do a pretty good job of solving problems and making things easy for users, we are less adept at helping people understand why and how our designs are the best approach. Being intentional about demonstrating this is the key to communicating that value.

This part of our communications strategy keeps us focused on using the tactics and messages that will help us convey this important piece of the puzzle. We want to be sure that our response includes examples, data, alternatives, comparisons, and any other tangible or visual demonstration of why our designs are the best choice for both the user and the business. Being able to keep that front and center is critical.

Your response is an opportunity to not only talk about why your design is better, but to also visually show why and how your designs will make a difference. Talk is cheap, but a picture is worth a thousand words. Every response should focus specifically on the differences between each design and express why your own solution is best. More than that, you must show your stakeholders precisely why that is the case. Being able to identify and express these differences is a key skill in articulating design decisions.

Prototyping FTW

One of the things that can be really difficult to understand until it's in a usable form is user flows. UXers spend a lot of time putting Post-it notes on the wall, discussing the right way to guide a user through the application, and then usually flesh those out in a series of static mockups to present to stakeholders. Often, what seems to make sense on the wall of a conference room has a very different feel when you're holding it in your hand.

A mobile app I worked on had a very complicated flow for users signing up for a series of special promotions because there were a lot of variables. Did the user arrive from a special URL or an email campaign? Were they paid subscribers? Did they have an an online account? Were they logged in? Depending on the combination of variables, the user might be funneled into one of a dozen or so different paths. Early on it was clear just how confusing these flows were, even to those of us designing them. After the team had agreed on a solution, I realized we were overcomplicating it and suggested a simpler approach, but my stakeholders weren't convinced it would cover all the cases.

Rather than argue about sticky pieces of paper on a wall, I instead jumped into prototyping mode and built a simple frame-by-frame demo of how it should work. The result was immediate agreement, like lightbulbs going off in everyone's head as they saw the difference. The original flow felt confusing and error prone as soon as we held it in our hands. The newer flow was simpler and obvious. So simple, in fact, it was hard to believe that we hadn't thought of it before. In this case, the most eloquent words might never have convinced anyone of the right approach. The best thing I could do was show everyone what it would feel like in real life. It wasn't enough to just talk about it; I had to actually demonstrate the effectiveness of my solution. Demonstrating your designs is the most important strategy you can have for articulating design decisions.

Tactics Are Actions

Now that we have our strategy well defined, the next step is to employ tactics to help deliver on that approach. When talking about design, I suggest five tactics to shape our response:

1. Show a comparison

2. Propose an alternative

3. Give them a choice

4. Ask others to weigh in

5. Postpone the decision

There is not one way to apply these tactics. You might choose to use one or all of them, depending on the situation. Your job is to decide which of these methods will create the best case for your designs and help you get agreement.

1. SHOW A COMPARISON

The first tactic is to show a comparison. You want to take your proposed design and the suggested changes and show them side by side so that the differences between the two are clear. The purpose is to provide a visual reference that leaves no question about which approach is the best. Too often, we talk about design in meetings using words that cannot adequately demonstrate the effect it will have on the user experience. The idea here is to find a way to make quick design changes and put both options next to each other.

I usually do this directly in design software by taking a screenshot of both ideas and dragging them onto the same canvas with a large dividing line down the middle. I may already know what the feedback is going to be and I've prepared both designs for discussion. Perhaps my stakeholder insisted on the change at a previous meeting. Now, I'm coming back prepared to make a compelling case with visuals that will show the differences and, hopefully, make my case. No matter how you do it, show both options in the same view so that you can discuss them without having to switch tabs or windows.

Show all the things

One of the sites I worked on had a two-level horizontal navigation, one below the other. The second level of navigation was a set of filters that, although useful, were not part of our goals for the project. They were simply an artifact of the design discussion, "Let's show all the filters!" However, one of our design goals was to fit as much content (in this case, news headlines) within the vertical browser space on a mobile form factor. So, we optimized the design of the content blocks to ensure that the headlines themselves were plainly visible, including removing many other elements that we might normally want to include, such as content tags or the author's name. As I was working on it, I realized that this second level of navigation was taking up too much space, so I redesigned it to make everything fit in one horizontal menu. The way that I did that, though, was by moving the filters into their own dropdown menu and prioritizing a few of the main-level items.

I redesigned the navigation to be one level because fitting headlines in the vertical browser space was an important goal for this project.

When my client saw it, he disagreed, asking, "How will anyone know what they can filter if they can't see the filters? We need to show all the filters so they're easier to access." But because I knew that fitting more content within the vertical space was a priority, I decided to simply show him the difference rather than argue about the discoverability. I grabbed screenshots of both designs, dragged them into Photoshop side by side and put a big line right down the middle. When he saw it, he agreed that a single level of navigation was the way to go. It was immediately clear by way of the comparison that the new design had helped us achieve one of our goals for the application. Not only was this technique effective, but it saved me the time and energy of having to describe a design decision that was better communicated visually.

When clients and stakeholders make suggestions about how to change your design, it's unlikely that you'll get away without at least trying it out and showing it to them. If you only show them their idea by itself, they're likely to believe it's the right choice because there is no reference to your original proposal. They may not remember the differences. However, comparing the two side by side in the same view is a better technique because everyone can see what was changed and it plainly tells a story about which design solves the problem in the best way. Showing a comparison is a really effective way to make your case.

2. PROPOSE AN ALTERNATIVE

The next tactic for responding is to offer an alternative solution that meets the need in a different way. In Chapter 4, we took the time to anticipate our stakeholders' reactions and preemptively prepared alternatives that could be used in this situation. Now is the time to bring these ideas to the table so it's clear that there is more than one way to solve this problem. Maybe you had a similar idea in the moment, some designs that didn't make the final cut, or their suggestion was close but not quite close enough. You might propose something completely different or even suggest something that meets them halfway. Whatever the case, proposing an alternative is a necessity in almost every situation.

It's rare for stakeholders to be in tune enough with the user and with interface design that they'd be proficient at proposing solutions that don't require some level of refinement. Even if their suggestions are really great, be sure to think critically about its implications and add value to the process to make it even better. That doesn't mean we should discount the stakeholders' input as irrelevant or value our ideas over theirs. Our job is to take these suggestions into serious consideration and then apply our own expertise to take it one step further. As the experts on design, this is where we add value the most.

Most stakeholders don't have the same depth of knowledge in technology or design that we do. They lack the vocabulary to suggest meaningful changes to our work in a way that makes sense to the end user. It's been my experience that when people use generic terms to describe a solution, it's a sign that they really don't know what the best solution is and that our alternatives are welcome. A common expression of this is with the use of the word "button," and yet a button is rarely the right solution to a complex design problem. Instead of adding the button, choose a more appropriate UI control, move it to a different position, or make it more subtle. There is always a more appropriate way of implementing stakeholder suggestions than to just take them at face value.

Stakeholder: Just put a big button in the header.

Designer: I'd recommend using a text link instead and adding an icon to emphasize it, rather than a full-size button, which will compete with the other options in the menu. This is also consistent with the other utility links we use elsewhere.

In fact, most stakeholders expect that we will bring our own suggestions to the table and that we're capable of offering solutions to the problems they identify. This is, in fact, why they're paying us. Don't be afraid of reprisal when you take their feedback and apply it differently. Even if they overrule you, you're demonstrating that you're intentional about your thought process and creating an awareness that these decisions aren't to be taken without consideration. A track record of being able to gracefully propose alternatives will win you the respect of your stakeholders as a trusted partner who is always interested in making their product the best it can possibly be.

However, when you're in the moment of a meeting, it can be difficult to propose the right alternative on the spot. Even with a set of prepared designs, the best answer sometimes still eludes us. This is why we have jobs: because it's really difficult to find the right solutions. A single idea in a single meeting is not usually going to be sufficient for creating the best possible user experience. Further, there is nothing more demoralizing than a change from a stakeholder you disagree with that you're unable to fend off. For this reason, try your best to suggest *any* alternative that will keep the decision open. Any solution you propose—even one that's not ideal—will create a conversation that demonstrates there are more ways to address this problem. Propose something, even if it's wrong. Hopefully, that will give you the space you need to continue the dialog without feeling like everything's going to be ruined unless you solve it now.

3. GIVE THEM A CHOICE

A third tactic is to give stakeholders a choice between something you know they want and the new thing they're suggesting. You want to present their suggestion alongside what they'll lose if we go down that path. They have to make a sacrifice. This is very effective if the thing they will lose is more important than what they propose.

In consumer behavior, the fear of loss is more powerful than the promise of gain. This is why we have coupons that expire, early-bird rates, and limited-time offers. The fear of missing out on a good deal overrides our sense of rational thought about whether we actually need what's being advertised. Give someone a $20 bill and they might hang onto it for a while, but deliver it with an ultimatum that it will disappear within the hour and I promise they'll spend it (perhaps on something frivolous). Without attempting to manipulate our clients into making rash decisions, we can use this tactic to our advantage and help people better see the design priorities in light of the entire experience. What is it that they will lose if we do what they're proposing? Capitalizing on the fear of loss can be very effective.

This tactic isn't meant to be a grab for control, the way a parent might force a decision on their child at dinner by saying, "You can't have dessert unless you eat your vegetables." Instead, it's an honest attempt to make stakeholders aware of the implications of their proposed choice. We need them to know that every decision affects everything else. Our job is to be attuned to those connections and communicate them when they're relevant to the discussion. Because many people want their ideas to be front and center in the design, it's often possible to point out that their suggestion will have a negative effect on the overall experience.

Here are some examples:

- *"If we add that new call to action, it's going to move the login form further down the page."* You know that they've explicitly asked that the login form be above the fold, and moving it could adversely affect conversions.

- *"Adding that will require some time, so if we do that, we won't be able to launch with the dashboard graphs."* You know that the dashboard graphs are a priority for this phase and that by comparison the stakeholder's suggestion isn't as important.

- *"If we put that new option in the menu, there will not be enough space for the existing items. We'll need to remove either Preferences or History."* You know that those options are part of the core feature set, whereas the new options add less value or even distract from the experience.

- *"Changing this text link to a button will compete with the other buttons on the page. If we do that, we'll need to remove or change the other buttons to accommodate it."* You know that the other buttons are purposely designed to attract the most attention and adding another will create too much visual weight.

- *"Moving the messaging to the right column means that we cannot support products with multiple options. Should we remove support for these products?"* You know that we have to support products with multiple options and, therefore, moving the messaging is not possible.

- *"Adding a logo here will distract the user from their profile tasks. If we have to add the logo, I'd recommend refactoring the design of the user's profile tasks to be smaller and more subtle."* You know that the user's profile tasks are the point of this view and that placing a logo in this space won't actually add any value to the experience.

In each case, we are emphasizing the trade-off. Not only does this allow stakeholders to see their feedback in light of all the other priorities on the project, but it also involves them in the decision process and empowers them with the right information. Any time you can allow someone else to agree with you in a way that makes it seem like their decision, do it that way. Think about what will be lost in the process of implementing your client's suggestion, be aware of all these connections, and call it out when you know it will negatively affect the user experience.

4. ASK OTHERS TO WEIGH IN

The fourth tactic is to solicit help from other people and ask them to weigh in on the decision. This is where the time and effort you spent building good relationships, creating a network of support people, and prearranging "ringers" is put to use. There are other people in the room who will agree with you, and you want to ask them directly to speak up. Creating a feeling of consensus around your designs will bolster your case and help your stakeholders to see that other experts agree with you. This shows your stakeholders that others are already in agreement with you; they just need to join you.

It also helps make your case without forcing you into the awkward position of outright disagreeing with a stakeholder. This is partly because you let other people do the talking and take the pressure off of you. But also, when other people are able to agree with you (rather than directly disagreeing with a stakeholder), you maintain a positive atmosphere rather than a flat-out accusation that one person is wrong. You're deflecting the disagreement with a stakeholder by instead emphasizing the agreement from other people.

Hopefully, you already know who you can call on to back you up, as we covered in Chapter 4. Even if you don't have a set group of support people, asking others to weigh in is still an effective tactic for pushing the conversation forward and getting more opinions out in the open. It's possible that the people you ask to speak up will agree with your stakeholder, and that's okay, too. Building the conversation around a collective group of thoughts is still more positive than two individuals in direct opposition. Your job is to funnel that energy to the right place.

When you ask others to weigh in on the conversation, it's important to remember to always ask directly and remain neutral:

Ask directly

> Call on people by name and ask them directly what they think. If you ask the entire group for feedback, few people will speak out in disagreement with the other person. You want to ask an individual person for an opinion. For example, "David, what are your thoughts on this?" or, "David had an interesting take on this issue earlier. David, do you mind sharing?"

Remain neutral

> Don't ask for your ringers' feedback in a way that reveals your true feelings about the stakeholder's suggestion. Instead, ask open-ended (not yes/no) questions using terms such as "opinion," "viewpoint," or "perspective." Ask for people's thoughts or reactions in a general way. For instance, "David, I'd be interested in hearing your perspective on this," rather than pitting him against another person, "David, do you agree with Susan?"

Stuck in the middle

At one of my largest clients, two different UX teams were coming together to collaborate on a special project for the first time. Each team brought a unique perspective, and both groups were opinionated. I was stuck in the middle, tasked with managing a conversation of competing priorities. When it came to some of the details of the UI, like specific colors and the placement of smaller details, I found that it was far more difficult to reach a consensus than I would have expected. The leader on one of the teams was more vocal and opinionated than the others. I knew that if I could get his buy-in, it would be easier to make a decision. He was my ringer.

I made a point to share my designs with him early on, and we discussed some of the details and landed on what we thought was the best solution. When it came time to meet with everyone else and questions arose, I called on him specifically to share his perspective. Because he was in a senior role and also because he was more vocal, he made the case for my design on my behalf without me having to be involved in the gritty details of outright disagreeing with the other people. He did the hard work of making a case for my designs, I stayed out of the relational complexity between these teams, and we kept the user experience right where we wanted it to be. Asking other people to weigh in is a great way to make sure you get agreement on the best possible user experience.

5. POSTPONE THE DECISION

Finally, if all the previous tactics have failed to move the conversation in a positive direction, suggest postponing the decision. Before you allow your team to make any decision that will negatively impact the user experience, wait until another time. That could be for just a few hours or even a few days—whatever it takes for you to take a step back, wrap your mind around the problem, and come back with a better solution. Too often, hasty decisions that seem like a good idea in the moment turn out to be poor choices when actually implemented. Build in some space for you to regroup and consider the best approach, even when you agree with what's being proposed. Anyone will appreciate that you want to take the time to do it right and verify that the suggested solution is appropriate. So ask for that space.

You can postpone the decision by leading with a "yes" by saying something like, "Yes, I see your point and we really need to find the right solution. How about I take the next few hours to work on it and then we can touch base again before the end of the day." The idea that you're postponing the decision doesn't have to slow down your progress. Iterating on your designs is a good practice anyway, so be prepared to pick up your stakeholder's feedback and run with it, even in the moment of a meeting. Don't waste time with this tactic by putting it out of your mind. Instead, seize the moment to capitalize on your own energy for defending your choices and make it happen right now.

Meeting adjourned

I was working on a small team once when one person's suggestion turned into a brainstorm and morphed into a solution that was so far removed from the problem it was hardly recognizable. That's my opinion, of course, but while I was watching the conversation play out, I saw the inevitable conclusion that the group-think generating this Frankenstein of a solution would eventually become something that was far from ideal. It was time to step in and do something about it!

I interrupted the discussion, saying it was clear that we needed to come to a decision and that design-by-committee was probably not going to help. Rather than waste everyone's time by continuing the discussion, I canceled the meeting right there and sent everyone back to their desks, only 15 minutes into an hour-long meeting. Meanwhile, I stayed behind in the conference room and cranked out several alternatives that would be more useful in leading the discussion, without five people looking over my shoulder and touching my screen.[2]

Before the hour was up, I called everyone back together to review the options I had just created. One of them seemed to work, was tweaked, and eventually made its way to production. The end result was a product that was better because I had the insight to stop the crazy train before it pulled into the station. Postponing the decision even for a few minutes gave me the space I needed to come back with a solution that would help ensure the best possible experience for the user without diminishing the ideas that had been thrown around in the moment. Plus, I saved everyone the time and hassle of wasted brain space that would only have resulted in rework.

You won't always need to cancel your meetings like this, but the point is that it's better to take your time (even just a few minutes) to get your designs right than it is to let a single bad decision unintentionally force you into a UX dead end. More likely, you can propose postponing the decision until your next meeting, which gives you the capacity to figure out a better solution in time. Don't be hasty and never be afraid to suggest delaying the decision.

---

2   Don't touch my screen!

To be an effective communicator, you need to learn to respond to people very quickly, in the moment of a meeting. The only way to get good at it is to practice, memorize your strategy (the answers to the Big Three), and apply these tactics on the fly. This response will form the basis on which you and your designs will be judged, so it needs to be purposeful and actionable. The more you practice, the better you will become.

The good news is that in addition to having a well-defined strategy and these easily applied tactics, many design discussions revolve around similar themes and ideas. You can capitalize on this by remembering and reusing similar, common responses every time. In Chapter 8, I share some of the most common key messages that are used to justify design decisions so that you'll have some premade templates for articulating your response.

[8]

The Response: Common Messages

He who wants to persuade should put his trust not in the right argument, but in the right word.
JOSEPH CONRAD

NOW THAT WE'RE KNEE deep in our response to stakeholders, let's take a quick look at what we have so far. Our objective is to get agreement from them. Our strategy for accomplishing that is to communicate that our design solves a problem, makes it easy for users, and is better than the alternatives. We'll communicate that using any of the tactics from Chapter 7. So now we need to identify the important messages that will help us to employ those tactics in our context.

Although every project is different and every client has unique needs, I've found that there are some ways of explaining design decisions that I seem to use over and over again. I often say the same kinds of things to defend my projects and I've compiled them here for reference. Some of them are similar or related to one another, but they should give you a good basis for the kinds of responses that are effective in design discussions.

These are the key messages that you need to communicate to deliver on your strategy and achieve the objective. With our strategy and tactics in mind, find the messages that apply most to your situation and modify them to accommodate your particular context. The goal for this chapter is to give you a list of common ways of describing design decisions that you can use and reuse at each meeting: a set of templates to give you a head start toward forming the best response.

I've organized them into four categories (in no particular order): Business, Design, Research, and Limitations. This is a list of reusable responses whether you are appealing to the business, pointing out important design logic, addressing research and data you have, or noting the limitations you face. Use these messages to make your case for a better user experience.

Business

One of the best ways to make a case for your designs is to directly connect it to the needs of the business. Here are three of the most common responses for appealing to the business:

- "Helps achieve a goal"
- "Facilitates a primary use case"
- "Establishes branding"

"HELPS ACHIEVE A GOAL"

Stakeholders always appreciate connecting your solution to the goals of the business. This is a solid way to make the case for your design through appealing to a nobler motive. This may very well be your answer to the question, "What problem does this solve?" because usually the problems we want to solve with the design are the same as the goals of the project or business overall. Whatever the source of the reasoning, always emphasize that your design is intended to help the company achieve its goals.

It can be difficult to know with certainty how a particular design will affect your goals, especially for smaller interactions that might not affect the overall use of the entire application. The point here is not to know with certainty. If we always knew with certainty what would definitely accomplish our goals, we wouldn't need to even meet. You need to have confidence that your experience leads you to believe with all reasonable certainty that this design is at least one step of a larger approach that will take you where you need to go.

To do this effectively, make this connection clear and provide an explanation for how your solution solves this particular problem. Because you've already written down each problem alongside your solution (as I recommended in Chapter 2), and part of your strategy is to appeal to a nobler motive, it should be a simple matter of making a statement that clearly communicates these connections. A pattern for expressing this is: "[design] will affect [goal] because [reason]." Here are some examples:

- "Moving 'Related Items' above the product description will increase product engagement because users will have more opportunities to see more products."

- "Putting 'Recent Projects' at the top of the home screen will improve data quality because users will have easier access to keeping their data current."

- "Removing the login requirement will reduce abandonment because users can bypass registration and still see promotions even if they aren't logged in."

That doesn't mean everyone will agree. After all, you might think that using a toggle switch for "Remember password" will improve engagement by keeping users logged in, but I might think that a tried-and-true checkmark will be a more effective solution. The purpose isn't to expect automatic agreement. The purpose is that we're being intentional and purposeful with all of our decisions, and this is one way we can communicate that to our stakeholders. As often as you can, connect your design decisions to the goals and objectives of the business.

"FACILITATES A PRIMARY USE CASE"

This might be the most obvious and common explanation for any design decision because everything we do is about designing around a particular use case, user story, or feature set. Depending on your stakeholders, they might not be aware of how we use these techniques to create a structure and logic to our decisions. Pointing out which use cases benefit from the decision is a good way of demonstrating your thought process and will get you talking through the decision in a way that makes sense to them.

Just as often, we try to optimize the primary use case by minimizing and limiting secondary or edge cases. For example, although any user is encouraged to maintain his account profile information, it is not the main purpose of the application. This informs our decision to put account management functions in a drop-down menu rather than a large call to action. Noting these justifications can help you keep people focused on ensuring that the primary use case is always optimized even in the face of other needs and features.

Even though designing for a use case may seem obvious, it's surprising how often teams can make decisions in a group setting that completely ignore the main use of the application. Because you've already identified that your decisions are tied to that case, remember to do a quick gut check to confirm that you haven't lost sight of it in the process of moving things around. It's always useful, even after a decision has been made, to circle back and double-check your decisions against the documented use cases for which you hope to design. When you find your team getting off track, bring them back by reminding everyone what the use cases are and how our decisions affect them.

"ESTABLISHES BRANDING"

Although it is less important to the overall user experience, I often find myself justifying design decisions based solely on the branding standards of the organization. Sometimes, things are the way they are because the company has a specific image it's trying to establish and our applications have to reflect this, as well. This is more true with the use of color, fonts, or language than with specific interactions but it's important to call out. If you chose that style because that's what the marketing department told you to do, bring that to the attention of your stakeholders.

Sometimes, application design can be a good opportunity to work with and help an organization develop their brand identity. Even though it's not usually an explicit part of the UX process, some organizations don't have standards that include styles for elements such as buttons, drop-down lists, and checkboxes. As a result, we might have a chance to help them evolve their standards documentation with our own style guide and move their visual identity in a positive direction. Marketing people probably aren't thinking about interface controls and are usually happy to have your voice in the process of updating those standards with a common design language. The standards they create will be based largely on their needs, like print ads and direct mailers. Helping them understand where we've run into problems can shape the conversation of branding to expand and include other elements that might not previously have been considered. The end result is better collaboration and a more comprehensive branding guide. That makes stakeholders happy, too.

Design

Often, we have design reasons for why we did what we did. I find there are three common ways of describing my decision for design reasons:

- "Uses a common design pattern"
- "Draws the user's attention"
- "Creates a flow for the user"

"USES A COMMON DESIGN PATTERN"

Designers spend a lot of time on other sites, apps, and devices learning about the newest useful design patterns, and so we naturally choose patterns that make the most sense to our audience and context. Every few months, new patterns emerge that challenge our thinking about device and system interaction while we all wait to see which ones catch on. It can be risky to choose a pattern that doesn't have a track record, but purposefully choosing a pattern because it is widely understood in the market is a great way to build a case for your decisions.

Your stakeholders are probably not aware of the concept of "patterns" in UI design, so you want to be careful not to make them feel like an outsider. Help your stakeholders understand that because this consistency in the experience is so important, changing an expected pattern in one context will have the ripple effect of needing to use the same pattern in other places throughout the app. It's not merely an isolated decision. We want to create consistency so the user will know what to expect.

Also tricky with patterns is that there is a lot of subjectivity in choosing them. Unless your project has a well-defined design language and robust style guide, you'll be on your own in making the initial choices about what patterns work well for your users until you can test them. And even then, there's a great deal of subjectivity. So remember that design patterns are meant to provide consistency and set a user's expectations about what interactions will take place. Beyond that, it's fruitless to argue over which one works without solid research to suggest otherwise.

"DRAWS THE USER'S ATTENTION"

There are parts of our design work that are more driven by intuition than others, and this is one of those blanket explanations that I find seems to explain a lot of my own choices in ways that I otherwise could not communicate. There's a lot of psychology that goes into the thinking about where users look, how they scan (not read) websites, and what makes them move from one place to another. Much of that knowledge is distilled into design practice through techniques such as the use of color, negative space, balance, or type size. These ideas can be incredibly subjective and difficult to justify to the average person, but often it is simple enough to explain that the combination of elements they see on the screen is meant to move the user from point A to point B.

Here are some examples:

- "The headline and call to action are arranged so that the user reads the headline first and taps on the call to action next."

- "The containers overlap to give the user a sense that they are connected as they scroll through the page."

- "The elements are arranged left to right and top to bottom, because our audience tends to scan the page in that way."

- "We used green because green means go or success, and the contrast will draw the user's eyes to that element."

It's important that we help our stakeholders understand the relationships between design elements and user action so that they can see the rationale behind our decisions. We need to communicate that we're not only putting things on the page in a way that looks good, but that we're trying to draw users into the application and lead them to action with an appropriate placement of design elements. Our decisions are based on getting the user to act, which is the ultimate purpose of any website or app.

"CREATES A FLOW FOR THE USER"

A lot of time and effort goes into creating user flows. We can spend days or weeks with a wall full of Post-its trying to find the best path for our users to navigate the application. That hierarchy is expressed in our work and influences how we structure the entire design. We define use cases, edge cases, error flows, and remove dead ends only to hear a stakeholder suggest a change that disrupts this flow, potentially sending us back to the drawing board. Occasionally, this happens without us even realizing it: we make a change in one place that affects something else down the line. Unintentionally, we've broken the path we so carefully tried to plan based on the whims of a well-meaning, but uninformed stakeholder. You need to pay careful attention to how your decisions will affect the flow you've created. Don't let your stakeholders break that without their first understanding why you did it that way.

> "Our checkout flow was designed so that each successive control for the next step is in exactly the same place and the user moves forward in a linear fashion. If we make the change you're proposing, it will break that flow on step 3 and cause the user to have to stop and go back, rather than quickly completing the step by moving forward."

> "Our signup flow requires only the email address to be submitted first, because we can reduce abandonment by not exposing all the fields at once and allowing the user to progressively add information to their profile later. If we add the additional fields to this step, it will complicate the process with validation rules and break the user flow if a mistake has to be corrected first."

Research

Using data, user testing, and other research is perhaps the most compelling justification for our design decisions. I've found three common responses useful when research is used to inform our choices:

- "Validated by data"
- "Revealed in user testing"
- "Supported by other research"

"VALIDATED BY DATA"

Using data to support your design decisions is the golden ticket to getting agreement because it is the most scientific way of demonstrating that your designs are having the intended effect. The importance of using data cannot be understated. Too often, companies have plenty of data to help them, but lack the time or skill to sift through it and draw meaningful conclusions, so find data that is useful to your context and allow it to help you make your case.

Designers sometimes have a difficult time wrapping their minds around a spreadsheet full of percentages and decimals, myself included. Hopefully, you have someone who can help you find meaning in the numbers or maybe you can get access to a slide deck in which the data was presented in a palatable form. Product owners and project managers are usually the ones who will help you with this effort, but it's entirely likely that you will need to do the work of combing through the chaos and drawing connections between elements of your design and the behavior of the user. It's not easy, but the good news is that this effort pays off in huge ways, because almost everyone is convinced by data.

There are two types of data we can use to talk about our decisions. The first is *existing data*: data we already have available that we can use to help us make decisions now. The second is *reflective data*, the data we collected after changing our design and comparing the before and after. With the first, you can make informed guesses. We don't really know if our proposed solution will help us achieve the goal, but we can use the data to make our best guess. The second is what we do after our informed guess: we check our changes and verify that the numbers are better. When you have that kind of information, it is more clear what the "right" answer is.

Using data is really compelling to stakeholders. For that reason, it's also important to recognize that looking at bad data will still yield the wrong choice, so we need to be really careful with this approach. What I mean is that data often tells us what the user did, but not why. We try to infer *the why* by looking at *the what*, and this naturally involves making assumptions. If we make changes based on a wrong assumption, we end up with a design that is likely to cause more problems than it solves. So, keep in mind that making decisions based on data can only be truly effective when taken as a measure of the project on the whole, in context, and without too many assumptions.

One of my former managers was a data-driven person. She and I could discuss different designs for hours, but if data supporting one side ever entered the picture, it was a shut and closed case. I quickly picked up on this and discovered that every time I gathered data to support my proposal, she would agree. It was a strange power because it became tempting to augment the numbers to support my case even if there weren't truly direct connections. This is the problem with data: nearly everyone is convinced by it, yet it can be easily manipulated. The key thing to remember here is that our goal is not simply to get agreement and have our way with the designs. Our goal is to create the best user experience and help our stakeholders to achieve their goals. Skewing a perspective on data to selfishly support our claims is not going to be effective in the long term.

To get the attention of your stakeholders, it's important to begin your response with a phrase that emphasizes your use of data, such as:

- "According to our analytics..."
- "We have data that suggests..."
- "We are tracking this metric and..."

It's usually enough to simply state with confidence what the data shows without the need for further discussion:

- "According to our analytics, 64 percent of users drop off at this point in the user flow."
- "We have data that suggests the phone number requirement is our biggest barrier to conversion."
- "We are tracking this metric and have seen a steep drop in engagement since making this change."

However, you should always be prepared to provide the data that you cite even if you don't have it on hand. I usually have the data in a separate file or report that I saw earlier, and I know I can share it with stakeholders when asked. It's usually enough to tell them you can send the report afterward, as long as you follow up. But it's a best practice to visually show the data in a simple way, right there and then, so that stakeholders can really latch on to the idea. Because many people are visual, showing a chart, image, or simple table will help bring home the importance of the data in this particular decision.

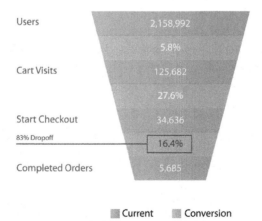

Having visuals available to show the data is a really effective way to make your case.

You must decide what kinds of data will be most relevant to your stakeholders and optimize your designs to improve those metrics. Using data to support your decisions is very convincing, as long as you've got an airtight connection and are making the right assumptions.

"REVEALED IN USER TESTING"

Often, we have experience watching people use our designs, and those insights inform our decision making. Being intentional about realizing when those studies are influencing our decisions will help us to communicate to our stakeholders, when appropriate. Demonstrating good design through a connection with a usability study is a very effective way of making a case for your designs because it shows that your ideas are working in the real world with real people. It has a human element to it that creates a story for our stakeholders, rather than the mechanical feeling that raw data provides. Depending on your stakeholders, using real stories of users might be even more effective than numbers and charts. Using the tactic from Chapter 7 for representing the user, tell your stakeholders a story about your users that will get them on board with your decision.

The challenge with user observation as a justification for design decisions is that it can be very subjective, based on what you remember of the session, and difficult to document for the purpose of meeting with a client. Usually, the way we bring these to our stakeholders is in the form of a memory—some special knowledge that might only reside in our heads; for example, "During our usability study last week, we realized that people were confusing the 'Okay' and 'Cancel' buttons because the design was too similar." Even though this statement is based on our experience with users, it is undoubtedly clouded by our own memory and conclusions from the study. Still, it's an effective way to demonstrate that you're interacting with users and improving your designs to accommodate what you've learned. That alone is very valuable to communicate.

The best way to communicate our insights from user testing sessions is to assemble a set of slides with quotes from a few select users and maybe even a video clip showing the problem areas. Edit the video from the session down to a few seconds or create a highlight reel of the most relevant parts from the study. This demonstrates that you value everyone's time by only showing them the important parts while also giving them the opportunity to participate in a real user session. Even though this requires advance preparation to put together, it's the only way to truly show your stakeholders why you did what you did, and it might be more necessary depending on the scope of the proposed changes. I'd even recommend showing them one or two complete user sessions, if you have the time. I find that this is often the first time my stakeholders have ever seen a user session at all! Any time you can get your stakeholders to see real people using their app, you create a connection for them to empathize with and be motivated to act on changes for the sake of the user.

Creating a New Case

"I find it difficult to enter the patient's history at this point because I don't usually have that information on-hand... I have to go back later to correct it and sometimes forget."

Including a short video clip or quote from a user session in your slides is an effective way to give stakeholders quick access to real users.

"SUPPORTED BY OTHER RESEARCH"

It's common for me to cite other, external research that I've seen when discussing design. I spend a lot of time consuming blogs, books, and podcasts. Often, this information influences my thinking in ways that are almost unconscious. I discover new best practices all the time and begin incorporating them into my work without even realizing it. I often don't even know this has happened until I am talking to stakeholders and parsing through my decision process on the spot. I find myself saying things like, "I read recently that..." and then have to backtrack to find those original sources.

As a result, I've developed the habit of saving useful research in a project folder or keeping a list in a shared document so that I can easily provide it to other people. As I casually browse other research, I copy links, quotes, and data over to a separate file that I can sort through later, if needed. Usually, my notes include the title, author, URL, and a description of the part that's relevant to my project or a short summary of the findings. This makes it much easier for me to make claims about other research because I can quickly send the reference to my client if asked.

It's actually pretty rare that you'll need to provide the original research as proof unless, of course, people disagree. Most of the time stakeholders take these kinds of statements at face value and trust you with the rest. Much like using analytics, this can be a dangerous power because if you're prone to overstate or misremember the data, you will still make bad decisions. For that reason, I don't recommend quoting another study without having the reference available. Sometimes, what you remember about a study and what the actual learning was is heavily influenced by your own perspective. It's easy to bend it to your advantage, so be careful.

Other times, though, having all your external references is critical to justifying your decisions. When the stakes are higher, it might be the only way to convince people that your design is the best choice. What can be unfair, however, is if your stakeholders aren't prepared to defend their own opinions against your prepared list of research. If you're not careful, it could feel like an attack. In that case, give them the opportunity to think about it and respond another time, send them your research in advance so they have a chance to review it, or bring research with you that presents both sides of the problem for discussion. You don't want them to feel like they were bullied into agreeing with you.

Taking hamburger off the menu

One of the mobile projects I worked on used the all-too-common "hamburger menu" for the primary navigation. During the course of a redesign, I tried several times (unsuccessfully) to convince my client to abandon the use of this icon as a catch-all for everything in the menu. My recommendation was based on research indicating that the icon is not as effective as the word "Menu," but simply telling the client this was not convincing enough. For one meeting, I collected as many articles as I could on the subject (a few of which disagreed with my perspective) and opened them in separate browser tabs to make my case. When we reached that agenda item, I presented my proposed design (again) and then carefully clicked through the tabs to give a quick summary of each post. When I was done, the client was impressed with my preparedness, admitted that they did not have a similar amount of evidence to support their opinion, and we restarted the discussion about changing the icon. The end result was to create an A/B test with our two proposed options in the hopes that it would further inform our decision making. Had I not been prepared with this research, we would not have been able to restart that discussion.

Hamburger menu icon

When using other external research to support your decisions, remember to:

- Make a habit of saving research to a separate document as you find it

- Note the title, author, URL/source, and date

- Write a short summary of the post or a sentence about how it relates to your project

- Provide the list of references to your stakeholders when they ask

- Try to find research to support other viewpoints for a balanced understanding

- Give your stakeholders the chance to consider it or respond with their own

User Generated Content

Why User-Generated Content Is More Important Than You Think

More than 8 in 10 say user-generated content from people they don't know influences what they buy and indicates brand quality, while 51% say it is actually more important than the opinions of their friends and family, and far more trustworthy than website content. 65% of users aged 18-24 considered information shared on social networks when making a purchasing decision (source: eMarketer). On top of that, 2/3 of consumers use search engines to help them research and make purchase decisions (source: eConsultancy). http://blog.hubspot.com/blog/tabid/6307/bid/31258/Why-User-Generated-Content-Is-More-Important-Than-You-Think.aspx

Millennials Trust User-Generated Content 50% More Than Other Media

Ipsos' study, however, reveals that millennials trust UGC just as much as professional reviews. UGC is also 20% more influential when it comes to purchasing and 35% more memorable than other types of media. http://mashable.com/2014/04/09/millennials-user-generated-media/

Millennials Love User Generated Content and Peer Reviews

The study, in full below, shows that millennials spend 18 hours with media per day and 30% of that time is spent consuming user-generated content. Real, local, peer reviews are even more important now for your business with millennials trusting almost 70% of all peer reviews. http://larchedigitalmedia.com/millennials-love-user-generated-content-and-peer-reviews/

Millennials Said to be Highly Trusting of User-Generated Content

http://www.marketingcharts.com/wp/online/millennials-said-to-be-highly-trusting-of-user-generated-content-41276/

When I find research that will be useful with my clients, I compile it in a document so that I can quickly reference the information in a meeting if I need to. Often, clients will ask me to share the entire document with them so that they, too, can use the information to convince other stakeholders.

Limitations

As often as we're justifying our decisions based on what we think needs to be done, we are also making a case for times when there are limitations that need to be taken into consideration. We can't always do what our clients want, simply because of other factors that are beyond our control or because we're trying to adhere to standards in design and programming. I've found three common responses for dealing with limitations:

- "Not enough resources"
- "Limited by technology"
- "Complies with a standard"

"NOT ENOUGH RESOURCES"

The unfortunate reality of design is that companies frequently do not have everything they need to realize their dreams for the app or website. There simply isn't enough money or people for everyone to be able to design and build anything they can think of. Taking these limitations into consideration is an important part of the decision-making process because spending too much time on something that's not possible is not an effective use of time. Although limits in resources are usually just a matter of money and people, there are four main areas that seem to affect web and application design more than others:

Support

There is a lack of support, infrastructure, or internal processes to handle the added requirements. Even if we can build and launch our project, there isn't enough internal support to maintain it over the long term. This could be because customer service isn't set up to handle the additional calls, that accounting doesn't have a practice in place for handling the payments, or that QA doesn't have the capacity to test another app. It's not as much about people as it is about process. The organization simply isn't equipped to handle what we want to do yet. These support roles are an important consideration for how we design, and factoring it into our decision process is an important point to clarify.

People

There are not enough designers or developers who can actually create it within the time and constraints given. Very simply, the things that we want to do require a larger staff that we don't have. This may not even be a budget problem, but one of hiring: we can't hire the right kinds of talent or we can't hire fast enough. Perhaps it is only a short-term problem, but not having enough people is a legitimate reason for scaling our designs. Always consider how your designs are affected by the current and future staff.

Money

The budget is insufficient for acquiring the services or technology needed to make it happen. No matter how much money you have, it's almost never enough to go no-limits on your product. There is always another piece of hardware or a hot new service we can use to augment our product and take it to the next level. But absent these resources, we must curb our designs to account for a limit in funding. Making this an explicit reason for your design decisions is important.

Time

There is not enough time to implement the designs, given the current requirements. And when we have limited time, we usually scale back our ideas to a point that's do-able. It's this perceived "downgrade" that is most important to communicate. Every stakeholder wants to build the biggest, best app as soon as possible, which is why so many teams begin with a minimum viable product and iterate over time. In theory, we should never be forced to tell a stakeholder that there isn't enough time because our process is such that we always create appropriate levels of work during each cycle. In reality, we are always scaling back ideas to fit the current calendar.

Telling your stakeholders that you're limited by resources will either result in sobering agreement or righteous indignation. Either way, it can yield a good outcome. On the one hand, they're apt to agree with you because they understand the realities of the resourcing situation. On the other hand, they might be compelled to fight on your behalf for additional resources to make it happen. The point isn't really the final outcome, though, as much as it is your ability to thoughtfully explain the reality and constraints within which you're working. We must always design around our limits in resourcing.

"LIMITED BY TECHNOLOGY"

Although we would like to think that we designers can create anything under the sun, the reality is that we're limited by technology. What's available to us will naturally force us to make design decisions that need to be explained to our stakeholders. Often, these constraints cannot be foreseen when creating the original designs, and it is only during implementation that we have to make these adjustments. Our stakeholders had certain expectations, but when it came time to make it happen, we realized that we had to make some sacrifices.

Sometimes, these limitations are straightforward and there's simply no way to accommodate their request. A common example in mobile app design is the size of the device screen: we simply don't have the space to do everything our clients want. Other times, there are more raw technical limitations. For example, I was working on a mobile web app and the client wanted to access the device camera in the browser. Although this is technically possible, support for it is not widespread and it was an easy decision to remove this from the scope. It might also be that there are other technological factors outside of your control that force your decisions. Perhaps the server simply isn't capable of doing what you need or the technology you want isn't cheaply or easily available. In these cases, it's appropriate to suggest that even though everyone agrees it's a great idea, we can't consider implementing those designs unless we have better technology.

It's not always simple. These can be the most difficult decisions to help other nondesigners (and nondevelopers) understand because the reasons are often highly technical. Stakeholders don't like (or understand) these limitations and might even be put off by the prospect that you can't do the same thing their competitor does. I imagine an executive pulling out his phone, showing you the way someone else does it, and then asking "Why can't we do that?" But these limitations are real, and we have to help our stakeholders see the constraints so they can be part of the decision.

"COMPLIES WITH A STANDARD"

Occasionally, what our stakeholders want us to do will go against the technical or social standards we've set for our application. We want our app to work in all browsers, on different devices, and for all people so we have to follow the "rules" that are set forth on the development side. This sometimes results in making changes to our design to accommodate these standards.

One example is designing for accessibility. When you're building an accessible application, it will inform decisions about the kinds of controls you choose and how those interactions are implemented in the design. We usually begin with a no-limits design that, as soon as implementation is underway, gets whittled down into what's actually possible, given our desire to make the app work for everyone. Even though nearly anything is technically possible, it might not always be recommended (or it might take too much time to accomplish), and so we must adjust our expectations to account for these needs.

Another common example is with standard HTML control types. Maybe the stakeholder wants a custom date picker, but the prospect of building and maintaining your own is out of scope. It's not always the right decision to "roll your own," so it's better to explain why using a standard control is better for both the user and the bottom line. Sometimes highly interactive page elements require programming hacks to pull off. In that case, you might need to move away from something too complicated if the goal is to build an application that's meant to work on different devices or browsers. In each case, we're trying to demonstrate that the standards put in place for applications have a natural benefit to our development process as well as the portability and accessibility of the application in the long term. These standards inform and influence our design decisions.

Appeasing the Natives

I was consulting with a nonprofit on a web-based mobile app. Although the app would run in every major mobile browser, the client wanted it to behave more like a native application. To that end, their team had designed a series of interactions and design patterns that, while natural for some native mobile apps, would actually have required us to overwrite native browser functionality and potentially break some web standards in the process. Not only did this present technical challenges with the implementation, but it also created a set of confusing interactions. For example, browser users would not be able to scroll up and down (scroll-jacking) and would only be able to navigate the website by swiping left and right. In the end, I was able to convince the client that valuing native browser behavior was more important than maintaining the perception of a native app in the browser. For the first implementation, at least, they chose to forgo all the customized gestural events and stick with tried-and-true (standards-based) HTML and JavaScript.

Hopefully, now you can see how design decisions across different projects frequently share a similar rationale and explanation. As designers and communicators, our jobs are made easier when we have this short list of common messages to pull from, using them as the foundation for our response. Use them as templates to help you jumpstart your response, no matter what the context.

Focused on our objective of getting agreement, we now have a memorized strategy, a set of actionable tactics, and a list of frequently used messages as the basis for our response. The next step is to compile all of these together and plug them in to a formula that will finally accomplish our goal. We are only one step away from delivering on our promise to effectively articulate our design decisions in a way that is compelling and fosters agreement. Next, we will assemble an ideal response.

[9]

The Ideal Response: Getting Agreement

Unless both sides win, no agreement can be permanent.
JIMMY CARTER

WE'VE NOW COVERED SEVERAL tactics for forming your response as well as some of the most common ways that we can respond to design feedback. If we combine all of these practices together, we can see how this will form the basis for a standard response to stakeholders that establishes a formula for success.

Every response to design feedback needs to hit on a number of areas if it's going to have the kind of weight it needs to be compelling and convincing. For UX discussions, I have a useful formula to help make our case to stakeholders. This is the *IDEAL Response*:

Identify the problem

We must always remain focused and ensure that our stakeholders are aware of the problem we're addressing; otherwise, the conversation can quickly become counterproductive. Very briefly state the problem that your design addresses for the purpose of getting everyone on the same page.

Describe your solution

This is where your specific design can be connected to the problem that you're trying to solve. Make a clear connection between what you did and how it addresses the issue. Without a clear solution, the design is useless and ineffective.

Empathize with the user

Stakeholders can forget about the people at the other end of our products. Our job is to represent them, to feel so burdened for them that we're driven to action. State how your solution solves the problem for a specific user by calling to mind the people at the center of your design process.

Appeal to the business

It's not enough to just fix stuff. All our decisions must be motivated in part by a need to grow the business or organization. This is where you describe how your decisions are meant to affect goals, metrics, or key performance indicators (KPIs). Bring it up, tie them together, and demonstrate the value.

Lock in agreement

After clearly making your case, directly ask for agreement from your stakeholders. You don't want to leave this conversation open ended, without resolution. Ask them directly, "Do you agree?" Put them in a position of needing to respond to you, and keep the project moving forward.

Getting Agreement

Getting this agreement is, of course, the entire purpose of this book. Because without agreement, everything you talk about with your stakeholders is just an IDEA. You can make a great case, argue your position, and walk away feeling confident, but without the agreement of everyone on your team, your project will not be successful. This is why locking in agreement is so critical, because it allows you to move from having something that's just an idea to something that is truly IDEAL.

BE DIRECT

To get agreement, you need to directly ask your stakeholders for their buy-in. The simplest way is to ask, "Do you agree?" Put them in a position of needing to respond to you before you move on. Further, it should be clear that you're asking them for a specific response (agreement) and that you expect an answer.

It's easy for a design discussion to casually devolve into a handful of random ideas until eventually the conversation feels like it should move on. However, if you don't have agreement yet, do not let the team move to the next item on the agenda. You need to be the one who pauses the chatter long enough to say, "Before we move on, are we all in agreement?" Getting that verbal confirmation is important to make sure this item doesn't come up again during the next meeting because someone forgot what was decided.

HIGHLIGHT THE BENEFITS OR CONSEQUENCES

In addition to being direct, phrase your question so that your stakeholders want to provide you with the answer that you need. In other words, make it clear what the right choice is by the way you ask so that they're compelled to answer with agreement. You can do this by highlighting either the negative effect of disagreement or the positive benefits of agreeing. For example, "Do you agree that we should improve conversion by removing these fields?" In this case, you're emphasizing that your solution will improve conversion. Your stakeholder is unlikely to disagree with a decision to improve conversion.

Security Blanket Statement

One of my clients made a unilateral decision to remove some user information from a form validation message because of a security concern, but I didn't agree that it was a valid concern. After making my case that this data needed to be displayed for the user experience, I asked for agreement by saying, "Do you agree? Or do you think we should purposefully hide this information from the user?" Phrasing my question in this way made it clear what I thought the right choice was, but it also put her in a position of needing to agree. No one wants to intentionally hide important information from users.

FORCE THEIR HAND

Finally, asking your stakeholders direct questions about whether they agree forces them to also be direct in their response. Sometimes, stakeholders are not forthright in their reaction, and we need them to tell us exactly what they think in order to accomplish our goal. If they disagree, we need to know and there should be no question about it. When you phrase your question to be direct and to emphasize the affect it has on the user experience, stakeholders are compelled to give you an answer that makes it clear which side of the fence they're on. If they're unsure of their position, they'll probably agree with you just so they can move on. If not, it creates an opportunity for you to continue the discussion and arrive at the right solution to meet everyone's needs. Either way, you'll have a definitive answer.

Putting It All Together

Now we begin to apply everything we've covered so far into one coherent response, which:

- Provides a natural transition using Thank, Repeat, Prepare

- Considers our answers to the big three questions

- Applies any number of the tactics necessary to make our case

- Takes advantage of common responses to design considerations

- Encapsulates all of them in the IDEAL Response so that we can get agreement

What follows are several case studies. These are examples of responding to stakeholder feedback using the IDEAL Response. My intent is to provide you with a handful of common situations and their responses so as to further demonstrate how you can articulate design decisions with your own stakeholders. I may or may not have found myself in these situations with my own clients. I can neither confirm nor deny the existence of these scenarios in real life! The names of design patterns and UI controls have been changed to protect their innocence.

For the purpose of simplicity, I avoid providing much context about the product or the conversation. These examples are common enough that you should be able to infer enough from their context alone. Focus not on the specific details of feedback in each case; rather, consider the application of how to communicate value to stakeholders in a way that appeals to their needs.

CONTROL OVER MY CONTENT	
Thank, repeat, prepare	Thanks for coming to me with your idea for being able to manually sort the content on your page. I know that you'd like some more control over how your posts are displayed, but we're intentionally limiting the amount of control we're giving content creators to help maintain some consistency, so let's talk about the best way to help you.
Identify the problem	Familiar and semi-familiar situations, with a reaction based on prior experiences Our challenge is that each view is supposed to be sorted chronologically so that users know to expect the most recent content at the top. This keeps the list of posts fresh and ensures that all the content creators are submitting new content each week.
Define the solution	Rather than give you the ability to manually sort all of the content, I would suggest adding a feature with which you can "pin" one article to the top of your stream at any time. If you were to pin a new one, it would replace the existing one. We'll add a special icon or visual clue to show that it's been pinned.
Empathize with the user	This will maintain the user's understanding of our content streams being sorted chronologically. The visual clues will help them know that this one pinned piece has been removed from the regular stream of content.
Appeal to the business	For you, it will highlight that single post out of all the others, giving it extra exposure for a longer period of time. Plus, it gives you a greater sense of control over how things are displayed without running the risk that everyone will start reordering their content.
Lock in agreement	Is that an acceptable solution for you to be able to choose one featured article at a time? Or do you still think we should allow everyone to do what they want with the sorting of their content?

"ADD TO CART" INTERACTION	
Thank, repeat, prepare	Thanks for sharing your thoughts with us about this project. Your insights are really valuable, and I appreciate you going through all of that with us. I'm going to go back through all of your points so that we can discuss them, but I want you to know that some of the things we decided on are rooted in an explanation that I think you'll agree with when we start talking about it. First, I want to review the new "Add to Cart" interaction.
Identify the problem	The issue we're trying to address is that when a user sees this interface for the first time, they're confused by the presence of two buttons and don't really know what each one means or which one they should tap.
Define the solution	Our solution is to consolidate those into one button labeled "Add to cart." Tapping on the single button reveals more options and gives the user the option to make the second choice after committing to the first rather than having to make all those decisions up front.
Empathize with the user	Keep in mind that our users are frequently ordering at their place of business. It could be a busy manager walking down the hall who notices that a light bulb is out and needs to order a new one on the spot. We don't necessarily have his full attention and need to present him with really simple options that don't require too much thought.
Appeal to the business	We believe our solution is going to increase conversion, because even though it creates an extra tap for the user, it makes the choice of adding an item to their cart much, much simpler. There is no question about what "Add to Cart" means because it relates to standard commerce. Very simply, more people are going to tap "Add to Cart."
Lock in agreement	I know the company has preferred the existing language, but we believe this new approach should be put into production with the next release. We might even consider A/B testing it with the existing implementation so that we can directly compare the results. We'd like to see conversion increase dramatically this year, and this is one of the most important ways to make that happen. Do you agree?

OVERBRANDING	
Thank, repeat, prepare	Thanks for your input on the logo and colors. I agree with you that we could adjust a few things to improve it. The challenge is that the marketing department is driving this effort, and we've had little input in final decisions. However, I think there are some points of discussion here.
Identify the problem	Marketing would like to brand this initiative separately from the rest of the product to create a campaign and awareness around it. The problem is that, in my opinion, our users will not understand the difference between these subbrands. They use the application for its utility, not for its branded add-ons, and placing these extra elements like logos and tag lines gets in their way.
Define the solution	My suggestion is avoid the use of a logo in this space and instead focus the branding effort on the use of color and copy to communicate the message. In this particular view, we could work with small icons to identify the add-on services or add a line of copy in a new color to highlight the value. This will save us a significant amount of space with minimal impact to the user. To do this, we'll need to go back to marketing and work with them on this solution.
Empathize with the user	From the users' perspectives, a subbrand like this is meaningless. They are primarily interested in completing their tasks and getting their job done. By putting a logo in their way, we are hindering their ability to use the application efficiently, and therefore, slowing them down. This is not only potentially frustrating to our users, but also risks conversion for paid services when users aren't able to get into the flow as quickly as they could.
Appeal to the business	Our goal for this initiative was to create a new revenue stream for add-on services when the user enters the flow. Although I know marketing wants to capitalize on this opportunity to create a new product with these add-ons, I believe that a branded approach does not provide value to the user (at best) and confuses them and slows them down (at worst). In other words, it might actually dampen our efforts at creating revenue from this channel.
Lock in agreement	I'd like your help working with marketing to remove some of the requirements for branding. I'm happy to coach them on some alternatives and help them understand the user's perspective. Do you agree that we should do our best to reduce the amount of branding for add-on services?

Thank, repeat, prepare	Thanks for your input. I really appreciate your viewpoint on these changes and I understand your suggestion about needing to add these new options to the main menu. However, I think there's a better solution we can discuss to make sure these new features have visibility.
Identify the problem	The problem I see is that we frequently add new options to the main menu and it's becoming a catch-all for links that we don't know what to do with. Secondly, these are time-based promotions rather than permanent offers so it's unlikely that a user will explicitly look for them in the menu since they don't view them a constant feature set.
Define the solution	My suggestion is focus our effort on highlighting these promotions in the content slots that we already use for other important messaging, like system alerts or the search suggestion text. When these new offers are available, we can display them in those content areas and have even more space for images and other content.
Empathize with the user	We don't want our users to be overwhelmed by the number of options in the main menu. Instead, we can provide more value to them by adding appropriate context-aware messaging that's relevant to their current task.
Appeal to the business	If we put these items in the main menu, it will actually backfire because the people will be less likely to find it buried in that menu. However, strategically placing them on the page in our existing slots will actually increase visibility for the offers and improve engagement for this initiative.
Lock in agreement	I'd like to move forward with the idea of using our existing slots and can mockup some examples for our next meeting. Do you agree that this will provide greater visibility as well as improve the experience? Or do you think it would be better to add to the menu and risk it getting lost with the other options?

BRANDED BANNERS	
Thank, repeat, prepare	Thanks for your suggestion to add the logo to the header of the app. I know you want to brand the experience and I agree that's important, so let's talk about how to best accomplish that.
Identify the problem	The challenge with an application like this is that we have a limited amount of space for the user to have access to everything in the navigation. Plus, we want them to remain focused on their tasks with as few distractions as possible.
Define the solution	The reason we chose not to include the logo in the header is because it does not actually provide any functionality for the user. By not including it, we have more space for the navigation options and a simpler interface for the user.
Empathize with the user	The logo doesn't directly provide value to the user after they're in the app. It only serves to reinforce the brand of a service they are already consuming. The user can more easily focus on using the application efficiently because they have one less visual distraction. The more we can remove from the interface, the more the user experience will be improved.
Appeal to the business	Branding is important, which is why we've worked the brand into our colors, language, and interactions throughout the app. We're also providing an "About" option with a page that has the logo and links to our other products. It's also worth pointing out that users are already invested in our brand because they signed up for the service. The login view also prominently displays the logo.
Lock in agreement	The marketing site is really the best place to communicate the brand with a logo, whereas the application itself is the best place to keep the user focused on the tasks. I'd like to propose we keep the user focused on using our application while logged in, but allow for more explicit branding elsewhere when it matters more. Do you agree?

PHONE NUMBER COLLECTION	
Thank, repeat, prepare	Thanks for your time and for sharing your thoughts with us on this new design. You made several suggestions for changes, which I've noted, and I'd like to go through each one so that we can be sure we're in agreement.
Identify the problem	The first thing you mentioned was the need to add a phone number field to the sign-up form. Our focus with this effort is to increase conversions on the form, so our design is optimized for that goal.
Define the solution	We removed the phone number field for a few reasons. First, it's a best practice to contact customers using the same medium that they contacted you. So, an online form submission warrants an email, rather than a phone call. Next, fewer fields on any form typically boosts conversion because users can complete it more quickly and don't need to think as much about what they're entering. But finally, I have some research showing that just the presence of a phone number field on a form will hurt conversion by more than 30 percent, even if the field isn't required.
Empathize with the user	The reason for this is because many users are wary of sharing their phone number for fear of being added to a telemarketing call list. Further, the presence of the phone field alone makes them skeptical of the company that is asking for it. Many wonder, "Why would anyone need my phone number for an online form?"
Appeal to the business	I know you'd like to have the user's phone number for your records, but it will be better for our goal of improving conversion if we remove it from the form. After a user has converted, we'll have plenty of opportunities to follow up with her, engage her in a relationship, and progressively add information to her profile. This will create more meaningful relationships with new customers and establish trust right from the beginning. Removing the field is the best balance of creating a great user experience while also achieving our goals for the business.
Lock in agreement	Do you agree we should not include this field in the form? Or do you think it's worth the risk of including it and probably suffering lower conversion?

TOO MANY MESSAGES	
Thank, repeat, prepare	Thank you for your time today. I appreciate your input on our project. You have a unique perspective on the business and I'd like to discuss some of your concerns as well as bring up a few of my own. But I think we're on the same page, as far as what we need to focus on.
Identify the problem	The problem we're trying to solve with this design is communicating the savings value to the shopper. Our approach is focused on high-lighting just how much people can save on these items without them having to think about it too much. The challenge with this current implementation is that the business has defined too many messages to communicate those savings all in one small space. Here we have the list price, percentage savings, dollar off, free shipping, and a "Great Value" flag. In addition to that, we're also tasked with including messaging around urgency with a timer, quantity available, and "Limited Time Offer."
Define the solution	Our solution is to apply some logic and rules regarding what messages are shown and when, so that we don't overwhelm the user with too many messages at once. For example, we should always choose between showing the percentage and the dollar off, but never both. In this case, we show the savings percentage because it's greater than 30 percent and communicates the value more than the amount of dollars off, which is only $3. Next, we will show the timer only if the value will expire within 24 hours, and we show the quantity available only when it reaches a certain threshold. Structuring our messages around this logic is the best way to communicate that value to the shopper, without creating a jackpot of showing all the messages at once.
Empathize with the user	Shoppers do not have time to read all the details, do the math, and figure out which items represent the best value. Showing them too many messages will only confuse them more because they won't know which message to focus on. Our approach allows us to have some control over which messages to present to them so that we can remove the burden from them and they can focus on purchasing the item. This will result in faster purchase decisions.
Appeal to the business	If we focus only on the most important, relevant messages for each item, we are more likely to increase sales and revenue on these items because they will be easier for the shoppers to read and purchase. Reducing the number of messages the user sees frees them up to make the purchasing decision faster, resulting in better conversion.
Lock in agreement	Having a laser-focused value proposition by not including so many different messages is the way to go. Do you agree that we should focus our messages in order to simplify the value for our shoppers?

CUSTOMIZE REPORTS	
Thank, repeat, prepare	Thank you for your perspective on the case list view. You have some great feedback, and I'd like to go through everything to be sure we're on the same page about what needs to be done.
Identify the problem	You mentioned that you'd like the ability to customize each report directly on the view of the graph itself. I agree that would be a great addition to the app.
Define the solution	We purposefully left out this idea because it wasn't within our scope for this phase of the project. The concept requires adding quite a bit of functionality and design effort to really implement it well.
Empathize with the user	We understand that although this feature would be useful for some users, the majority of people using the application do not require this level of customization. For the time being, the interface will be simpler without it.
Appeal to the business	If we stay focused on finishing the case view in its simplest form as is, we'll be able to complete this core feature set within our timeline and get this view to users sooner. Afterward, we can collect additional feedback from users and make a plan to implement your idea.
Lock in agreement	Are you comfortable with us moving forward without that feature for now? Or would you prefer we reprioritize our tasks and adjust timelines to accommodate this feature?

I WANT A NEW WIDGET	
Thank, repeat, prepare	Thank you for your thoughts on the dashboard. Yes, I agree that a new widget showing the overall totals would be useful, but that wasn't in the original designs, so let's discuss the best solution.
Identify the problem	The problem is that the graphs need to take up the full width of the application because we have less control over the display, given that it's a third-party solution. Also, we already are including widgets for the current status as well as follow-ups, so there just isn't very much space available to add another one. The current arrangement of widgets is designed to optimize the application for reducing late follow-ups.
Define the solution	I would recommend replacing either the Current widget or the Follow-up widget with a new Totals widget, if that is the priority now. We can use the existing slots for the new widget without modifying the design and we keep the interface simpler by not adding one more thing.
Empathize with the user	The challenge with this approach is that we've already reviewed the needs with our internal users, and they agreed that our current widgets were the most needed in this first version. I don't want to add one and create clutter or information overload for them. At the same time, I want to satisfy the request for what they expressed they needed from this dashboard. I know Hannah is expecting to train her staff based on our current designs.
Appeal to the business	To be practical, even just swapping one widget for another will slow down our progress because we don't have a design for the new widget and it will need new support from the developers. From our perspective, that could delay the release a week. Maybe more. And even though the Totals widget is nice, it does not help us accomplish our goal of reducing late follow-ups. If we remove one of the existing widgets in favor of a Totals widget, I'd suggest modifying our objectives, too, because we'll need a new target to focus on with a different arrangement of widgets.
Lock in agreement	Would you like to add this Totals widget by swapping out one of the others? If so, I can adjust our timeline, go back to our users with this change, and then we should discuss what our new goals are for this phase.

USERS TOLD US	
Thank, repeat, prepare	Thank you for your time today and for sharing your feedback with us on these new designs. I've taken notes on everything you suggested and I'd like to go through each one to be sure we understand. With all of our designs, we are taking into consideration both the needs of the business and the users. I think it will help the discussion for you to understand our thought process on some of these areas.
Identify the problem	Your first suggestion was that we change the input fields on the medical history form. This is an interesting part of the application because it has the highest abandonment rate compared to the other parts of the app. About 40 percent of users drop off before completing this section. We'd like to solve getting users through this step so that we can make sure they make it to the subsequent steps and complete the process.
Define the solution	Our solution was based on an assumption that the field labels were confusing to the average person, so the first thing we did was to update the names with more user-friendly language. But next, we spoke with some of the call-center associates who helped us understand that many users simply don't have the details of their medical history with them at the time, so requiring all these fields before moving on forces them to abandon the site.
Empathize with the user	To make it easier for our users, we've removed many of the required fields on purpose and allowed them to indicate which information they have and which information they will provide later. This allows them to complete this step for now, even if their data is incomplete. We can prompt them to complete it the next time they log in or send them an email notification after a few days. The user will have a greater sense of control and be more likely to get to the next step because of these changes.
Appeal to the business	What that means for us is that we will see significantly higher submission rates because more people will be able to make it to the next step. Not only that, but we'll have more accurate data because some users were filling in fake information just to move forward. But the bonus is that we'll see fewer support calls because users will be able to complete the application now without assistance. That will save us real money in the call center. We're already storing the data as it is entered, so we can still go back and complete their profile with them when they're on site, if needed. There's no risk of losing information.
Lock in agreement	We'd really like to see huge gains in the number of clients that are able to complete their profiles and believe this is the best way to accomplish that. Do you agree that this is the best solution? Or would you prefer we revert to the old designs?

Following a formula for responding to stakeholders might seem like a contrived way of creating a natural conversation. The purpose of the IDEAL Response is to provide a framework and structure that reminds us to hit on all the important parts in our reply. It is not meant to force you into a way of talking that comes across as mechanical or is too strict to be normal speech. I've found that keeping the IDEAL acrostic in my mind is a memorable of way of making sure that I've covered all my bases. Whether you form your response in the exact same way each time is less important than making sure you've addressed everything you need to. Remember, the key is to respond to stakeholders in a way that appeals to their needs and makes the best case for your design decisions. Use this framework as a tool to help you communicate to stakeholders, keep your sanity, and deliver the best user experience.

[10]

Meeting Adjourned: The After-Party

*The single biggest problem in communication is the illusion that it
has taken place.*
GEORGE BERNARD SHAW

WHEN THE MEETING IS OVER, you still have plenty of work to do. The
time immediately after a meeting is nearly as important as the meeting
itself, so don't rush off and leave everyone behind. Wait and talk to people afterward to debrief and gain insights that weren't apparent at the
time. Informally have one-on-ones with people who can help champion
your cause and then follow up quickly while it's still fresh. This time
immediately following the meeting is your best defense against making
a decision that could ultimately spell disaster for the user experience
of the project. Plus, you might be able to correct some concerns even
if you think the decision has already been made. Let's quickly review
some of the things you'll need to do immediately after the meeting:

- Stick around to chat with people.

- Follow up quickly with your notes.

- Apply filters and remove the fluff.

- Seek out individuals who can help you.

- Make decisions when there is ambiguity.

The Meeting After the Meeting

The meeting after the meeting may be more important than the meeting itself. People hang around, casually discussing what just happened. But it is in these informal environments that some people will tell you how they really feel about the project or what they think needs to be done. For whatever reason, people don't always speak up and say what they're thinking in front of a group. Usually it's because the purpose is to allow the boss to have his or her say, but sometimes it's because what people are thinking might be unpopular or risky and they don't want upset the status quo. And so they'll wait until the meeting is over, pull you aside, and tell you what they think. It is amazing how many decisions are made immediately after a meeting is dismissed. This is your best chance to wrap up any unfinished business and work with the influencers to get the approval you need.

POST-MEETING POPULARITY

Sometimes, the hallway outside a meeting is the most productive place. I was in a meeting with an executive to review the implementation of a design that had been previously agreed upon. The meeting itself was fine. There were no huge hang-ups and nothing major to report. But immediately afterward, once the executive had left, everyone stuck around specifically to talk to me.

One person asked me to keep her in the loop in the future so that she could back me up during our next meeting. She wanted to help me succeed and was willing to be direct about it. Another person wanted to rewind to an earlier decision and give me permission to move forward, even without explicit approval from that executive. He wanted the project to move forward and was willing to stick his neck out for me. And a third person apologized for being absent from my other meetings, asked to meet with me directly to share her concerns, and promised to be more involved going forward. All three of these conversations might not have happened with the same degree of urgency if I had rushed off somewhere else.

Always make plans to stick around after the meeting, chat with people, thank them for their participation, and see what happens. I promise that just as much will get done in the hallway as it did during the actual meeting itself.

Follow Up Fast

As soon as possible (preferably within an hour or at least within a day) send a follow-up to the entire team. It doesn't need to be written perfectly; the purpose is more functional than poetic. You need to follow up while it's still fresh on everyone's mind, including yours, before anyone has a chance to forget and disagree with the decisions they've already made.

A quick follow-up demonstrates that the meeting was a priority to you, so much so that you're not going to do anything else until it's settled. Second, it values the participants because it shows that you're doing the leg work, keeping them informed, and making the best use of their time. Next, it shows that you're listening. You're not just going to throw away all of their feedback: you wrote it down, are taking it seriously, and are concretely communicating it to the entire team. And lastly, it gets everyone on the same page about what was decided so there is no confusion going forward. You're creating a record for everyone to see and giving them the opportunity to reply if they have any additional insights.

This written record has proven to be invaluable to me months later, when new people on the project want to know who or when we made decisions. A quick search reveals my notes or communications and I'm able to avoid a rediscussion. I've also had managers hang on to these communications and use them in other meetings to update different stakeholders. Some might even copy and paste it into a different communication to their own boss. The use and reuse of the follow-up cannot be understated.

The follow-up should include a few things:

- First, thank the meeting attendees for their time and participation. People believe they're very busy, and we need to appreciate that they're taking the time for us.

- Second, recap everything that was discussed. This can just be a simple bulleted list with the decision noted. Having a simple list makes it easy for them to share with other people.

- Last, focus on actions, next steps, or expectations. You want to always (as much as possible) communicate what's going to happen next. This helps people see that the meeting was a good use of their time because it's moving things forward. It also offloads the burden from you and allows the entire team to participate in the next steps.

Don't be afraid to assign tasks to other people, even those outside your immediate influence. It's common in meetings for one person to volunteer to investigate something, seek information from another person, or agree to take the conversation elsewhere. The follow-up is the perfect place to remind everyone who is doing what. Be as specific as possible. Note the item in question, mention to the person who will be responsible for it, and provide dates or a general timeframe for when we will know more. Ask direct questions, too, so that there's no ambiguity about what items are still open. List important decisions and make it clear why the decision is being made.

Here's an example of what a follow-up might look like:

> Thanks, everyone, for your time today! It was a very productive meeting, and I appreciate you all being available. Here is what we discussed:
>
> • The carousel on the home page moves too fast. Jon is going to change it to 100 ms.
>
> • The price for items in Best Sellers seems too small. I will check to make sure it's consistent with the others and adjust as necessary.
>
> • The category tree appears to be using the wrong data. We have an email out to Abdul to address this.
>
> • Stan is concerned the CTA for membership is too large and uses the wrong copy. Jennifer is checking with content for correct copy. I will forward the usability study that informed this.
>
> • The release date has been approved, pending QA. Jon is going to email us tomorrow with a status update.

The key here is to keep your update as short and specific as possible without leaving out any important information. Your stakeholders should be able to quickly skim without becoming bogged down in the details.

Apply Filters

Another post-meeting strategy is to use your best judgment to filter out all the unnecessary information that isn't worth repeating to the entire team. This can be difficult to assess, but it's necessary if we expect to communicate without too much clutter. The general idea is that there are plenty of things that are said in a meeting that do not need to be reconsidered, rediscussed, or rehashed again. Much of it will be obvious, but some of it is more difficult to discern.

For example, when most of the people in the room nod their heads at the right solution, but one or two people still have questions, allow them to speak their minds. Let them talk, listen to them, apply all the same skills you have learned so far. But, when it comes time to writing your notes or creating the follow-up, use your own discernment to decide if it ever needs to be mentioned again. Some stuff can safely fall off the radar, and no one will ever notice.

Other times, you may have a colleague or stakeholder who is saying or suggesting things that are totally off the wall. Related to the idea that people like to hear themselves talk, some people will just riff on an idea. They might call it brainstorming, but it's clear to everyone in the room that this person is going off on a tangent. It's okay, though. Allow them to speak and make them feel valued. The important thing is that you recognize these situations and account for them in your follow-up by discreetly excluding their suggestions.

IGNORING "INNOVATION"

Once I was in a meeting with a client, discussing the idea of an interactive map of the client's retail stores. The existing map was nothing more than a static image with labels that the user could pinch and zoom. While reviewing some of the map designs, the project manager went off on a tangent about how these maps weren't innovative or forward thinking, that he would have expected more from us and wanted to know where our "out of the box" ideas were. He then began pontificating on a 3D virtual reality map with which the user could walk down store aisles and, using augmented reality, see all the details of each product on shelves with pop-overs and animations. Although he meant well, I knew better than to spend time on this idea, and I was able to remove that part of the meeting from my follow-up notes.

There are a few flags to watch out for. You need to quickly assess several things about the person:

- *What are this person's intentions?* Some people are just throwing out ideas casually and don't actually have any intention of them going anywhere. They're comfortable with the idea that it never progresses beyond the initial suggestion.

- *What is everyone's opinion of the person?* Sometimes, you can tell that everyone else on the team doesn't take this person seriously. You can tell by the way they react, either with rolling eyes, groans, or polite compliance. Understanding relationships and influence is important to applying these filters.

- *Do other people agree or disagree?* It's often clear that no one else agrees with this person and even if there isn't a decision, you can safely ignore that idea. Read the room and make a judgement call.

- *Is this person influential enough to matter?* It might seem trite, but some people simply are not influential enough for their opinion to matter to us. Figure out who's who and then use that to inform your decisions for following up.

- *Is this person likely to bring it up again in the next meeting?* If so, you'll need a way to politely defer the decision and communicate later. You actually don't want it to come up again, so be sure to address the idea before that happens.

The point here is that it might be possible to just ignore the suggestions offered by some people and not allow them to cloud your judgement on the project. I don't mean to suggest that we should disregard certain people as irrelevant; rather, we must learn to understand when their comments don't align with the objectives of the project. If they aren't influential, no one agrees with them, and they aren't likely to bring it up again, it's a safe bet you can just move on and never mention it again.

NEVER MENTION IT AGAIN

I was in a meeting with five or six people, and there was one woman who was particularly charismatic and full of energy. She wasn't from the same team, but she was an influential person and asked to be included. Overall, I'd say that although everyone enjoyed working with her (she was a fun person to be around), she had a reputation for being, well, sort of crazy.

During the course of the meeting, another person was commenting on an interaction and making suggestions when she jumped in with an idea. Her idea took shape as something completely off the wall, virtually impossible to pull off or at least incredibly unrealistic, and the entire conversation shifted briefly to this wild brainstorm. I didn't participate; I just took notes and asked questions. Others chimed in, but it seemed clear to me that no one else really thought this was a must-have item. Her feature request was outside the scope of the project, although "revolutionary" and definitely forward-thinking.

After the meeting, when I was writing my follow-up, I came to the section of my notes with this idea. Rather than have it live to see the next meeting agenda, I chose to simply leave it off the follow-up entirely. I emailed everyone in the room, including her, a bulleted list of what we had talked about, but her idea was purposefully missing. After that, I never heard another thing about it. No one else on the team mentioned it, and she never brought it up to me.

In this particular case, I had to use a keen sense of understanding the dynamics of the relationships at play in the room; otherwise, I might have stumbled into a request that had the potential to completely distract us. Yet, it's important to point out that I did two things to make her feel good about it in the moment: I asked questions and I wrote things down. She had no idea *what* I was writing down; it didn't really matter. What mattered was that I respected her enough to listen and take notes. I made her feel valued. Even if she had noticed that I left her idea off the follow-up, she knew that I had at least considered it. I don't know for sure, but my guess is that she either didn't read the email at all or never even noticed that her idea was missing.

Overall, you must learn to filter out all the cruft that can cloud your decision making. It's too easy to think that everyone's opinions and ideas need to be incorporated into our designs, but that's not true. It's actually a dangerous path. Use your skills in listening and relational discernment to remove the stuff you don't need, keep the most important things, and follow up quickly with what's being done.

Seek Out Individuals

Just like the meeting after the meeting, there might be some people with whom you'll want to talk. You might offer to follow them back to their desk, walk them to their next meeting, or invite them to continue the conversation later over coffee. It's important that you ask right after the meeting, while everyone still has their brains in gear and is thinking about your project. When they get back to their desks, it will be a lot more difficult for them to make time for you.

The purpose of these one-on-ones is to give people an opportunity to share their thoughts and opinions outside the constraints of a meeting where other people are listening. You can use these interpersonal relationships to collect more information about the project, gain insights about team or company dynamics that you might not otherwise know about, and build new relationships that can help you get what you need in the future. These people are the influencers on your project, and they can become part of your coalition for influencing the next meeting and the next round of design revisions.

Meetings are usually a good time to see people who you don't normally interact with regularly. They might be from another department or team, and so they don't get to see everything you're doing. I find that I'm always pleasantly surprised when someone I don't know well comes to my defense and expresses agreement with my proposal. You want to always be intentional about seeking these people out and finding ways to connect with them more regularly to keep them in the loop and have the opportunity to help influence your work.

This is not a formal mentor relationship as much as it is an opportunity for you to involve people from other areas who you know are smart and can help champion your cause. It's one thing for your boss to hear you defend your designs, but it's quite another thing for him to hear other people outside your team agree with you. That sort of contribution is extremely valuable in design.

Do Something, Even If It's Wrong

When I was a kid, my dad and I built a treehouse together. I remember one time while he was holding up a board, he dropped his tools. He was standing on a ladder, holding this heavy piece in place, and unable to do anything himself. I didn't know what to do and just stood there looking at him in indecision. Should I try to help him hold the board? Should I jump down and get the tools? What should I do? After a few seconds of agony, he yelled to me, "Well, do something! Even if it's wrong!" This was actually a common phrase of my dad's. The sentiment is that sometimes it's not clear what we should do, but it's almost always better to do *something* rather than nothing.

I wouldn't suggest applying this logic to too many of life's important decisions, but it's often the case that meetings end without any clear resolution to some of the most important questions for our designs. Sometimes, even when we press hard to get people to make decisions, we still can't get agreement or move forward. Perhaps no one is willing to speak up in front of other stakeholders. Maybe no one really cares about one particular element. What's common is for no obvious solution to appear to be the right course of action. No one is really sure what to do, and so no one does anything at all.

In these cases, I recommend simply making a decision yourself and communicating it to the rest of the team in your follow-up. It's better to do something (even if it's wrong) and give your team the opportunity to speak out for or against your choice rather than deal with stale decisions and a stagnant design process. Sometimes, you just need to decide and tell everyone else what you're going to do to get them to speak up.

There's a similar idea called the McDonalds theory, proposed by Jon Bell. If you've ever had the experience of standing around with friends trying to decide where to go eat, then you know this feeling. Everyone is trying to be polite and no one seems to really care which restaurant you go to. As a result, you all continue to stand around and not go anywhere. According to Jon's theory, you should suggest eating at McDonalds—make the decision for the group—and suddenly everyone will have an opinion about where to go. Jon Bell says, "Anne Lamott advocates 'shitty first drafts,' Nike tells us to 'Just Do It,' and I recommend McDonald's [sic] just to get people so grossed out they come up with a better idea."[1]

A developer friend of mine, Mark, does the same thing with styling CSS in his projects. Because he's not a designer (and not very good at CSS), he wants to be sure the designers will make it better. However, he's had too many experiences when his CSS was seen as "good enough" and never polished to the degree he knows it should be. Rather than have to explain to everyone what needs to be done, he simply applies appalling colors to every element: bright red, hot pink, or putrid brown to be sure that anyone who sees it will insist that the designer restyle it appropriately. Often, the best way to get people's attention is to make a bad decision.

---

1   McDonalds Theory, Jon Bell, Apr 29, 2013. *http://bit.ly/1EnqiOD*

The same thing happens with design decisions and business. No one is quite sure what the right solution is, and everyone wants to be polite. These are your designs, after all, and they may not want to hurt your feelings. If you're faced with indecision or ambiguity, take the lead and make the decision for everyone. Find the choice that you believe is best and then communicate that to the team. Be specific, provide examples, and give them a deadline. Say something like, "If I don't hear back from anyone by the end of the day, I'm going to move forward with this design." You may not hear from anyone, but sometimes people will suddenly have stronger opinions and allow you to discuss the right solution. It's not a perfect science, but it's a great way to keep your designs moving forward. Remember: do something, even if it's wrong.

It's important to keep in mind that even when the meeting is over, your work is not done. Often, the most productive parts of the meeting happen after everyone has left the conference room. Don't miss out on this opportunity to finalize decisions and get buy-in from people after the fact. Keep these tips in mind for when the meeting is adjourned:

- The time immediately after the meeting is a great opportunity to hear what people really think.

- The faster you follow up, the more you communicate urgency, value, and decisiveness. Do it now.

- Filter out any clutter or unnecessary recommendations from your notes that you know do not need further action.

- Stick around to chat, follow people back to their desks, and get the last-minute buy-in you need to move forward.

- If there's ambiguity, make a decision and communicate it to everyone else. That might be the only way to move things forward.

The thing with meetings and design decisions is that they don't always go the way we want. Even with the most eloquent response and the best follow-up, we might still need to make changes to our designs that we disagree with. But if you walk away from a meeting feeling like all is lost, don't worry. It's still possible to save the day and rework your designs to meet everyone's needs without totally losing it. You just need to learn how to recover from disaster.

[11]

Recovering from Disaster

In every difficult situation is potential value. Believe this; then begin looking for it.
NORMAN VINCENT PEALE

AFTER EVERYTHING WE'VE COVERED, I want to be honest and say that sometimes no matter how much we try, we will still need to make changes to our designs that we disagree with. It could be that the people we work with are not willing to budge on their opinions despite our expert suggestions. Or, it's possible that we just haven't done a good enough job of making a compelling case for our designs. In this chapter, I propose some options for dealing with changes we disagree with and hopefully recovering from a UX disaster. The purpose is to ensure that we maintain the integrity of the user experience even in the face of disagreement about the right solution.

We'll cover the following:

- Ways to comply with the request without going overboard

- Seeing the opportunity in these changes, no matter how terrible they might seem

- Deciding to choose your battles and earning a deposit in the bank account of trust

- Learning to recognize when you're wrong and correcting yourself

- Creating purposeful distractions without being underhanded

- Setting expectations properly about what our stakeholders can expect going forward

First, let's uncover the root problem that landed us here in the first place.

How Is This Possible?

Being asked to make changes that we disagree with is the very thing we're trying to avoid. If it's still happening, we need to correct the problem. The first step to addressing a problem like this is to understand the reason it happened in the first place and what could have been done to avoid it. We've gone to great lengths to listen to and understand our stakeholders so that we can appeal to their needs with our response. If they still disagree with us or continue to insist that we make a change, there are a few reasons why, which we'll look at in the next few sections.

THEY HAVE A SPECIFIC NEED THAT ISN'T BEING MET

Some people—especially executives—simply want to know that the thing they're interested in is available and accessible to them. This is not always user-centered in the way we would like it to be, but is driven in part by their own needs. Perhaps it's something that high-profile clients or other executives request. As long as they know where it is, they're usually satisfied. They might even be perfectly happy to jump through a few hoops to get to it, if they know what to expect. I worked with one person who loved to look at all the social media chatter about the app and insisted that we add it to the home page. In reality, he just needed quick access to it. Helping him to bookmark it with a vanity URL that he could remember addressed his needs. However, it's not always that simple. If you suspect there's an underlying need that your stakeholder isn't expressing, you'll need to work harder to uncover their motivations and find a way to address their needs to overcome the objection.

THEY WANT TO KNOW THEY'RE BEING HEARD

It's also possible that our stakeholders simply want to know that their ideas and suggestions are being heard and taken seriously. Occasionally, people insist on a change because they don't think we're listening to them. As figures of authority, some stakeholders may just want to exert their power. I don't mean that our stakeholders would be so arrogant that they'd purposefully push their own agenda at the expense of the team or user experience. I think this can happen unconsciously when they don't feel that we've done a good enough job of explaining why their suggestion doesn't work. If this is happening, we need to communicate to them how much we value their input and feedback. They might have felt like we shrugged off their suggestion without taking it seriously. But more important, we did not help them understand why our solution was preferred. You'll need to go back and ask them to explain their perspective again.

THERE IS A MISUNDERSTANDING

If you're confused about your stakeholder's insistence on changing something that you've recommended against, it's possible that you're simply not on the same page. There could have been a miscommunication: your stakeholder didn't understand what a carousel was, wasn't listening close enough, or misunderstood the context. Clearing up the miscommunication is usually sufficient. Other times, the stated goal of the project has changed and morphed over time, and we're now solving different problems than the ones we originally set out to solve. This is quite common, and a stakeholder's suggestion for changes is often a reflection of these moving objectives. Getting to the root cause and clearly redefining the goals will help guide you back to a healthy place.

YOUR DESIGNS ARE NOT THE BEST SOLUTION

I know it's hard to believe, but it's possible that your design is actually not the best choice. In fact, you could be wrong. We will look at understanding when you're wrong later in this chapter, but it's important to realize that our stakeholders and leaders have been placed in authority for a reason and they are usually ultimately responsible for our successes and failures. They have expert knowledge in different areas and insights into the business that we don't have. Just because we disagree does not mean that we're right. In the same way that our stakeholders extend trust to us for recommending the best solutions, we also must learn to extend that same trust to them when it comes to the final decision. It may not be easy, but it's our reality. Our leaders and managers might know something, perhaps intuitively, that we don't. They've been tasked with making the final call, and sometimes we need to lean on them and go with their vision.

THEY ARE COMPLETELY UNREASONABLE

Some people are just totally unreasonable, and no matter what we say, they will always insist that we do it their way. This is actually less common than you might think, but it does happen. Usually when we think that our stakeholders are being unreasonable, it's actually that we just don't see things from the same perspective as they do, and it's possible (even likely) that we would make the same decision if we were in their shoes. Still, there are definitely people who we just can't please, no matter how much we try. They believe their ideas are best, they do not trust their team, and they'll push for their agenda no matter the cost. These are the most difficult relationships to manage, but I've found that even unreasonable people can eventually come around to our way of thinking. It just takes a lot more effort and relational capital to make it happen.

Making Changes You Disagree With

In the event that you're faced with the challenge of incorporating a change you disagree with, I have a few simple suggestions that might help you address it without ruining the experience for the user. In most cases, we don't need to make the changes exactly as they've been prescribed. As we saw in the previous section, sometimes people just want to know where to find the thing they need, regardless of the specific suggestion they make for designing it. Executives, in particular, tend to make requests to satisfy their own needs. Often, just helping them know where to find the thing they value (even if it's not in plain sight) is sufficient for dealing with these requests. To help you do that, I'll describe some simple tactics for dealing with this feedback in the next few sections.

MAKE IT SUBTLE

The goal here is to take the request and reduce it to something more palatable for the user experience. If the stakeholder wants a button, make it a text link. If they suggest a menu, hide it off canvas unless the user explicitly asks for it. If they want it at the top, put it at the bottom, out of the way. Do whatever it takes to appease your stakeholders while also preventing the request from becoming a distraction that will cloud the usability of the app. It's often possible to minimize the impact these requests have by making them more subtle.

MAKE IT AN OPTION

Often, these changes don't need to be publicly accessible if it's just something your boss or team needs to see. I've successfully argued for adding stuff like this as an option that isn't turned on for everyone, either based on user login and permissions or even once as a cookie that was set after following a specific URL. I limited the audience so that it didn't affect usability for the general public. If creating an option is viable for your project, see if your stakeholders are willing accept that as a possible solution.

CAREFULLY CONSIDER PLACEMENT

Depending on the technology you're using and the kind of app you're working on, you might be able to avoid including the proposed change in every view, particularly if the change involves a new navigation item. The same is often true if it involves the home page. In those cases, you might be able to include these elements on only one view rather than all of them. Offer to add the element to the footer, to some other out-of-the-way page, or in a way that is not exposed by default in the primary template. Always keep in mind how the placement of the change will affect the rest of the app and look for an opportunity to minimize its visibility while still making a point to accommodate the stakeholder's suggestion.

The hidden menu

I once had a boss who was very much supportive of my user-centered approach to design, but he also had specific needs for the website that he felt were important and he wanted me to add several things to the home page. I disagreed that these elements were important. They were essentially links to other external resources: a customer portal login, some financial documents. What I found was that as long as I could teach him where to go to get what he needed and that he could be empowered to also tell others how to find those resources, he was completely fine with me putting them in a less accessible place. In fact, that's what I did. I "hid" his things in an out-of-the-way menu and showed him where to find it. "Go to this page, click this link, and then choose from those options." It was simple enough for him to remember and that's all he really wanted. Carefully choosing the placement and working with him to find an appropriate solution helped maintain the integrity of the user experience.

PLAN A SPACE

It's a good idea to always plan a place where you know you can easily add or remove elements that might be requested from time to time. I'd even recommend having several areas where content can be added and removed on a regular basis to accommodate changing needs. Many stakeholder requests are temporary or seasonal: a special promotion, announcements, or a new initiative. If you have planned for screen real estate (such as a container, sidebar, or flexible content area) where you can include these elements without disrupting the user's flow, the conversation becomes a lot easier to manage. Accommodating changes like these is all about expectations. If you expect these requests are coming and have already planned a space to add them, it's simple to accommodate.

I've purposefully planned multiple areas on a home page where I knew I could add elements, as they were requested, with the goal of removing them after a period of time. I also purposefully chose a different area with each request, based on its needs, so that we weren't blindly dropping irrelevant content or functionality into the same black hole each time. This kept the home page fresh and interesting because new content was moving in and out, so it was more effective at attracting the user's attention, too.

In other cases, I've used an "About" view of a mobile app as a place to put content that the business wants but no users really need ever see. One app had a small info icon in the navigation. That icon linked to a page with content about who built the app, in partnership with others, with a goal of doing something, links to the blog, and on and on. As more ideas for business-related content emerged, I was able to move some of those elements to the About page and keep it out of the user's way.

On a website I maintained long-term, I planned several areas (in orange in the adjacent figure) where I could add content that I knew would be requested from time to time. These spaces were not part of the original design or requirements. By planning it out in advance, the conversation was easy to manage without feeling like everything would be ruined. Rotating the location and changing the design each time also kept the website fresh and gave stakeholders the sense that I was tailoring it to their needs. Some of these areas were conditional (based on a login or cookie), others were time-based and automatically removed upon expiration. When stakeholders came to me with a special request, I already had the rules and patterns in place to accommodate their needs.

These are simple approaches to what I assume will be simple requests. A lot of the more common stakeholder suggestions are driven by a need to show something that we weren't aware of in the beginning. Obviously, these suggestions aren't going to work with more difficult requests for user flow tweaks or complicated interactions, but they're valid options for times when someone just needs their "thing" to be included and you have to find a way to make it work.

Making Lemonade

It's not always the case that one person's "bad idea" will turn out poorly and ruin everything. Usually, it's our poor execution of that idea that causes these changes to create chaos. Rather than try to fight it or do the difficult work of making it better, we often just give in, shrug our shoulders, and add the thing that person wants exactly as it was proposed. However when we do that, we're missing a huge opportunity to improve the design in a way that we had never thought of before.

All design has constraints and limitations. Our challenge has always been to build websites or apps that are easy to use, yet are required to support a certain feature set, user story, or major constraint such as the limited viewport size of mobile devices. We relish in these challenges. This is what gets us out of bed each day: making great stuff with constraints. If our projects had no constraints at all, it might be theoretically easier but it would not be nearly as rewarding. The fact is that these constraints make us better designers. They are the reason we have a job; other people can't figure out how to make it all work given the same requirements. And so, when directed to implement a design decision that we don't support, it's important that we don't give up and just paste it on top of the interface—tempting as that may be.

Making these changes is an opportunity to find the best possible way to implement that idea. It's a new constraint that you are tasked with incorporating into the project. Our stakeholders expect that we'll "figure out the best way to do it" because that's what we're being paid to do. In fact, our goal should be to take this constraint and actually use it to improve the experience rather than muddle through and hope we don't break it. We need to flip this attitude on its side and see the opportunity in the mess. We can improve the app and manage the conversation with clever solutions and creative thinking.

In my experience, one person's suggestion is a gold mine of other ideas waiting to be excavated. The changes your stakeholder proposes should spark a conversation that leads to an even better solution. Your job, as a communicator, is to lead that conversation to a place that will yield the best results for your application. You can do that by asking questions, understanding their perspective, and listening: all the skills we've covered in these pages. Involve other people. Ask them how they would solve the same problem. Propose an alternative; even a bad alternative should start a conversation about solutions. You see, this is an opportunity for you to both practice your skills as a communicator as well as effectively lead a discussion on maintaining the right user experience.

UNCOVERING OTHER PROBLEMS

Occasionally, having a stakeholder insist on a change can lead you down a path to improving the app in a way that you never expected, solving problems you might not have uncovered otherwise. A mobile app I designed displayed demographic data in both a list view and a bar chart view, controlled by tabs. Originally, the two views were distinctly different, but over time as the team moved things around, the two views unintentionally became similar without us even realizing it. Finally, the client asked us to add an additional field to the bar chart and we realized that we could combine both views into one. What started out as two different ways to show the information merged into one consolidated view and a simpler experience for the end user. Had we argued against all these changes, we never would have arrived at a better solution.

On another project, one of my stakeholders requested changes to some interactions on form validation and messaging. Although her intentions were well placed, I thought the changes would degrade the experience for the user. Rather than blindly comply, our team did some quick user testing to ensure that what we were doing would work. By observing users perform all the tasks end to end, we discovered a completely different flaw in the user flow. As it turned out, neither my suggestions nor those of the client would work. Being open to changes in one part of the app revealed a flaw in another. Because of our timeline, we might not have uncovered that problem as soon if I hadn't been open to the suggestions from my stakeholders.

Seeing stakeholder requests as an opportunity for change or a challenge to solve for is a much healthier approach than groaning accommodation. Plan for these changes, *because they will happen.* If you already know how you're going to address them—for example, with preplanned real estate, an extra user study, or a reevaluation of the approach—you'll be in a much better position to ensure that you're creating the best user experience even in the face of difficult changes. Your stakeholders will appreciate your effort, your attitude will help you stay on track, and in the end the user will thank you for it.

The Bank Account of Trust

As you consider the different ways to approach stakeholder feedback, it's important to realize that every relationship involves some give and take. It's simply not possible to have a healthy relationship with other people if that relationship is only one-way. You can't expect that other people won't suggest changes. Consequently, you must be prepared to deal with them. It's much better to anticipate these changes and know how to react before they even occur.

Purely from an economic standpoint, your job as a designer is already established as a give-and-take relationship. You receive money in exchange for providing designs. Beyond that, for the relationship to not only function but to thrive, you also need to keep your stakeholders happy. That's more than just a purely economical transaction. This happens by building trust, demonstrating your expertise, managing their expectations, communicating effectively, and (of course) delivering what they expect. In those areas, there is also give and take. Think of it like a bank account: every positive experience working with you is a deposit and every negative one a withdrawal. In his book *The 7 Habits of Highly Effective People*, Stephen Covey calls this the "Emotional Bank Account."[1] Your goal is to maintain a positive balance with them at all times.

---

1   Covey, Stephen. *The 7 Habits of Highly Effective People*. Fireside, Simon & Schuster, 1989: p 188.

For every time you agree with your stakeholder, you make a deposit. When the metrics improve as you promised: deposit. When you show them an incredibly beautiful design they love: deposit. But when we disagree, we begin to see withdrawals. When you miss a deadline or fail to follow up on feedback? Withdrawal. You refuse to make a change because you believe it's in the best interest of the user? You might end up being right, but at least temporarily, it's a withdrawal of trust. At the end of the day, your relationship with stakeholders can be measured by the balance you have in this bank account of trust. Their willingness to trust you when it matters most is dependent on having a positive balance.

As a designer, that means that sometimes you have to relent and allow your stakeholders to make changes even when you're opposed to them, maybe only because you need to make a deposit. The important thing is that you're learning which battles are worth fighting. You're taking stock of the big picture and choosing to only make a fuss about the ones that matter most. You're focused on your goals, the problem, the users, and seeing to it that the areas where you disagree can still allow you to deliver on your promise of building the best possible interface. It's a balancing act, for sure, but one that you will always be learning to manage. You must constantly be balancing the needs of the user with the needs and requirements of your stakeholders. When those two things collide, you have to make difficult decisions about where to draw the line. But realize that you always have a choice about where that line is. In many ways, as the designer, you get to draw (and redraw) that line at every meeting and in each conversation. The outcome of the project is dependent, in large part, on your ability to effectively manage these conversations and find the best solutions, given the constraints of working with real humans.

The long-term goal of building trust with stakeholders is to come to a place where their default response is to assume that our choices are right rather than questioning our decisions from the beginning. My clients know that I have opinions and can express my perspective. Over time, they learn to trust me and shift from a position of assuming that my choices are questionable to assuming they have purpose. On a phone call recently, one of the stakeholders questioned a design element but then deferred to me, "I know Tom usually has good reasons for his choices. Tom, what's the reason you did it this way?" When you can get your stakeholders to approach your work with this perspective, you set yourself up for long-term success in building great user experiences you can be proud of.

When You're Wrong

One of the keys to good communication is building trust with the people whose support you need. It's not enough to only be good at telling people why you believe you're right, although that's important. You also have to build rapport, trust, and develop a track record of making good decisions. The more people see that your designs accomplish their goals, the more likely they'll be to defer to your judgement when the time comes. This only comes with experience and by building good relationships.

However, something strange happens when you're wrong: there is potential for that trust to be broken. The metrics don't improve like you'd hoped, you miss a target deadline for the release, or your designs are found to be difficult for users. It's difficult when you express confidence in your decisions and then watch as your assumptions come crumbling down. Hopefully your decisions won't cause critical damage to your product, but in any case when your designs are shown to not be the right solution, it creates a tension that can be awkward to handle. You have a choice: own up to your decisions, or ignore, deny, or absolve yourself of any involvement.

Although being wrong might seem like it would tear down trust, it's actually an opportunity to build more trust by admitting you made a mistake. It seems counterintuitive: we've let them down and now we're supposed to admit it. How does that build trust? In a court of law, admitting to a crime means that you are prepared to bear the punishment. You've broken the trust of the people and now you have to pay for your mistake. But in the world of relationships, people are far more forgiving than you might expect. People appreciate honesty more than smoke and mirrors. They prefer transparency over a cover-up. The way they know they can trust you is when they see that you'll own up to your mistakes. Honesty is truly the best policy. It may be tricky at first: it will create difficult conversations. But in the end, you'll almost always come out on top when people realize you're a trustworthy person—that even when you screw up, you're there to admit it, fix it, and move on.

In a worst-case scenario, your mistake will cost your company money. It's possible you could lose your job for a major flub, but I don't believe you should ever fear that sort of reprisal for being honest about what happened. It's really challenging to hire and keep good people. If you've done a good job of building relationships and establishing value at your organization, there's very little chance you'll be let go just because one of your designs didn't meet expectations. So don't fear your job and try to protect yourself, because you'll only end up creating a self-fulfilling prophecy.

Move on

The best thing to do is just get it out of the way so that everyone can move on. Rip off the bandaid of your pride and set things in motion to fix it. Be direct and clear about what happened. You need to clearly state, "I was wrong" or "I made a mistake," but also be quick to get to the solution and focus on action instead of excuses. Tell your stakeholders what needs to be done to correct the problem and outline a clear plan for doing so. Most stakeholders are results oriented, so quickly admit your mistake but jump directly to the solution. When you make yourself part of the solution, you're also making yourself indispensable: they need you to help correct this problem. And because the blame lies with you, communicating a sense of urgency and willingness to go above and beyond on correcting the issue will help establish the trust you need to move forward.

The reasons why something went wrong are not nearly as important as fixing the problem. Don't obsess over rehashing the history. This usually sounds like excuse-making. Instead, gloss over the why and get straight to the fix. If people want or need to know the history, they'll ask and you'll have the opportunity.

The blame game

It's also important to recognize that often people just want to know who to blame for the problem. It might seem unfair, but some people want a scapegoat so that they can talk about it with their bosses if it comes up. A good stakeholder will own the mistake with you, as the person who oversees the decisions on the project. But even if they don't, you'll get a swifter resolution if you own up to what happened and move on. As soon as the source of the mistake has been identified, everyone usually feels better about moving on.

Fall on your sword

There are also cases in which you, as a leader, will need to own up to mistakes that might not have been completely within your control, just for the purpose of moving on. Teams can get so hung up on asking, "Why did this happen?" that it derails the project even more. Although it's unlikely that you're solely responsible for a failure on a project that involves a team of people, it's still worthwhile to admit your part (however small) in getting the team to where it is now. This can sometimes result in you falling on your sword and taking the hit for the team. It's not always advisable, but in tense situations in which everyone is pointing fingers, it might be the best way to move on.

KNOWING WHEN YOU'RE WRONG

The most difficult part of admitting when you're wrong is even being aware that you're wrong in the first place. It can be easy for our own arrogance to get in the way of seeing the problem. As designers, we see our designs as our baby—this perfect thing that we created and are sending out into the real world. It's really difficult to see the flaws with it, even when people point them out to us. We are often in denial about the fact that our work doesn't work. How, then, do we know when we're wrong? There are three red flags and they all conveniently line up with the three things you need to be a successful designer. How to know when you're wrong:

The problem still exists

> While we try to solve problems, it's not a given that our designs will always work as expected. If we find that the problem still exists, we're wrong and we need to change something. I've actually witnessed designers who were in complete denial that their designs were to blame for an unsolved problem. "I redesigned it and it's much better now. If conversion hasn't improved, there must be some other issue." No matter how great *you* think your designs are, if the problem still exists, you're wrong.

Users don't get it

> Because we want our designs to be easy to use, we need to see that they're actually making it easier for people. If not, we're wrong! I've worked with designers who were so convinced that their interface was easy to use, that no amount of failed user testing would have convinced them otherwise. They usually blame the users. "This

interaction is common on mobile devices now. If the users don't know how to use it, they must not be familiar with modern design patterns." Guess what? The user is not to blame here: your designs are.

Everyone is against you

We can be really arrogant about how elegant our solutions are, especially if we're the only designer on the project. We feel justified that "no one else knows good design," and so even in the face of opposition, we insist we're right. But when a majority of people disagree with your decisions, it's a sure sign that you're doing it wrong. "I know you all disagree with this decision, but *from a design perspective* this makes the most sense, so you need to trust me and my expertise." Although we do want everyone to trust us with difficult decisions, it's not true that you're always right just because you're a designer. Take stock of the room and be smart about how you're perceived when you push for something. When you own the company, you can take those risks. But until then, allow other people to influence the project, too.

However it comes about, when you see that you're wrong and you're willing to admit it, go straight to the business of reconciling the project. Focus on action, propose a solution, communicate urgency, and be willing to hustle. Your reaction to a mistake will speak volumes about you as a person and set you up to build trust with everyone on your team going forward. Recognizing when you're wrong and proposing a solution is one of the most important ways you can recover from disaster.

Painting a Duck

Half the world is composed of people who have something to say and can't, and the other half who have nothing to say and keep on saying it.
ROBERT FROST

Yet even after all of this, it's still possible that you'll be unhappy with the outcome. The truth is that the world is full of unreasonable people who will want what they want, no matter what we think, and much to the detriment of the user experience. This can be more common in executive-types who have the authority to just tell us what to do and lack the perspective that we have on the project, but it can happen at any level of the organization.

This attitude is heavily influenced by *Parkinson's Law of Triviality*, which states that people in a meeting will spend a disproportionate amount of time on issues that are not central to the project. According to Wikipedia, "Parkinson observed and illustrated that a committee whose job was to approve plans for a nuclear power plant spent the majority of its time with pointless discussions on relatively trivial and unimportant but easy-to-grasp issues, such as what materials to use for the staff bike-shed, while neglecting the less-trivial proposed design of the nuclear power plant itself."[2] This gave rise to the term "bike-shedding" in software development.

Although I've participated in plenty of meetings in which bike-shedding was a problem, there's a derivative of this attitude that seems pervasive in design meetings where feedback is always expected, regardless of the quality of the designs being presented. I'm not exactly sure what it is, but some people like to give feedback even when they have none to give. Why? I think some people just want to sound smart (perhaps to other people in the room), but for most people the reason we're meeting is for them to give feedback. It's as if they wouldn't be getting their money's worth of our time if everything we did was great. "What's the point of having a meeting if there isn't something to change?" It is for these people that I suggest *painting a duck*.

According to Jeff Atwood of Stack Exchange, a duck is "a feature added for no other reason than to draw management attention and be removed, thus avoiding unnecessary changes in other aspects of the product."[3] The idea originated from a story out of Interplay Entertainment, a gaming software development company.[4]

The story goes that one of the designers on an animated chess game was tired of all the changes his stakeholders wanted. It seemed as if no matter what he did, they always had one more change. To solve this problem, he created the Queen character and animations exactly as he wanted them to be, but with the addition of a pet duck. He was careful to make the duck obnoxious and overdone, flapping around on the screen while also not disturbing the Queen. According to the Coding

---

2   C. Northcote Parkinson's 1957 Parkinson's Law of Triviality. *http://bit.ly/1iuD1dW*

3   Atwood, Jeff. Coding Horror Blog, "New Programming Jargon." July 2012. *http://bit.ly/1JfEtrg*

4   *http://www.interplay.com*

Horror blog, "Eventually, it came time for the producer to review the animation set for the queen. The producer sat down and watched all of the animations. When the animations were done, he turned to the artist and said, "That looks great. Just one thing: get rid of the duck.'"[5]

I apologize if you're so distracted by this duck that you're unable to concentrate on reading.

I don't mean to suggest we should deceive or manipulate our stakeholders, but there is a truth to this story that bears considering for our work. Some people aren't going to be happy no matter what we do, and we need to find a way to work with them without compromising the integrity of the user experience. The duck might be an extreme example, but it makes a good point: that all relationships are about give and take. We need to be able to recognize situations in which it's appropriate to offer solutions that we rightly know our clients won't accept, even if it's just to keep their focus on the primary objectives. Painting a duck or even purposeful bike-shedding might seem like a waste of time (and it is!) when we should be focused on solving real problems. But if the alternative is addressing changes from an unreasonable person that might impact the effectiveness of our apps, it might actually save time and energy in the longrun to find a creative way around this problem.

People ask me if this really works. They also often ask, "What do you do if they *like* the duck?" My clients have asked me if I've ever painted a duck with them. Of course I have! But practically speaking, painting a duck more commonly takes the form of presenting clients with multiple alternatives that I've carefully curated. It's about controlling the order in which designs are presented or including designs that I know they won't accept. I can always present one extra design that I'm pretty sure they won't like if it means they'll be more likely to agree that my proposed solution is best. It's not quite as sneaky as it sounds. In other situations, the duck might be a poor font choice or unnecessary visuals (like icons and graphics) to demonstrate that simplicity is better. Even though the story itself is fun, in my experience a real duck tends to be

---

5   Atwood, Jeff. Coding Horror Blog. "New Programming Jargon," July 2012. *http://bit. ly/1JfEtrg*

more of a jumping-off point to turn the conversation toward a better solution rather than an outright deception. You will need to decide just how far to take your ducks with your own stakeholders.

Managing Expectations

An important part of your relationship with clients, bosses, and stakeholders is managing their expectations of you, of the project, and of the outcomes. **Your ability to properly set, adjust, and communicate expectations is more important than your ability to crank out killer designs on a daily basis.** This is especially true when you're faced with making unexpected changes or taking the project in a different direction based on stakeholder feedback. More than just making their changes, you must help them understand *how* it will be done, *what* your thought process and approach will be, and *when* they can expect it to be finished. Setting those expectations at the outset (and all through the process) is critical to getting stakeholder support and buy-in over the long term.

I mention this in a chapter about recovering from disaster because it is in these moments of trying to right a wrong that we most need everyone to understand the situation. I've seen projects fail, not because the designers had bad ideas or didn't work hard enough creating innovative solutions, but because they didn't communicate expectations and eventually lost the support of everyone who mattered most.

The most memorable example was Jim. I had hired him to lead the design effort of a new product. As a concept, this web service had no track record, questionable internal support, and virtually no budget. Our job was to build something out of nothing, to create value in an area that hadn't been explored before. It was new, exciting territory, but we faced an uphill battle of helping other people understand and support our vision for the product.

Jim was young and inexperienced, but he had good ideas and was talented at expressing those ideas in the browser. He understood the vision for the product, had experience with similar services, and all the energy of a nuclear power plant when it came to executing that vision. Jim was also extremely opinionated, quite arrogant, and had a difficult time seeing anything wrong with *anything* he designed. To make matters worse, his communication style turned out to be defensive and terse, if not downright rude. When the platform was being tested with real users, we got a lot of great feedback. People were interested in our idea, but didn't understand the vision. They were willing to try it, but questioned the approach. Complicating matters was the fact that this new platform affected how everyone in the organization posted content to the website, as well. Not only did we have a problem of helping people understand our vision for the new initiative, but we also had a lot of people upset by how their workflow had been changed.

Jim's approach to addressing these challenges was not ideal. His attitude was: "The system is easier to use. Don't they understand that? The things we're doing are innovative and unique! Why can't they see the value in that? The new features are geared toward an audience of young social media techies: why does it matter if the old people don't get it?" Because he was unable to reconcile these questions, he was usually perceived as writing off other stakeholders. When someone would ask him about it, he would become defensive and basically tell them that they were wrong, they didn't understand, or they weren't the target user. It was a relational disaster.

When I finally pulled the situation into a triage of prioritizing changes and reevaluating the project, his work habits had devolved into a cycle of trying to pump out as many new features and fixes as possible. He was working overtime to get everything done, because he believed the problem could be solved by spending more time on it. If he could deliver on the features, he thought, then everyone would be happy, but no one was happy. Why? Because time and time again, Jim wasn't able to deliver on his promises. He was terrible at helping people understand his workload, any reasonable timeline, and he believed he was faster and better than he actually was. The relational fallout was worse: no one got on board with the project despite the fact that we really did have some great designs and a well-built system. People became frustrated, moved on, or demanded something completely different. "Just give me back the old site," they'd say, "because at least that worked and we knew how to use it."

In an unfortunate turn of events, Jim lost his job because his project was essentially a startup within a larger organization, and when the product proved unsuccessful, there was no more money to fund it. But, even though the product itself died, I was faced with the challenge of inheriting a new custom-built content management system for the website that everyone was still unhappy with and which had a mile-long list of bugs and missing features. I had to take ownership of this new project, in addition to all my other responsibilities and without the full-time support I'd previously had from Jim. If Jim couldn't manage it all, how could I?

I decided to approach the problem differently. I saw it not as a matter of the number of hours I needed to put in, but of relationships and conversations to manage. It was more about the people than it was about the problem. I immediately started aggressively pursuing everyone that had been put off by Jim's attitude. I listened to them, made notes of their suggestions, and created a publicly visible list for everyone to see what was on my plate. I invited several key people into different conversations to help prioritize the needs in a group setting; this way, everyone could see how each person's changes affected others. I attached priority values and time estimates to each task. In some cases, where it was appropriate, I outright refused to pursue an idea.

The end result was a well-structured conversation: everyone was on the same page, everyone knew where we were going, and everyone supported my effort to make it happen. I didn't stop there. I moved quickly to implement the schedule as fast as possible. As people saw that I was making good on my promises (even if it was at a slower pace than we would have liked), they learned to trust me and I quickly gained support for the new system. When I couldn't deliver, I let them know ahead of time and let them help me reprioritize things. They were part of the decisions, they had visibility into the project, and they felt ownership with me.

Whereas before two people might have met in the hallway and grumbled about Jim or the missing features, now they would defend and support me in similar circumstances. They would say things like, "I was in a meeting with Tom and he has plans to make that happen," or "Tom has been really open to suggestions. You should go ask him about that." Overall, I was putting in fewer hours than Jim but making better progress. Because I still had all my other responsibilities, I had no choice but to make it work with less effort. In a short time, I accomplished more (and built more trust with people) than he had been able to do during his entire tenure of full-time employment. What's interesting, too, is that while he was still on staff, I was dealing with most of the relational fallout from his poor communication style. As his boss, I had to calm people down, and I was constantly apologizing for his behavior. It was so distracting, in fact, that I had a difficult time getting anything else done. After he was gone, I got more done by myself than we had both been able to do when he was on our staff. The time I spent dealing with the aftermath of his mistakes was more than the time it took me to properly manage expectations and do the actual work. So I will repeat myself: **Your ability to properly set, adjust, and communicate expectations is more important than your ability to crank out killer designs on a daily basis.**

I don't know for sure, but I suspect that Jim (like many other designers) believed that his designs would speak for themselves. That interpersonal communication, as a skill for designers, was wholly unnecessary because our designs are, in and of themselves, a communication medium. He was the expert, but his arrogance clouded his ability to value the stakeholders on the project. He was good at solving problems and he was very user-centric in his thinking, but he failed to realize that without the support of everyone else on the team, he was not going to be able to succeed. In an extreme sense, he lost his job because he was a terrible communicator. This is a lesson that every designer needs to learn, though hopefully you won't have to be fired to learn it. **The way you communicate with and manage relationships with stakeholders is critical to your success as a designer.**

Over, but Never Done

Our journey of meeting with and communicating to stakeholders has come to an end and yet it is a process in which we are constantly involved. By now, the meeting has concluded, you've already done a great job following up with everyone on the team, and you're well on your way to executing your vision for building an incredible user experience. Hopefully there aren't too many changes that you're concerned about, but even if there are, you're well equipped to find solutions that will benefit both the user and your clients. The culmination of everything we've covered together should prepare you to articulate design decisions, communicate with stakeholders, *keep your sanity*, and still deliver the best user experience.

Before we close this book, though, I'd like to provide two more things for you to use in your design practice that can help you succeed in building great products. The first is Chapter 12, which is a resource to give to your stakeholders, teammates, and clients. It was written for nondesigners and is meant to help them understand and work with us more effectively. The second is an approach to design that values the needs of our stakeholders by learning to design with and lead from a place of vision rather than only focusing on what's realistic and possible given our constraints. The final chapter, Designing for Vision, is meant to help you communicate the most value to your leaders through creating and pitching product designs that purposefully defy the limits of your organization, your current project, and even your own thinking.

[12]

For Nondesigners

What we do see depends mainly on what we look for.... In the same field the farmer will notice the crop, the geologists the fossils, botanists the flowers, artists the colouring, sportsmen the cover for the game. Though we may all look at the same things, it does not all follow that we should see them.

SIR JOHN LUBBOCK[1]

THERE ARE OTHER PEOPLE in the organization besides designers who are interested in learning to talk about design. Stakeholders from every level see a gap in communication with their own team and seek out resources to help them work with us and make better products together. It's no secret that designers have a difficult time getting around in today's organizations. In particular, the designer-developer relationship can become particularly tenuous when these two people don't see eye to eye.

I've had teams ask me, "How can we work together more effectively?" Executives ask me, "Can you teach me to work with our designers?" These people understand the value of having good working relationships, and the key to maintaining it in a technology-driven sector is to focus on clear communication. Most often, people become upset and projects become difficult when two or more people fail to communicate. Miscommunication results in missed expectations. Missed expectations leads to disappointment and distrust. We want to prevent this from happening!

---

1   *The Beauties of Nature and the Wonders of the World We Live in*, 1913

Even when communication doesn't appear to be constrained, the way you approach and talk with designers has an impact on their productivity, attitude, and creativity. More than just clear communication, you need to be sure that you're getting the very best from designers.

This chapter is devoted to helping the other people in the designer's path to better understand, communicate with, and thrive on teams with designers. Whether you're a developer, executive stakeholder, product owner, project manager, marketing type, or customer advocate, this chapter is for you. If you're a designer, tear out these pages and hand them to your boss or favorite developer. (Or you can read along and pat yourself on the back as I affirm you and call out your suspicious quirks.) The goal for this chapter is to bridge the gap and help everyone on the team be more effective at communicating with one another. **We want you to learn how to get the very best out of us**.

To do that, we'll:

- Identify several key areas where stakeholders can help us be more successful

- Provide a list of tips for working with designers on a regular basis

- Make a checklist of questions that most projects need in order to start off on the right foot

The King and the Blind Man

Once there was a king who had a blind man as an advisor. When the king was returning from a hunt with a large party, he became very thirsty and spotted a field of watermelon. He called to his servants to fetch some to quench his thirst, but the blind man began to laugh.

> "Why do you laugh?" asked the king.
>
> "Good king, there are no watermelons here!" he replied.
>
> The king was surprised, "You're blind! How do you know there are no watermelons? I can see them with my own eyes. You cannot!"
>
> And the blind man responded, "My lord, one does not require eyesight to know these things. The season of watermelons is over. There may be some left rotting in the fields, but all the good fruit has already been harvested."

You see, the king saw watermelon, and that's what he wanted, but the blind man knew better. It seemed so obvious to the king that this was the solution to his thirst. It was also so unlikely that the blind man could understand the situation enough to help him with his problem. Yet the blind man's perspective allowed him to help the king and ultimately spare him from collecting rotted watermelon. I suppose there are worse fates!

Obviously, this is an amusing illustration, but the point is this: you have people on your team to make you successful, to help you do your job better, and to provide a perspective that you don't have. There might be times when it seems like the designers don't know what they're talking about or couldn't possibly contribute meaningful solutions to difficult problems, but that's not true. Designers are problem solvers, whether it's addressing business concerns or proposing coding solutions. I've seen designers turn heads when they make suggestions that everyone else thought was outside their realm of understanding. So in order to make the most of your time with designers, you need to remember the Four "izes":

- *Realize* we are good at our jobs.

- *Prioritize* our needs so that we can get to work.

- *Authorize* the entire team to move quickly.

- *Recognize* that we are people, too.

REALIZE THAT WE ARE GOOD AT OUR JOBS

One of the biggest challenges we designers face is with other people believing and trusting that we're actually good at what we do and that we make good choices. What's strange is that so many of those same people will also compliment our work when they like it. However, when people disagree or question our design decisions, there can be a lot of distrust—or at least a lack of complete trust. Many people see the designer's role as merely to make things look nice, and they often aren't afforded the opportunity to have a seat at the table when it comes to decision making.

As you work with the designers in your life, realize that they're actually good at their jobs and that their job is more than just making your project look pretty. They are equipped to find design solutions to business problems. You hired them and have them on your team for a reason:

because they're experts in design and are better at it than you are. They have expertise in understanding what makes things easy for users. They're trained in usability techniques and best practices. They know the right patterns and UI controls. You need to trust them to do their jobs without telling them how to do it.

In fact, design is really difficult. It seems easy and simple to you because you only see the final result. There is a lot that goes into the design process: defining use cases, mapping flows, writing requirements and a ton of ideation and iteration on wireframes and prototypes. You aren't seeing everything we threw away or the time and angst we put into finding the proper solutions. By the time our designs get to you, we've been working diligently at checking all the different angles. There's far more to it than just putting some elements on a page.

If we're coming to you with our proposal, you can assume that we believe it's the best solution. You don't need to ask us if we like or not: we do! We made it! If you disagree, it's absolutely appropriate for you to engage us in that conversation, but don't begin with a posture of skepticism about whether we know what we're doing. Instead, draw out our decision process, seek to understand our perspective, and ask a lot of questions to be sure you're on the same page.

Also, because design can be complex and many elements are interrelated, realize that any changes you suggest will affect the rest of the project. There's a ripple effect that may require us to rework the other parts. It's not isolated. Many stakeholders make well-intentioned suggestions, expecting the changes to be simple or only take a few minutes. It's not unusual to hear, "All you have to do is move this over there, right?" But the process of updating one part of the design requires that we step back and evaluate our decisions. Moving one thing requires that we also move another. Sometimes, changing elements can break the flow of the application. Not always, but often. So, you need to realize that your suggestions are more than they seem and that they may not be as easy as they appear. Even simple changes will require a certain amount of rework.

PRIORITIZE OUR NEEDS SO THAT WE CAN BE SUCCESSFUL

Easily the biggest blocker on any project is not giving designers everything they need to do their jobs. When you ask us to design something, we need a lot of things from you to be able to do that effectively.

It's much more than you expressing your vision and letting us loose. We need business requirements to be documented and timelines to be established. Technical needs, too, are critical: access to servers, contract approvals, or sharing your analytics and data. Often, we need permission and access to other people within the organization: gatekeepers, domain experts, and customer service advocates. We can't work unless we have these things from you, so make it a priority to track down what we need. Let us help you be successful by equipping us with what we need to get the job done. Do the work necessary to set things in motion so that we can hit the ground running.

This means that you have to prioritize our needs in order for us to get stuff done. You should be prepared when you meet with us. Review the designs we sent you in advance so you know what your feedback is. There's nothing worse than someone showing up, saying they didn't have time to review our work earlier, and then riff on a handful of knee-jerk reactions from seeing our work for the first time. No, we need you to be better than that. Value our time in the same way we value yours by being prepared.

You should have already jotted down your list of questions or concerns. You might even find some reference material, like other apps or data from a different project that will help us understand your perspective so that we can deliver what you need. Most important, do this within a reasonable window of time. If you take too long to review and respond to our work, it might shorten the time we have available to implement your changes. We lose time waiting on you and then we're rushed to get it done. You're not going to get the best from us in that scenario. Please value our role on your team by prioritizing our needs so that we can be successful.

Usability Testing and Research

One resource that we often need but don't get is permission and budget for doing usability testing. We need to check your project with other people to verify that it will work as expected. This isn't a focus group; we're not asking users what they want. This is taking the time to observe people using our website or app, and then taking notes about ways we can improve the experience. It's task-based and mostly observational. We don't do this enough because we often don't have permission to spend our time on it. It's not expensive, and the results will more than pay for themselves in uncovering problems earlier or optimizing tasks for a better app. Give us permission, the budget, and even encourage us to do more usability testing.

AUTHORIZE THE ENTIRE TEAM TO MOVE QUICKLY

Projects become stale or move slowly when decisions aren't made quickly. The best thing you can do for the project is to make quick decisions, stick to those decisions, and empower other people to make decisions on your behalf. This will allow your entire team to move quickly and deliver the best product with a great user experience. I can't emphasize this enough. The main difference between a scrappy startup and a bureaucratic behemoth is how quickly they make decisions and move forward. It has little to do with talent, resources, or ideas, and everything to do with the team's momentum. Projects fail or languish when the leaders don't make decisions or don't stick with the decisions they made. This is completely within your control.

You can make us successful by being decisive: make decisions, stick to them, and move on. Being wishy-washy or delaying a decision will cost you real time and money. We will either be waiting idle for you to make up your mind or we'll be working and reworking our designs to accommodate the changes. It might seem like waiting a few days for the next meeting is completely appropriate, but in those few days we could be already working on the next thing or finding the flaws with our current thinking. The best projects I've worked on were those where we met with stakeholders *daily*. That's right, *every day*. I would spend the day designing, show my work to the client in the afternoon, get immediate feedback, and then do it all over again. That sort of rhythm is empowering and exciting. Sometimes, I propose daily design reviews with larger clients and they groan. Why? Because they already have too many meetings and can't seem to wrap their minds around a process that iterates and moves so quickly. Yet, it is these projects that always take longer and yield inferior results. When stakeholders are involved only once a week (or less!), I can anticipate that it will take almost twice as long as needed.

The better you are at making good, fast decisions, the better off we'll be. Not just more productive, but also happier and more satisfied with our work. We feel good about what we do when we know things are moving forward. It would be better to do something (even if it's wrong) and keep the project moving rather than do nothing and flounder in ambiguity. Indecision and changing decisions are the killer of an effective design process, so authorize your designers and your entire team to move as quickly as possible. I promise that whatever you risk in the process of empowering them with decisions will be made up for in morale, speed, and momentum.

Empowering the team

One of the best ways you can keep your project moving quickly is to authorize us (the designers!) to make decisions and extend a reasonable amount of authority to us. Let us make some of the calls. When you're unsure what to do, allow us to inform the decision. Trust us when we make a good case on our decisions, even if you disagree. Ask us what we would do and then let us make the final call. This level of empowerment will result in a better product, happier teams, and quick movement.

I recognize that not every product decision can be entrusted to the designers. There are other factors, business considerations, and even other teams or people involved. However, often those other considerations cloud your own judgment and prevent you from seeing that the simpler, more obvious solution is really the best. In my experience, the designer's recommendations often come back as the solution we eventually land on anyway. I've worked with large clients whose multiple teams and executive meetings slow the process for weeks at a time. We might toy with a handful of ideas, perhaps even implement the one that the VP liked best, only to eventually (months later) rework the design to accommodate our original recommendation. What seems like a great idea in a meeting isn't always what works best in practice. Not always, but frequently enough to be a memorable waste of time.

The best website I ever built was one in which I convinced my boss to let me disappear for three months to work on it alone. It was risky. Other stakeholders in the organization felt left out and complained. People were really worried I would screw it up. No one except my boss saw my work. At the end of three months, I emerged from my hiatus with a finished product that was infinitely better than the existing site. Were the other stakeholders happy with what I did? Not all of them. Did it solve all of the problems we had with the old site? Somewhat. But that didn't stop us from putting it in production and immediately iterating on making it better. You see, had I involved the others from the beginning of the process, it might have taken me a year to arrive at consensus. For this project, we chose to value doing something rather than nothing. We refused to let perfect be the enemy of good. That kind of trust and empowerment is rare, but you'd be hard-pressed to find a faster way of getting things done.

My challenge to you would be to purposefully allow your designers the freedom to make design decisions. Start with some low-risk decisions at first but quickly work your way toward larger overall product vision. Begin by agreeing with them as frequently as possible, until you feel you can let them decide on their own. Find the level at which you start to be uncomfortable giving over control, and then push past it just a little. I believe that the sweet spot of good leadership empowerment in decision making is just past your point of comfort. Leaders should always be just a little uncomfortable giving over decisions to their team.

RECOGNIZE THAT WE ARE PEOPLE, TOO

One big missing ingredient from stakeholder-designer relationships is the recognition that we're all people. We need to remember that the people we work with are human. We need to focus on the relationship and communication. But mostly, we need to be kind, use helpful language, and create a conversation that yields positive results.

This is going to seem obvious, but designers are people, too. In business culture, projects and deadlines are often (unintentionally) valued more than the people delivering on them. Remembering that your team is made up of people who have lives, families, and interests beyond the conference room is important in any organization, and it's no different with designers. All of us have different personalities, original ideas, and a unique perspective on life. There are other things going on in their lives besides this project. Someone is caring for an ailing mother, another has to shuttle kids from school to sports, and someone else will go home lonely. This human-centered leadership approach is nothing more than remembering and recognizing that the people you interact with are real: they have feelings, they can be built up and encouraged or they can be torn down and discarded. You can ignore them or you can show an interest in them. As you can imagine, you'll get the best results when you approach people with a mindset that recognizes their humanity. So as often as you need to, stop, look around the room, and remember one thing: they are human.

After you've done that, the next step is to focus on building good relationships. Although it's important to recognize how our specific roles as designers shape our identity, the foundation of good communication is a good relationship. No amount of organization, management, or empowerment is going to make up for a personal/relational disconnect. Too often, meetings are about projects, projects are about tasks, and tasks are tedious and unhuman. The end result is a robotic approach to projects that has no flesh, no excitement, and no life. So, in addition to being organized and making projects a priority, you also need to work hard to establish a rapport that will speak more for you than the words that come out of your mouth. Be kind and get to know us. Show a genuine interest in us by asking questions about our hobbies, pets, or favorite sports team. You don't need beanbags and foosball tables at your office; you need to be nice and interested in people. It doesn't take much to create a sense that you truly care about the people you work with.

Use helpful language

Recognizing that we're all human, then, naturally leads us to a place where we are better equipped to use language and communication styles that are helpful when discussing design. When you provide feedback for our designs, focus on the designs themselves and not the designer who created them. Don't be terse and don't attack our work. Instead, ask lots of questions in an effort to understand our perspective and approach. Be direct but be kind. Focus on the problems and potential solutions, not on the people and their decisions. Design is already a difficult thing to talk about because people (designers) can get wrapped up in their work. When you criticize people for their decisions, you back them into a corner and cause them to become defensive. Design, more than many other disciplines, has the propensity to be divisive and polarizing. Recognize this at the outset and strive to use words that will help the conversation along rather than pit people against one another. The way you choose to talk to designers about their work will have a dramatic effect on their ability to be agreeable and productive for you.

Also, be patient when things change. We can't always know how our designs will work in the real world, and so it's natural that we need to modify our work even after it's in production. It's common for us to believe we've made all the right choices with our designs, but when we test it with users for the first time, we find that we made the wrong assumptions. Those kinds of challenges are part of the process. In fact, I always feel a little self-conscious and sheepish when I have to go back to the developers and ask for a change. Even though this is part of the design process, I'm admitting my mistakes and taking the blame for something I caused. Because it's my fault, it can be hard to own up to it, but that's necessary if we're going to create a great user experience. You should expect, even encourage us, to embrace these unexpected challenges and help us to prepare the rest of the team for the changes. As much as possible, support us through these changes and clear the path so we can feel good about doing the right thing for the user and the product.

Ten Tips for Working with Designers

To briefly summarize, here are 10 short tips to help you work with designers more effectively:

1. **Focus on what works.** Remove the word "like" from your vocabulary and always talk about what works or doesn't work. Your personal preferences are less important than the needs of the user or business.

2. **Don't provide solutions.** Tell us about the problem you see and describe the issue that needs to be addressed, but don't tell us what to change first. Let us find the solution.

3. **Ask lots of questions.** This is the key to seeing from our perspective and understanding our motivations. Ask questions to uncover our thought process.

4. **Don't claim to be the user.** The truth is that every user is different, and you don't represent the target market any more than the designer. Claiming to be the user of your app or website does not add value to the conversation.

5. **Let us explain our decisions.** Don't offer your own perspective and walk away. Allow us the time and space to form an adequate response.

6. **Empower us to make decisions.** Even if you disagree with our choice, learn to trust us in areas where we have more expertise than you.

7. **Use helpful language.** It can be difficult to receive feedback without becoming a little defensive. Avoid harsh or extreme language and focus your feedback on the designs, not the designer.

8. **Ask if there is data.** We should all use data to support our decisions, but just because the designer doesn't have data doesn't mean he's wrong.

9. **Be prepared.** Review our work in advance and have a list of questions or concerns ready. Don't wait and provide knee-jerk reactions in the moment. Your feedback should be purposeful and thoughtfully considered.

10. **Give us what we need to be successful.** Whether it's logins, access to analytics, or permission to do usability testing, we need things from you to work effectively. Make it a priority.

Design Project Checklist

To help everyone be better prepared, here is a checklist of the most common website and app project needs. If every stakeholder provided these things at the beginning, projects would move faster and create a better-quality experience every time. I use this list with my own clients to ensure that we have what we need at the beginning of every project. Following a checklist like this ensures that everyone is on the same page and makes ongoing communication about the project much easier. It establishes a good foundation for talking about design decisions going forward.

This is just a tool and should be used with a degree of flexibility appropriate to the project, company, or team. Some of these aren't necessary for every project; some projects might have additional needs; and throughout the life of a project, these things naturally change as the team settles into a rhythm. Use this as a guide, but don't be afraid of changing it (or your answers) as the project progresses.

MANAGEMENT VISION AND GOALS

☑ What is the purpose of the website or app? Define the primary use or need. Why does this website or app exist?

☑ What is the overall vision for the website or app? A clearly defined vision helps us understand how this project affects the future roadmap.

- ☑ What are the short-term goals for the business overall? What does the business want to accomplish, and how does this project fit with those goals?

- ☑ What metric can we track? How will we know we've succeeded? We need a way to measure our success.

- ☑ What is the strategy for accomplishing the goal? This is *what* needs to be done to accomplish the goal: the tasks, tactics, or deliverables for the project.

- ☑ What are the business requirements for this project? Having documented requirements at the beginning is important, but we can also work together to create them.

USERS OR CUSTOMERS

- ☑ Who are the users? What do we know about them? This could be a starting point for writing personas and user stories.

- ☑ What is the primary problem we want to solve for them? What are the biggest pain points for users right now? This might not be the goal of the project right now.

- ☑ How do users interact with the site or app? What is their context/location, device type and size, entry and exit points, or frequency of engagement?

- ☑ What is the plan or budget for usability testing and/or user interviews? We need to work with real users in order to design for them.

WORKFLOW AND COMMUNICATION

- ☑ What tools should we use to communicate? What is the best way to get answers? Everyone has different preferences about email, text, video, and phone.

- ☑ What should our meeting cycle look like? We'll want both short, frequent updates, as well as longer, in-depth progress reports. For example, 30 minutes daily, plus a weekly hour-long (or more) design review.

- ☑ What is the timeline for the project? How frequently can we release? Establish a pattern for when tasks should be completed. Take the deadline and work backward on the calendar. This can inform resourcing or scope, too.

☑ Who makes the final call on decisions? Identify one person over-all and/or assign one individual per role, for Business, Product, Design, Engineering, or Content. No committees.

ACCESS TO INFORMATION AND PEOPLE

☑ What technical resources will we need? Who can provide us with access? This includes login credentials, email accounts, VPN, or access to servers.

☑ What existing data is available? Access to analytics, usability stud-ies, A/B tests, or any business reports or slide decks.

☑ Is there an existing website or app that we can use for reference? Is there another product that we can use as a basis for this project?

☑ What is the org chart for the company? What people are import-ant for our project? A list of relevant people, including: names, titles, relationships, and areas of expertise along with contact information.

☑ Do we have permission to work with these people? Necessary intro-ductions or permissions need to be given for us to contact other people in the organization.

DESIGN AND TECHNICAL REQUIREMENTS

☑ What design guidelines already exist? Branding guidelines, logo standards, design language documentation, style guides, or visual UI libraries.

☑ What is the tone or style of the design? This might be defined by the design guidelines. If not, we can discuss.

☑ What are our ground rules or design goals for guiding the design? A short list of limitations, best practices, or focused priorities to guide design decisions.

☑ What other websites or applications are similar or relevant? A list of competitors, similar or unrelated products that are of interest.

☑ What technical requirements will influence the design? Accessibility, browser/operating system version, device or viewport size support, responsive/adaptive/mobile.

A Seat at the Table

The way that businesses approach design has changed dramatically. Design used to be something that only made the company look professional or projected an image for the product or brand. Today, design is being used to solve real business problems, and more and more companies are seeing that value. Entire organizations are pivoting to make design the center of their process because they recognize it's good for the bottom line. The most famous and popular products now are those that are well-designed and provide a superior user experience.

To meet this demand, a lot of companies are hiring designers, building teams, and modifying their processes to more clearly value design— yet, a lot of these same companies still fall short when it comes to delivering a product. Initially, it might seem like their designers aren't talented enough or there's a disconnect between customer needs and the design team. This is what leads managers and developers to seek out resources (like this book) to learn how to better talk about design or to improve their communication and working relationships with designers. I wrote this chapter because difficulty working with designers is a real concern, and every stakeholder can benefit from understanding their designers. But when it comes to overall business practice, there is an underlying issue. Better communication will help, but it's not the main problem.

Companies that struggle to incorporate design thinking into their organization have one problem: they don't have designers at an executive level. The problem of delivering poorly designed products isn't one of talent, but of design leadership. These companies lack a vision that's inclusive of the user experience. They have talented designers, but not design-thinking decision makers. Companies that consistently fail to deliver the products that they believe they should offer need a new seat at the table: a designer.

Think about the most popular products, websites, or apps with which you're familiar. Who started the company? Who is its CEO? In most cases, the people leading the organizations that create great products are people with a design-centric mindset, even if they aren't technically qualified as a designer. They are designers in their own right, but they surround themselves with other talented designer-types, too.

These organizations don't need to "pivot" to make design the center of their culture, because design is already valued at the highest level. They simply *are* organizations that value design.

If you're serious about wanting your company, product, or service to be known for great UX, put a designer at an executive level. It's no longer adequate to hire a contracted freelancer through a sales manager to create your website. You can't just invite the designers to a meeting, inspire them with your vision and then wait for them to bring back the best product ever. You are going to fail if the only designer you have sits at a desk with the marketing people down the hall. Designers need to be involved at the highest levels of the organization if you expect to succeed in a marketplace driven by design. They need to be empowered to make difficult decisions, they need the autonomy to create the best product, and they need to sit in the C-suite, right next to the other executives.

How can you do this? In an ideal world, you'd have the authority, money, and time to create an organizational structure that reflects these values. Create a role for chief design officer or vice president of design. Involve them in all the details, let them decide on product and design direction, and give them a team. Unfortunately, that's not something every company can do easily. More practically, designers and executives need a deeper level of engagement and trust. The people designing the products, website, or app need to be meeting with the CEO. They need frequent communication with other executives. This might just be about proximity: give them a desk in or near the executive suite. It's amazing how much easier design and communication is when a VP walks by your desk occasionally to say hello. This is "management by walking around" (attributed to Hewlett-Packard[2] and described in the book *In Search of Excellence*[3]).

One of the best (and simplest) models I've seen was a former employer who moved the creative director to a desk with the other executives in an open-office environment. Just sitting next to one another greatly

---

2 *https://en.wikipedia.org/wiki/Management_by_wandering_around*

3 Peters, Tom and Robert H. Waterman, Jr. *In Search of Excellence: Lessons From America's Best-Run Companies.* 1982.

improved their thinking, made a political statement about their values, and firmly established the organization's vision. The designers and artists weren't off in another room; they had a seat at the table.

The only way to truly incorporate design thinking into your company values, processes, and products is to put designers in positions of authority. Everyone says they want to be like Apple, but few are willing to make the leadership choices required to create that kind of environment. If you find that your team isn't living up to your expectations for creating great products and designing incredible user experiences, take a look at your own part in that process. Before you go through another reorganization or replace your design director, take a serious look at the people in authority (yourself included) and ask if they're really equipped to lead a design-centric product company. If not, you have an open seat at your next meeting that needs to be filled.

The fact that you've read this chapter speaks volumes about your desire to work more effectively with designers. When you follow these best practices, you create an environment in which designers are free to create, are comfortable expressing themselves, and feel empowered to design great products. Whatever your role, I hope that you'll apply these principles in your practice on a daily basis so that you can get the most of the designers on your team and deliver the best possible user experience.

[13]

Designing for Vision

An artist is not paid for his labor but for his vision.
JAMES MCNEILL WHISTLER

BEFORE WE CLOSE OUT THE BOOK, I want to emphasize how important design is to organizational and product development. Most of us consider ourselves designers of the things that our company produces: web designers, interface designers, or product designers. But in our roles, we shape the vision and perception of the entire organization with our work. We are more than just designers of things; we are designers of the business. In a very real way, we are *business designers*. I am amazed at the power we designers have to shape the organization, and yet how few designers actually realize or use this power to its fullest extent. The fact is, design has the power to change the future, to influence people, and to benefit you and your career. Our fate is in our own hands when we understand that we can inspire people with our creativity. Imagining the future can earn your team praise, get the attention of stakeholders, and give you a shot at actually making something meaningful.

We need to recognize that we have the power to imagine the future, the ability to create something that didn't exist before, and the ideas to inspire the entire organization. We can use these tools for good, for the betterment of the product, and the satisfaction of our own work. Learning to talk about our designs extends beyond the conference room; it begins with purposeful habits of practicing creativity and staying inspired. Few other jobs have the same ability to create excitement around something that doesn't exist, and so for this final chapter, I'd like to go on a journey of discovering just how powerful it can be when we design for vision.

Recognizing Our Power

You have more power than you realize. Designers have the skills and ability to cast a vision for a preferred future—a future that doesn't exist yet and won't exist without our help. Our role should not be to just iterate and moderately improve an interface, but to create an awareness of incredible new possibilities. We have the power to influence the future with expressions of our ideas that make the future seem real, attainable, and exciting.

You see, most people can't do what we do. They don't think visually, and, even if they did, they lack the skills to put pen to paper and sketch out something that looks like what's in their head. This makes us special; we have unique skills that most other people around us don't. We can choose to use them in a way that will benefit our organization and our own careers.

Our value as designers is not just locked up in the day-to-day mechanics of pumping out new wireframes, theming an app, or brainstorming ideas. Sure, those things are valuable and that's probably the main reason why we have a job, but it's not the only way (or the most important way) that we are valuable. We create more value when we help other people see the future; when we take ideas born out of a simple conversation and provide the context or skin it needs to feel real.

This power is the reason we keep photos and video of special moments: because the visual representation of those moments suspends our memories of those events. We are transported into those moments again and again when we look at them. Naturally, we want to share those moments with other people so that they too can experience what we did. We post on social media and relive them over and over. Those images, those visuals, are as much a part of the experience to us as the experience itself.

IMAGES MAKE THE UNREAL REAL

When you build a house, you start with an empty plot of land and it's difficult to visualize how you will live there, but after you see the drawings of what it will look like, you grow excited and anxious. When you see your baby on an ultrasound for the first time, tears well up inside you because it hits home that this is really happening. Things that exist only in our mind become something completely different when they're expressed visually.

We can make these images

A friend wants to start a new business, but the website you create for her is what will really make it feel like a legitimate enterprise. Your boss jotted down some ideas at lunch, but you can take those ideas to the next level. In the middle of the night, you had a crazy idea and you can flesh it out to show to other people. We have what it takes to create the images that make the unreal real. Most people can't do that.

Right or wrong, sometimes the visual of a product alone sets our expectations about it: making promises about functionality, telling us how we'll be better with the product in our lives, and asking us to try it. Attractive visual design has become the hallmark of good products. In fact, we might be influenced more by the way a thing looks than the way it actually works. That's how much power design has. When we see something that's well designed, we might think the product itself is great before we've even tried it. The point is that our designs have the effect of making people believe in what we've created, even if it only exists on paper. That gives us a lot of power when it comes to our designs. We can use this power for good, to move our teams and projects forward into a preferred future, and to create a new reality that didn't exist before.

The reason this is important to communicating to stakeholders about design is because we have the power to inspire people with our work. Expressing a vision for what the future could look like to stakeholders gives us the opportunity to earn their trust, demonstrate commitment, and get them genuinely excited about what we're doing. It's a huge deposit in the bank account of trust. Often, these inspirational designs will help our team move forward because our stakeholders will be on board with the vision. They'll see just how excited we are to work on this project and they'll want to help us accomplish this vision. With a vision of a preferred future, it's easier to get support, funding, research, and any other resource you might need to accomplish your vision. Your stakeholders will be saying, "This is awesome. What do you need to make this happen?" It puts you in a position of *making* the future happen rather than waiting around for someone else to tell you what it is.

Here are just some of the reasons how designing for vision can improve our careers:

It gives us a creative outlet.
> Designing for vision provides an environment for us to express something that we might not otherwise have the opportunity to express.

It creates a conversation with other people.
> Our designs get them dreaming about where we're going, what's possible, and what's ideal without any of the usual constraints.

It brings people together.
> Individuals are no longer stuck obsessing over one little thing; the entire team can get a sense for where we could or should be headed.

It builds credibility.
> People see you as a thinker, a visionary, as someone who is interested in providing long-term value, not just value for the immediate need.

It lives beyond us.
> These designs can be so exciting that they get passed around to other people in the organization. Long after we're gone, they still might be hanging onto that vision of the future.

And so, for these reasons, our ability to create visuals that communicate beyond words has the power to bring people into a world that didn't exist before. We can show them what the future is like before the future has even been created. A picture is as close as you can get to being in this new future without actually being there. People can become really excited when they see what it will look like. This is what it's like designing for vision.

Practicing Creativity

Designing for vision requires that we are purposeful about practicing creativity on a regular basis. You've got to step away from your project and dream a little bit now and then, even if the idea never sees the light of day. Sometimes, the prospect of making one...more...control...seems mundane and boring. If you're bored of your day-to-day job, this is a way to make it exciting and fresh.

FIND INSPIRATION

One of the missing ingredients for learning to design for vision is a lack of inspiration. Some people might consider pursuing inspiration a waste of time compared to the act of simply getting things done. But when the goal is to create something completely new that didn't exist before, it's almost impossible to do that well without an external, aspirational, creative stimulus that models how we might approach our own endeavors.

The easiest and most practical thing you can do is to simply look at other people's products. Find designs that you like, discover how they might be applied in your context. Download and use as many apps as possible. Collect a repository of favorite websites that you can reference when the time comes, browse through pattern libraries, try new open source tools, read case studies, go to a conference, read a book—there are almost too many resources to help you find and create inspiration that you have no excuse, other than the practice and habit of making it happen.

SEE UX EVERYWHERE

There are models everywhere—including those outside the world of tech—that can influence your thinking and passion for designing digital products. We tend to see the world through our lens of UX and may comment on the usefulness of everyday objects as a matter of pride. Turn those powerful observational skills into an opportunity to find patterns in the real world that will inform your designs in the digital realm. Ask yourself this: how does the design of this thing apply to my current project? Is there something it does well that I can use? Start seeing everyday objects as opportunities for learning and inspiration in your own work.

USE A DIFFERENT CANVAS

An alternative way to get the most out of your creative mind is to stimulate it in a different way. Pursue a different artistic endeavor; try something completely different from your usual design-a-thing day job. Find something that allows you to create, express yourself, and sink into a mode of creating so that the worry of delivering melts away. Without hard expectations about what you create, you'll be free to think more clearly and enjoy the process. This could be cooking, landscaping and gardening, painting, photography, or any other creative hobby that interests you and will spur you to greater comfort with your creative self.

You might even do something out of your comfort zone, something that you're not at all interested in or are not particularly skilled at. Being uncomfortable has the fortunate side effect of causing us to see things in a different light, to approach problems in a different way. When we have no bearings on how to behave or what to do, we have no choice but to be creative and make it up as we go along.

For me personally, I am restoring a classic car as an act of deliberate creativity. For several years now, I have been working on a 1969 Triumph GT6+, a small British sports car. Prior to starting this project, I had very little mechanical knowledge. In fact, on the day the car arrived at my house, a neighbor stopped by, pointed to the distributor on the engine block and said, "Wow! You don't see those anymore." I had no idea what that part was, so I just laughed uncomfortably and replied, "Yep, you sure don't!" But since that time, I've completely dismantled the entire vehicle, cleaned and painted each part, and am now meticulously putting it all back together.

In the process, I've learned a lot of about engines, but I've also learned a lot about design. I'm inspired by the engineers who created these cars before there were computers. I'm amazed at the ingenuity of working within such limitations and I'm baffled that humanity figured out how to make a car in the first place! But building a car has given me a way to step away from my desk, to pursue something creative that is 100 percent outside of my comfort zone. I rely on other people for advice and tools. I am constantly reading and learning about these old cars. It's a slow process, but one that has freed my mind and given it new places to go, be inspired, and enabled me to return to work, armed with fresh ideas.

The takeaway here is to find something that can add to your fulfillment of designing interfaces and push you to greater limits of creativity.

Before (top) and after (bottom) photos of the frame and engine from my GT6. I didn't know much about cars before starting this project, but the process has given me a creative pursuit away from the screens and digital interfaces of my daily life.

IDEATE AND ITERATE

Ideation and iteration are both important to ensure that we're practicing creativity. Generating new ideas should be one of your primary outputs. Iterating on those ideas, then, gives us a chance to refine and mature them. These approaches are important when working on visionary vaporware that has no current basis in reality. Thinking of a single new idea and expressing it in a mockup isn't too difficult, but it's far more difficult to come up with five completely different or derivative ideas. That's what we need to do regularly: learn to generate as many ideas as possible and iterate to make as many different versions as possible. Set a goal for yourself to create at least five completely different designs. Don't reuse elements; create new ones. Begin with a blank canvas each time. Then, approach the same problem with a different use-case. Go about creating each one by setting the previous design aside. The more ideas and versions you have, the better. The exact quantity you produce or the fidelity of these ideas isn't important. The goal is to make it a habit of thinking differently about our projects and forcing our brains to learn (and relearn) how to design.

Making It Happen

Practically speaking, designing for vision is creating visuals that express your vision of a preferred future. You design mockups of your product, website, or app, but instead of being constrained by all the limitations you know you have (engineering, marketing, support), you create what you believe to be the best possible product and illustrate that with some form of interactive prototype or static mockup. You can then show or present these designs to your team or executives to inspire them to want to achieve the same goals. The purpose is to create a conversation that results in the organization chasing after something that is bigger than the current vision (perhaps even impossible), but is inspiring and motivating.

However, frozen in the day-to-day maintenance of our jobs, we often overlook just how influential our ideas can be. It's hard to think about vision and the future when there are so many other things to do.

> Documentation needs to be written. The mockups need to be updated. And I have to get ready for a meeting this afternoon. How could I possibly take the time to design for something that doesn't even exist? That isn't even part of my project?

It can be hard to see the value of creating something that's not on everyone's radar. No one is expecting you to do this. No one is explicitly paying you to create visionary, inspirational stuff (usually). It's sort of above and beyond your normal activities and so it can be a challenge to find the time to create things just for the purpose of inspiring others. But the long-term benefits of being purposeful about this direction are well worth it.

We have to be purposeful about making the time and space to do this every so often, whatever is the most efficient for you while not interfering with your regular work day. The following sections offer some tips for setting aside the time you need to design for vision.

FIND A DIFFERENT ROUTINE

One of the most important things you can do is to find a completely different time and space to go dream about the future. You want to break from your usual routine so that your brain isn't even in the same mode that it usually is when you're pumping out UI controls on a daily basis. Finding that routine is about looking for a different *time, space, activity,* and *materials* that will help you to relax, free your mind, and get down to the business of creating things.

Time

You might want to limit yourself to a certain block of time each week to be sure that it doesn't interfere with your work. It can be easy to get carried away and spend all your time making stuff that doesn't pay the bills. So set aside a specific window of time that you think will be helpful. A former boss of mine let me spend every Friday on these kinds of endeavors, but you might be even more limited than that. Set aside one or two hours each week. One hour is more than enough time to mock up an idea if you remove the usual constraints. It's just enough time to get your thoughts flowing, but not enough to disrupt your daily work.

If that still seems like too much, set aside 15 minutes every day. Just 15 minutes. It's not enough time to get any serious designs made, which is why it can be so effective. You're forced to come up with ideas and solutions quickly because there isn't enough time to think deeply about any one concept. The focus is more on ideation. Set a timer and begin sketching your ideas. Jot them down before the timer goes off. Each day you'll have these small snippets. Which ones do you go back to? Which ones seem to have the most potential? At the end of a few weeks or months, you'll have some really great concepts that you can further refine into expressive mockups.

Space

The space where you work is also really important and affects how you work. Our brains work themselves into routines (and ruts!) based largely on our physical location. We condition ourselves to work when certain factors are present, many of them being physical: the chair, the window, the position of your desk, even your position in relationship to other people. Part of your challenge might be to find a different physical space where you can go. If you want to create something different, you'll need to go somewhere different. A new space can inspire thoughts and ideas that you wouldn't normally have. New spaces have new sounds, new visuals, and unexpected stimulations all around you that contribute to your sense of creativity.

I personally find it difficult to get work done if I'm not at my desk, but because I occasionally travel, I've taken to listening to music almost constantly while I design. As a result, I usually can't get any serious design work done unless I'm listening to music piped through headphones. I've learned that this is the way I work now. So if I want to do something out of my normal routine, I have to go somewhere other than my office: a different room in my house, a local bookstore, or a park. The exact location doesn't matter as much as the change of routine. If you expect to create something that isn't routine, you must change your current routine. Go find a new, perhaps unexpected, place to let your brain percolate thoughts and come up with better ideas. You'll need to learn what works for you, but the process of searching for new, interesting places to create will yield better discipline and a different way of designing.

Activity

Sometimes, the best way to come up with better ideas and create better designs is to actually not do any designing at all. That is, change your activity to give your brain an opportunity to relax and wander. Do something that would wholly prevent you from even accessing a computer or any of your usual tools. For example, rather than sit with your laptop at a coffee shop, go for a walk in the woods, hike in the mountains, do yoga, pull weeds in the garden, go jogging, sit on the beach, watch the sunrise—do something that will allow your mind to be still, listening and thinking to what the future could be.

When I get stuck trying to figure out how something should work, I go run. Fresh air, no screens, my brain is free, and my mind wanders. I usually don't even pay attention to what I'm thinking. I'm not explicitly trying to solve problems, but it's during these moments of thinking of nothing that the solution presents itself without me even trying. Not always, but often. And even if I come back to my desk without having come up with the best idea ever, I am usually better prepared to tackle my work again.

Your brain's ability to solve problems while doing a different activity is a common yet remarkable phenomenon. Remember that great idea you had in the shower? Or that thing you fixed while sitting in traffic? It turns out that we all have better ideas when we're relaxed: doing a simple task and letting our minds wander.[1] Anything that you can do that is relaxing and pleasurable will allow your brain to also relax and come up with ideas or solve problems you never thought possible.

You won't be able to actually create something tangible from a change of activity like this, but it will force yourself to be unencumbered and think freely about how to solve some of the difficult problems you face. When you're out in the woods, you don't have your computer. You're forced to just *think* about all the hard problems. When you return, write down you thoughts, sketch out your ideas. Make a record of what you learned in the hopes that it can turn into something worth communicating to others on your team. A change of activity yields a change of ideas.

Materials

Lastly, I recommend changing up the kinds of materials and tools you use to force you into new habits and new ways of approaching your work. The simplest method is to bring along a pad of paper and a pencil, even if you're not the type to draw or sketch. Often we design based on what we already know we can do with our tools. Our ideas are limited to the tools we have in front of us. When something is a little more time-consuming to express with existing tools, we become stuck, waste time, or avoid that idea altogether. Changing the materials you use is a great way to discover new approaches because you're not limited by your typical toolset.

Once I was designing a UI that needed some specific icons, but I was tired of reusing similar icons over and over. I had developed a habit of just searching common icon libraries and grabbing something I liked. I needed to find something with a more unique personality, so I went outside with sidewalk chalk and drew my icons on the driveway. I then took photos of each of them, imported and traced them, and placed them in the project. There was nothing artistically innovative about

---

1   Widrich, Leo. "Why We Have Our Best Ideas in the Shower: The Science of Creativity," February 28, 2013. *http://bit.ly/1JfExHs*

the resulting icons, but I accomplished my goal of creating something unique that communicated the style and tone of my project. Changing materials gave me more opportunities to create a better vision.

I would also highly recommend removing Internet access from the equation when you're trying to find new ideas. It's too easy to search and copy other ideas. Although there's nothing wrong with that, in terms of generating new ideas for your own product (taking someone else's idea and expressing it in your own context), I personally find it more helpful when I'm untethered from the online world and forced to use my own brain capacity for all of my thinking. It's about reducing my dependence on screens or tools for finding solutions to problems. I have access to too much information. Often, my access to infinite amounts of knowledge hinders my own ability to truly be creative and solve problems with good, old-fashioned thought. When I intentionally put myself in situations in which I can't access those screens, I have no choice: I'm all on my own.

So, set aside your computer, phone, and tablet for the time being. Grab some paper and a pencil and start scribbling down things that will help you create the next version of your product. Write words, draw boxes, and generate ideas that can contribute to your vision of what the future can look like.

For one project, I designed a set of icons using sidewalk chalk, took photos, and then traced them on the computer. The result was something that was truly unique and refreshing to work on.

Another time, I tried designing icons in the snow. This didn't yield a real icon set for a project but it was an excellent exercise in expressing an idea with a very limited toolset.

Making Stuff Up

When it comes down to it, designing for vision is really just about making stuff up. There is no magic, except in your design's ability to inspire people. Other than that, it's just a collection of visionary vaporware that has no basis in anything real. You are just making things up, expressing them in a tangible way, and then using imagery to create an excitement and urgency about the future.

If we take that a step further, I'd suggest it's as important to create a fake product with your designs and mockups as it is to create the version 2.0 of your current project. You probably have a pretty good idea about what version 2.0 is going to be like, but what are the products, opportunities, or niches that no one is even thinking about? What would the 4.0 version look like? We are too encumbered by the limits of our bosses and developers. What would you design if you had unlimited resources? What's the right thing to build? Is your current product even the thing you should be working on? We need to be designing more 4.0 versions of our products and 1.0 versions of things that don't even exist yet.

It's a good practice to create a product that doesn't exist yet. Look for opportunities within your organization and express them as best as you can. Don't wait for someone else to come along and pitch the next big thing. Take ownership of your skills, create something from nothing, and give people a reason to get excited.

Don't limit yourself.

Forget all the business requirements, legacy ideas, or engineering questions. Just create something that makes sense to you.

Start from scratch.

Don't reuse anything from an existing project or copy and paste from a template. Design this thing from the ground up, with only raw materials.

Don't obsess over the details.

It doesn't have to be perfect; the purpose is more about communicating a concept than it is about what's realistic and final.

Make lots of different versions.

The more different ways you can approach the problem, the better. When you think you've finished, try it again. It's a good habit to force yourself to make just one more iteration.

This extends, too, to new designers who are looking to build their portfolios. Often, entry-level designers have nothing to show for their skill and are looking for opportunities just to gain experience. This is a great opportunity to find something that you think needs to exist, and make it happen. You don't need an internship or a school project to help you create something; just go create it and build the case for it yourself. Make up a business, design an app for a new product, or imagine what interfaces will be like in the future. Don't wait for other people to give you something to do; go create something for yourself and demonstrate your skill.

When I worked in the electronic-payment services industry, I had an idea for a new kind of loyalty card that our company could use and resell as a value-added service. It had nothing to do with my job. It was just an idea. But I spent some time (not a lot of time) creating mockups and designs that demonstrated what this new service might be like. I shared my ideas with my boss, who then sent it to the CEO and a few other executives. During my tenure, that idea never saw the light of day and I have no idea if it was ever even pursued as a product. However, it *did* create a conversation around our current thinking on loyalty cards, established my name with the CEO, and circulated a document that other people would later tell me they appreciated.

More recently, one of my retail clients had mentioned the need for their customers to easily reorder items that they had ordered in the past. During one of my purposeful creative pursuits, I created some designs for a standalone app aimed at power-users specifically for this purpose. I made some mockups and a simple demo showing how this system would work and shared it with the stakeholders on the project. Unknown to me, another team at the company was already working on something very similar. Although my own expression of that idea didn't cause them to stop what they were doing, it did create a "great minds think alike" conversation during which our combined efforts were validated. I gave them something tangible and sharable that they could use to influence the thinking on their own initiative. It may not have been completely original, but it did demonstrate that I was willing to think beyond their immediate needs and contribute long-term value. My role was more than delivering the day-to-day designs they expected. I also contributed ideas and designs to another project that was outside my current scope. It gave me another platform on which to communicate with them about design.

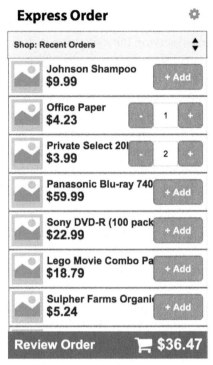

I created a very basic prototype of a reordering app to express a vision for this opportunity. Then, I recorded a two-minute screen-capture video presentation of the idea. Even though my client was already working on a similar concept, it created a conversation that added value to the relationship.

You see, even when our ideas fall flat or aren't entirely useful, they still create value for us as far as learning to communicate about design and build the kind of momentum we need to be successful. When we make things up, we show that we're thinking, we're invested in the success of the organization, and we're smart enough to communicate our ideas to people in a way that's compelling. This sort of commitment is invaluable to organizations.

Taking Your Ideas to the Right People

Relationships are everything. Who you know will greatly influence the opportunities that are available to you. Working with and communicating with people will determine how likely they are to help you and connect you with those opportunities. It's one thing to have great ideas and to even be able to express them in meaningful ways, but it's another thing entirely to have an audience of people who are there to support, encourage, and help you on your journey. Even if you're capturing that vision of a preferred future, it's not going to help you if there aren't people with whom you can share that vision.

The good news is that our skill in design can help us establish a connection with the people that make decisions. Like I've said before, everyone wants a designer on their team. Everyone needs something designed. You need to find opportunities to get in with the right people who have the power to make your vision a reality. You can take advantage of your success in articulating design decisions to influence these decision-makers.

This isn't about selfishly pursuing one-way relationships. It's about finding the opportunities to create your own success with people who can (and want to) support you. Usually, this is your boss: your direct report. Often, it's a peer or other colleague who recognizes your talent and makes a personal connection with you. Sometimes, it's an executive who periodically needs your help, which gives you access to them on a regular basis. Be on the lookout for people who have influence, build into those relationships, share your ideas with passion, and allow them to help you.

How can you do that? The best opportunities to build these connections are when someone needs a "favor" from you. When your boss asks you for help putting together a presentation, do it. If there's a critical bug that needs to be addressed, be the kind of person who sees the urgency and pitches in without complaining. When the product owner comes to the team with a last-minute missing requirement, step up and support her by making it happen. The more often you can help other people, the more likely you are to get help when you need it. These kinds of situations are major deposits in the bank account of trust. The way to get what you want is to help other people get what they want.

In these relationships, keep your ideas, designs, and vision handy. Eventually, you'll have an opportunity to share your ideas with someone who can make your vision a reality. They'll be surprised, delighted, and impressed that you can create that level of vision and communicate it so tangibly. Having an audience of people who can help you execute your ideas is a necessary part of designing for vision.

More Than Pixels

The things we create convey a message to our audience. These pictures possess a quality that gives them a voice and breathes life into what is otherwise just a collection of pixels. Our brains perceive them as having more qualities than they actually have: intelligence, purpose, even a soul. That's because our designs reflect who we are. They are a mirror of our own existence, a reflection of our ability to create and to be the created. As much as we try to design toward the personas of our users or the brand of the organization, our work is still a reflection of us: our style, tone, and personal touch is everywhere. Just as we are drawn to people who are like us, so too we design interfaces that reflect our own shape and personality. This is perhaps why it's so difficult to talk about design: because we are so intimately knit up in all that we create that we cannot stand back far enough to see what it really is. It's difficult to know if what we're reflecting in our designs is what we ever intended in the first place.

Our skill at creating an experience for users that is both delightful and accomplishes business goals is something that few people can do. And even though we do our best to evaluate it, measure it, and improve it, I'm not sure we can ever have a complete picture of what we've created. No matter how much information we have, our ability to understand and talk about our designs is limited to our own unique perspective as the designer. When you hear your own voice on a recording, it sounds strange, "That's not what I sound like, is it?" When you see a photo of yourself, you might think, "That's not how I really look from that angle, is it?" Likewise, when we watch our designs operate in the world with a life of their own, we might react, "That's not how I really meant for it to be used, is it?" We can't always see ourselves (and our designs) for who we really are.

In this book, I've written a lot about how we should communicate to our stakeholders. The whole thrust of this content is to convey how critical it is to be able to explain yourself to someone who might not understand UX design. You cannot and will not be able to really succeed as a designer unless you learn to talk to people in a way that makes sense to them because *your designs do not speak for themselves*. But more than that, product design is bigger than any one person's skill at communication. Our ability to create incredible user experiences is influenced by the constantly changing world around us: other people are involved, external factors are beyond our control, and our life and relationships make us who we are.

Design is volatile and changing, but being a better communicator is something that we can always have. Our designs may get discarded, but we can still talk about them and learn from them. That website will eventually shut down, but we understand the problem that it solved at the time. We may take another job, but we still carry these skills with us. No matter where life and work takes us, we can always rest in the knowledge that in any situation, in any role, and with all people, we are prepared to bring our ideas to life through the power of articulating design decisions.

[*Index*]

materials, forcing new habits using new, 237–239
McDonalds theory, 187
meeting, keeping on track, 91–92
messages
    case study, 173
    conveying to audiences, 244
messaging
    about, 143–144
    business, 144–146
    dealing with limitations, 149–156
    design, 147–149
    research, 149–156
metrics
    establishing for projects, 29, 127–129
    in bank account of trust, 198
    when designers wrong, 199
miscommunication, 24–26, 89, 191
mistakes, making design, 199–203
misunderstandings clearing up, 191
mobile devices. *See also* iPhone
    growth of, 17
    revenue generated by, 13
The Mobile Moment (Wroblewski), 13
money, budget is insufficient, 158
motive, appealing to nobler, 127–129
moving on, being wrong and, 200–201

N

needs
    not meeting stakeholder, 190
    prioritizing designer, 213–214
Nest, 15
neutral, remaining, 140
nondesigners. *See also* stakeholders
    asking about data, 221
    authorizing team to move quickly, 216–217
    being patient, 219
    being prepared, 221
    design project checklist for, 221–223
    developing rapport with, 111
    empowering team, 217–218, 220
    funding for usability testing and research, 215–216
    having designers and executive level, 224–226

prioritizing needs for designers, 213–214
providing resources, 221
realizing designers are good at their jobs, 213–214
talking to, 1
tips for working with designers, 220–221
treatment of designers, 218–219
using helpful language, 219–220, 221
working with designers, 211–213
notes
    hand written, 58–59
    taking, 89–95

O

objections
    overcoming, 190
    writing down, 67
One-Tap Add, 32
option, making disagreeable changes, 192–193
orientation, toward others, 116–118
overbranding case study, 169–170

P

Parkinson, C. Northcote, Law of Triviality, 203
patient, being, 219
patterns, using common design, 147
pause, purpose of, 88–89
Peele, Norman Vincent, on difficult situations, 189
people
    dealing with unreasonable, 202–205
    describing problems, 87
    designing for, 5
    design project checklist about accessing, 223
    identifying to support decisions, 71–72
    not enough, 158
    taking ideas to right, 242–243
personal devices, 16–18. *See also* mobile devices
personal, getting, 47–48
Peters, Tom, In Search of Excellence, 225

[*About the Author*]

Tom Greever helps companies and organizations design better websites and apps. He is the UX Director at Bitovi, a frontend design and development consulting company, and has worked with both small startups and large corporations across many different industries. You can hire him to design your app, train your team, or speak at your next event. He lives in Illinois with his wife and five kids. He is probably cleaning up the house right now.

Follow him on Twitter: *https://twitter.com/tomgreever*

Keep up with him on his website: *http://tomgreever.com*

Have it your way.

Get even more for your money.

Join the O'Reilly Community, and register the O'Reilly books you own. It's free, and you'll get:

- $4.99 ebook upgrade offer
- 40% upgrade offer on O'Reilly print books
- Membership discounts on books and events
- Free lifetime updates to ebooks and videos
- Multiple ebook formats, DRM FREE
- Participation in the O'Reilly community
- Newsletters
- Account management
- 100% Satisfaction Guarantee

Signing up is easy:
1. Go to: oreilly.com/go/register
2. Create an O'Reilly login.
3. Provide your address.
4. Register your books.

Note: English-language books only

To order books online:
oreilly.com/store

For questions about products or an order:
orders@oreilly.com

To sign up to get topic-specific email announcements and/or news about upcoming books, conferences, special offers, and new technologies:
elists@oreilly.com

For technical questions about book content:
booktech@oreilly.com

To submit new book proposals to our editors:
proposals@oreilly.com

O'Reilly books are available in multiple DRM-free ebook formats. For more information:
oreilly.com/ebooks

Get even more for your money.

Join the O'Reilly Community, and register the O'Reilly books you own. It's free, and you'll get:

- $4.99 ebook upgrade offer
- 40% upgrade offer on O'Reilly print books
- Membership discounts on books and events
- Free lifetime updates to ebooks and videos
- Multiple ebook formats, DRM FREE
- Participation in the O'Reilly community
- Newsletters
- Account management
- 100% Satisfaction Guarantee

Signing up is easy:

1. Go to: oreilly.com/go/register
2. Create an O'Reilly login.
3. Provide your address.
4. Register your books.

Note: English-language books only

To order books online:
oreilly.com/store

For questions about products or an order:
orders@oreilly.com

To sign up to get topic-specific email announcements and/or news about upcoming books, conferences, special offers, and new technologies:
elists@oreilly.com

For technical questions about book content:
booktech@oreilly.com

To submit new book proposals to our editors:
proposals@oreilly.com

O'Reilly books are available in multiple DRM-free ebook formats. For more information:
oreilly.com/ebooks

CPSIA information can be obtained at www.ICGtesting.com
Printed in the USA
BVOW11s1153170216

437059BV00003B/7/P